WAITING FOR CO...
A CRITIQUE OF LAW AND RIGHTS

The enactment of the Charter of Rights and Freedoms in 1982 was celebrated as the harbinger of a new dawn in Canadian democratic politics. In this book, Allan Hutchinson contends that it was and continues to be a serious mistake. In his central argument he shows that, far from enhancing civic life, the Charter has attenuated both its practice and potential. He extends his argument to rights litigation in general, showing how 'rights-talk' actually betrays the cause of democracy.

Although primarily focusing on Canadian cases and writings, Hutchinson raises concerns that stretch well beyond Canada's boundaries. He condemns the assumptions and institutions associated with liberalism generally and shows how even critics of constitutional decision-making remain within flawed liberal premises. The book's *coup de grâce* lies in its analysis of some leading decisions of the Supreme Court of Canada, revealing the extent to which the Court has tendentiously interpreted many supposedly fundamental rights and freedoms. Thus exposing the constitutional enactment of rights as an elaborate legal mechanism that lulls citizens into political quietism, Hutchinson champions a style of politics that engages the virtues of democratic dialogue over the vices of rights-talk.

With this work Hutchinson has created a powerfully deconstructive exposé of the unfulfilled promise of the Charter, offering constructive suggestions for a change of democratic focus. This is a persuasive and vital critique, whose influence will reach beyond law schools into the heart of contemporary political debate.

ALLAN HUTCHINSON is a professor and associate dean, Osgoode Hall Law School, York University.

ALLAN C. HUTCHINSON

Waiting for Coraf: A Critique of Law and Rights

UNIVERSITY OF TORONTO PRESS
Toronto Buffalo London

Toronto Buffalo London
Printed in Canada

ISBN 0-8020-0672-8 (cloth)
ISBN 0-8020-7625-4 (paper)

Printed on acid-free paper

Canadian Cataloguing in Publication Data

Hutchinson, Allan C.
Waiting for Coraf : a critique of law and rights

Includes bibliographical references and index.
ISBN 0-8020-0672-8 (bound) ISBN 0-8020-7625-4 (pbk.)

1. Canada. Canadian Charter of Rights and Freedoms.
2. Civil rights – Canada. 3. Democracy – Canada.
I. Title.

JC599.C2H88 1995 342.71′085 C95-930070-8

University of Toronto Press acknowledges the financial assistance to its publishing program of the Canada Council and the Ontario Arts Council.

For
My Mother and Father

Contents

Preface xi
Acknowledgments xv

1 **Waiting for Coraf: Liberalism and the Charter** 3
Waiting For Coraf 3
Liberal Legalism 7
Liberal Empires 12
The People's Package 15
Critical Resistance 20
Taking Democracy Seriously 24

2 **Indeterminately Speaking: From Axiom to Action** 28
The Identity of Rights-Holders 29
The Contents of Rights-Talk 35
The Scope of Rights 38
Competing Claims of Rights-Talk 44
Rights and the Public Interest 48
Indeterminate Endings 55

3 **The Crisis of Legitimacy: Daydream Believing** 57
Democracy and Adjudication 57
The Formalist Faith 60
The Beatification of the Charter 66
Formalism Re-Visioned 75
Nocturnal Fantasies 79
A Critical Awakening 84

4 **An Abstraction of Vision: A Miserable Existence** 88
A Flight to Abstraction 90
Begging the Question 95
The Invisible Woman 102
Slouching toward Gilead 108
Through the Law Darkly 114
Concrete Closing 121

5 **The State of Rights-Talk: Private Rights and Public Wrongs** 123
The Corporate Age 125
Riding the Dolphin 128
The Liberal State 131
The Rock and the Hard Place 137
Another Fine Mess 143
Cutting Edge 147
Bright Lights 152

6 **Down the Yellow Brick Road: Rights Talk Back** 154
The Pragmatic Turning 155
A Crafty Suggestion 160
Getting on the Relational Track 165
Doing the Right(s) Thing? 172
The Democratic Gaze 182

7 **Talking the Good Life: From Rights-Talk to Democratic Conversation** 184
Toward Dialogic Democracy 185
Freeing Speech 190
The Liberal Impasse 194
Commercial Speech 198
Democratic Dialogue 202
A New State of Affairs 206
The Fourth Estate 210
A New Citizen 214
Lasting Words 217

8 **In Waiting** 221
Democratic Action 221

Postmodern Promptings 224
A Tragic Farce 228

Notes 231

Cases 263

Index 267

Preface

Before I completed the final draft of this book, I was invited to South Africa to talk about constitutional rights and to meet with African lawyers. It was a compelling and memorable trip: South Africa is a country and society that sears a profound mark on the mind. In professional terms, it presented me with the ideal opportunity to put my critical views to the acid test of political extremism. In the face of almost overwhelming support for a constitutionally entrenched and judicially enforced Bill of Rights by black lawyers, progressive academics, and liberal politicians, I felt that my opposition would meet its most sustained and penetrating challenge. Institutional oppression and personal suffering is so endemic in South Africa that people's appeal to the rhetoric of rights seemed almost natural and irresistible in its logic and cogency. However, my exposure, admittedly brief and limited, to the South African experience and the inspiring example of a few like-minded sceptics – Dennis Davis and Justice Poswas, to name but two – convinced me that such constitutional reforms were not the best way to achieve social justice: the short-term fix of liberal reform would not compensate for the long-term debilitation of the democratic cause. Rights-talk has had its day.

The attraction of rights-talk in South Africa and similarly straitened societies is obvious: it promises immediate and real relief from the grotesque abuses that people endure on a daily and continuing basis. The allure of North America and other advanced societies is seen as a shining example of the benefits and protections that constitutional rights can achieve. Yet, as I hope to show in this book, the light that those societies emanate is more diffuse and less ennobling than appears or is suggested. To be blunt, rights-talk flatters to deceive. The achievements of Canadian society are less uniformly good than is often conceded and they are more often brought about in spite of, not because of, the constitutional commitment to judicial rights-talk. Of course, it is better to be a citizen of Canada than of South Africa. But it is smugly offensive to observe, as former prime minister Brian Mulroney did, that the existence of the Charter of Rights ensures that 'we live in the kind of a democracy for which we are all thankful.' In spite of this country's natural and economic wealth, the anguished lives of many poor, Native, gay, illiterate, unemployed, female, and alienated Canadians stand as stark testimony to the fact that rights-talk dazzles rather than illuminates the critical eye of the liberal reformer. The Charter cannot be an empowering force for the egalitarian good when far too many still live in society's penumbral regions.

While in South Africa, I gave a series of seminars at various universities on the critique of constitutional rights in Canadian law. After one such event, in which I had argued strongly against the constitutional entrenchment of a Bill of Rights, one puzzled academic asked whether this meant that I was in favour of torture, arbitrary detention, surveillance, and the like. At first flabbergasted, I soon became angry at such a ludicrous and malign interpretation of my remarks. The fact is that I am not only appalled by the use of such inhumane instances of official power, but I am convinced that the practice of rights litigation falls well short of its promise to prevent such degradation. For example, despite its claim to be the standard-bearer of rights, the record of the United States on issues of race and violence is less than exemplary; it remains one of the most divisive and troubled countries in the world. Moreover, a constitutional dependence on judicial rights-talk as the exclusive bridle on governmental abuses of power obscures and, therefore, is indifferent to the many systemic ways in which oppression is woven into the social fabric of people's lives. The structured complexity and distribution of power in modern states demands a political response that is equally sophisticated and pervasive in its breadth and depth. Rather than settle for the attenuated discourse of rights-talk, people must aspire to a truly democratic polity that will enable and oblige them to become full and contributing citizens in an expansive civic dialogue over the terms and conditions of social life and personal living. Accordingly, this book is unapologetic in its commitment to championing a style and substance of politics that take seriously the virtues of democratic dialogue over the vices of rights-talk.

When asked whether he spoke Spanish, one of P.G. Wodehouse's characters answered, 'I don't know: I've never tried.' Canadians would do well to cultivate a similar open-mindedness and confidence in themselves when it comes to democratic conversation. The continued accumulation of elite power in the name of popular democracy is to be deplored. My proposal to abandon rights-talk and give democratic dialogue a real chance will only ring hollow and naïve to those latter-day aristocrats who crave the privilege to decide what is best for others. In working toward the social and material conditions for such conversations, much will have to be confronted and altered that is inimical to a truly just and egalitarian society. In so doing, people will learn that conversation and debate are not only some of the great pleasures of the good life, but that they are also its necessities. For too long, Canada's constitutional talk has been uttered by its political and judicial elites in an institutional accent and idiom that make it next to impossible for ordinary Canadians to participate: democracy has become more of a stylized exchange in which the powerful speak as often as they want and the powerless listen as best they can. This is the perversion of democracy, not its perfection.

Nevertheless, while I am an unapologetic advocate of unmodified democracy, I do recognize that I am not writing in a sociopolitical vacuum and that Canada has already made a constitutional commitment to an entrenched bill of rights. Unlike in the United Kingdom and South Africa, the political debate in Canada is not about whether to introduce constitutional change by way of rights-talk, but how to put an institutional discourse of rights-talk to progressive ends and effect. Consequently, while this book is devoted to demonstrating how the theory and practice of rights-talk betrays the cause of democracy, I concede that it might not be possible to ignore entirely constitutional litigation in a society that is already pervaded by rights-talk. Mindful that there is no 'outside' from which to work, there may be occasional strategic advantage in making 'inside' resort to the courts in the struggle to advance the project of progressive justice. However, it is a very dangerous two-edged sword that must be wielded with extreme caution and self-conscious scepticism.

Acknowledgments

While it almost goes without saying that this book would not have been completed without the assistance of many people, it would be inexcusable not to thank and mention some of them by name. Some of the work on which I have drawn in this book began life as joint projects with friends. I am particularly grateful to Pam Carpenter, Lisa Fishbayn, Robert Maisey, Patrick Monahan, and Andrew Petter for their generosity, insight, forbearance, and friendship: they prevented me from making even more gaffes than I otherwise would have done and made the whole business of scholarship much more fun. I have been most fortunate in working with talented, imaginative, humorous, and dedicated students who have made an invaluable contribution to the finished product; these include Jonathon Anschell, Adam Bernstein, Richard Epstein, Sue Hodgson, Blair Holder, Tom Lacerte, Moonlake Lee, Maureen Lennon, Evan Siddal, Anne Werker, and Laura Young. In the same way, I have had the definite pleasure of working with Carole Trussler, Rose Della Rocca, and, especially, Wendy Rambo, who have endured my eccentric work habits and taxing demands with an enviable professionalism and friendly equanimity. Also, I want to thank my colleagues and friends at Osgoode for contributing to an academic community that generates all the intellectual diversity, political tension, and institutional support that allows someone like me to thrive. Finally, I owe special debts of appreciation to Robert Maisey, who went above and beyond the call of friendship by reading the whole of the completed manuscript in his own rigorous and insightful way, and, in particular, to Andrew Petter, whose intellectual influence and personal example remain strong throughout.

Although there is much that is new in this book, it is the accumulated result of more than seven or eight years of research and publication. My ideas have gone through many twists and turns in that time; no doubt, they will continue to develop and change after the publication of this book. This way of proceeding has meant that as well as rewriting and re-editing older arguments and ideas, I have written a considerable amount of new material. As such, I hope that this book represents a more original and less patchwork effort than might be expected. In completing the final version of the book, I have drawn freely on ideas and material that was previously published in the *Harvard Law Review, University of Toronto Law Journal, Texas Law Review, Stanford Law Review, Law and Society Review, University of British Columbia Law Journal, Ottawa Law Review, McGill Law Journal, Canadian Business Law Journal, Yale Law Journal, British Journal of Law and Society, Michigan Law Review, Southern California Interdisciplinary Law Journal, Literary Review of Canada, Canadian Lawyer,* the *Globe and Mail,* and the *Toronto Star.* Many thanks to all editors and staff for their support.

Of course, life is much more than work. And work is much less than life. I am lucky to be part of a family that gives a broader meaning and value to both my work and life: my mum and dad, Marie and Charlie Hutchinson, have always shown me what it means to work hard and love unconditionally; my daughters, Katie, Emily, and Rachel, love me enough to put up with a father who is often more distracted than he might be; Katie, Chris, and Daniel Carpenter have increased my family in affection as well as size; and Pam Marshall endured me in ways that only she could – 'You showed me what it's all about.' Thanks and love to all.

Allan C. Hutchinson
31 December 1994

Power of some sort or other will go on
In games, in riddles, seemingly at random;
But superstition, like belief, must die,
And what remains when disbelief has gone?

– Philip Larkin

WAITING FOR CORAF: A CRITIQUE OF LAW AND RIGHTS

1

Waiting for Coraf: Liberalism and the Charter

What are we doing here, *that* is the question. And we are blessed in this, that we happen to know the answer. Yes, in this immense confusion one thing alone is clear. We are waiting for Godot to come ... Or for night to fall ... We have kept our appointment, and that's an end to that. We are not saints, but we have kept our appointment. How many people can boast as much?

– Samuel Beckett[1]

Samuel Beckett was always a man ahead of his time. He would have understood well the disconcerting dilemma of Canadian lawyers and constitutional scholars. His tragicomedy of existential despair, *Waiting For Godot*, is a threnody of hope postponed and abused, but never abandoned or extinguished. The wretched Vladimir and Estragon are waiting on a road, beside a blasted tree too frail for a gallows, for the inscrutable Mr. Godot to come. Through a series of desolate encounters in which Nothing happens, the Chaplinesque tramps continue in their daily round of abiding anguish and unrequited anticipation. The bewilderment and frustration of waiting seems to become life's reluctant ambition and dubious achievement – 'I wait, therefore I am (perhaps).' In this minimalist drama, Beckett suggests the predicament of human living in which the responsibility of ennobling opportunity and the burden of enervating risk combine in the god(ot)-less search for meaning in an abject and alienating world. As such, it captures neatly the perennial predicament within which Canadian lawyers and academics are squarely caught.

WAITING FOR CORAF

In 1982, the new Charter of Rights and Freedoms became part of

Canada's Constitution. Although some worried that 'Canada was in danger of becoming a rights-ridden country,'[2] most heralded the Charter as a symbolic distillation of all that is estimable and esteemed in Canadian political life; it was to be the legal jewel in the constitutional crown. As part of the patriation of the Canadian Constitution, it promised to make good on Canada's traditional commitment to being a just and ordered democracy. In particular, the Charter proposed a framework of rights within which the relations between individuals and the state could be monitored and structured. Of course, while the Charter crystallized the debate around rights and placed it at the constitutional heart of democratic affairs, it was not Canada's first encounter with the political and legal ramifications of rights-talk. Throughout the common law and in public law generally, lawyers and judges have attempted to identify and refine a style and substance of rights-talk that can bring the existential search for legal truth and social justice to a successful and satisfying conclusion. Nevertheless, the entrenchment of a judicially administered Charter that took constitutional precedence over the legislative enactments of a democratically elected Parliament was a seminal and sustaining event in Canadian political and legal life.

Nevertheless, as even its most enthusiastic supporters might concede, the impact of the Charter has been more than a little problematic and the performance of its judicial interpreters has been less than exemplary. The Charter's vaunted claim of being the authoritative voice on the potential and parameters of responsible government in a constitutional democracy has not been made out. With over a decade of judicial experience and jurisprudential reflection behind it, the whole of the Charter enterprise remains in serious need of political justification and jurisprudential support. However, as the flawed nature of the Charter's character becomes more apparent, its many supporters content themselves with reassuring each other that its real potential has not yet been fully actualized. Like Beckett's vaudevillian vagrants, Canadian constitutional scholars exist in that precarious purgatory between the unfulfilled hope of formalist salvation and the compulsive fear of nihilistic damnation. They live and wait in that demi-world of exquisite perdition in which it is uncertain whether the real Charter of Rights and Freedoms (CORAF, hereafter called Coraf) will or will not come. It is as if only the will to believe in Coraf and its imminent arrival is all that keeps society from an anomic abyss: 'In the meantime let us try and converse calmly, since we are incapable of keeping silent.'[3]

Within the context and confines of this self-imposed purgatory, it is crucial to its judicial and juristic inhabitants that a viable and legitimate mode of rights-talk be attainable. Without the possibility of effecting a legitimate practice of Charter adjudication – determinate in scope, objective in operation, and progressive in outcome – the struggle to establish a constitutional order that is worthy of a democratic polity is lost. It is feared that, without such an order, Canadian society would be cast adrift on a sea of ideological wrangling with only scholarly impostors to map the charts, judicial tyrants to plot the course, and lawyerly swabs to crew the voyage. More pertinently, the increasingly desperate nature of the legal community's yearnings for theoretical and practical relief from this dystopian vision ensures that its members will regularly be beguiled by the barest hint of Coraf's impending sighting. Without some sign of its likely arrival, mainstream lawyers, judges, and scholars will succumb to the insidious fear of self-doubt and begin to question their own authority: 'We always find something, eh Didi, to give us the impression that we exist.' Consequently, in the long night of rights-talk, constitutional law and scholarship sleep-walk a thin line between a dream of deliverance and a nightmare of inconsequence. It is a tired and tiring prospect: 'Don't let's do anything. It's safer.'[4]

This jurisprudential desire for a good night's constitutional sleep has deep cultural roots. More than most continents, North America is a land of dreams. It exists as much in the ideological geography of the imagination as in any political gazetteer. One particular dream (or nightmare) that has withstood the reality of waking history is about 'a government of laws, not men.' Although this constitutional vision is predominantly American, it has retained a firm grip on the Canadian popular and legal psyche; it has been a major source of governmental authority and legitimacy. There is a long-standing belief in the United States and Canada, especially in these post-Charter years, that Law is more than the sum total of extant laws: it is felt to be the expression and repository of a political wisdom that transcends the bounds of its own temporary articulation.[5] Democratic law-making cannot be left entirely to its own promptings, but must be judged by its willingness to conform to the dictates of a higher law. Whereas Reason and Natural Right used to hold considerable sway, recent invocations of these transcendent authorities are of a more specific and prosaic nature. Recognizing that, whatever else it might be, law is a human activity, contemporary legal theorists strive to explain and justify the delicate and elusive relation between law's immanence (the idea of law as the rational embodiment of an indwelling necessity) and law's instrumentality (the practice of using law as a democratic tool for social engineering).

Although this challenge is most pressing in constitutional matters, its demands colour all facets of the legal enterprise. At the heart of the matter is the vexing question of normative authority in a world in which people not only have the full prerogative to make new laws, but also the power to remake the very concept of law itself.[6] Despite the institutional commitment to democracy and the regular incantation that 'the life of the law has not been logic, but experience,'[7] lawyers are still deep in philosophical sleep. Detached reason remains the touchstone for valid knowledge about individuals, their collective predicament, and the legal order. In the struggle for social justice, abstract reflection is often given priority over democratic engagement. Although this preference seems to speak with the almost mystical accent of bygone days, it remains the dominant idiolect of modern jurisprudence. For instance, in the influential Dworkinian Empire of Law, the princely judges must leave it to philosophical 'seers and prophets ... to work out law's ambitions for itself, the purer form of law within and beyond the law we have.' While such imaginings may occasionally elude lawyers' grasp, they are not left to their own devices because their 'god is the adjudicative principle of integrity.'[8] Thus, it is recommended that if law is to perfect itself and operate as a guide for the anguished democrat, lawyers must become philosophers.

Under the spell of this ambition, Canadian legal practice and constitutional scholarship is characterized by an abiding and sustaining faith in the realization of the Constitution's philosophical ideal. There persists the bedrock belief that the vital process of rights adjudication under the Charter and elsewhere can be carried out in a manner that is consonant with the demands of a political commitment to democratic governance. In the name of constitutional legitimacy, it is insisted that the use of rights-talk by courts must satisfy the three cardinal virtues of democratic operation:

- *It must be determinate* (i.e., a general enumeration of rights and their informing values can be made so that they are capable of being applied directly and distinctively to the concrete resolution of particular disputes).
- *It must be objective* (i.e., the enumeration and application of those pertinent rights and values must not be reducible to the opinions of sitting judges or academic commentators, but must be governable by

principles and values that inhere in the law itself, Canadian constitutional traditions, or some other independent source).

- *It must be progressive* (i.e., the rights articulated and the results achieved do not uphold the status quo for its own sake, but are based upon a commitment to improving the lot of the least advantaged in society and allow for the serious possibility of social change).

Occasionally, some judges and jurists are foolhardy enough to insist that all three virtues can be effectively accommodated in a theory of judicial review. However, wary of overreaching themselves, most contemporary protagonists are content to ground the political legitimacy of judicial review on two, rather than three, of these conceptual virtues. Suitably humbled by the historical record, they are less idealistic and more pragmatic in their aspirations than earlier generations. Nevertheless, the formalist faith remains the dominant credo of constitutional scholars. They contend that, whatever the dubious merits of Charter adjudication to date, a proper appreciation of what judicial review under the Charter entails would allow its performance to meet the minimum standards of constitutional rectitude and get over the threshold of political integrity. In short, behind the prosaic and flawed actuality of constitutional law stands the immanent perfection of Coraf, as yet only barely glimpsed and imagined, but soon to arrive in all its resounding constitutionality and redeeming amplitude. By adopting this objective theory and determinate practice of judicial review, the judicial arm of government can further the progressive campaign of social justice by ensuring that the have-nots are protected and better able to participate in the process and benefits of democratic politics. It is an affirmation of liberal legalism on a magnificent scale.

LIBERAL LEGALISM

The sonorous and majestic ring of the Rule of Law has resonated throughout the centuries. It has operated as a potent call to moral arms, a clarion call for constitutional justice by a whole host of political actors and combatants. At times, the Rule of Law has been used to legitimize and galvanize a challenge to entrenched power; at other times, the ruling elite has relied on it to sanction its power and resistance to would-be usurpers. Like any ideal, it only exists in the political consciousness and conscience. But, like every other ideal, it exercises a tenacious grip on the imagination and actions of its adherents. Indeed, its ideological attraction and political durability are largely attributable to its political plasticity, its facility to accommodate itself to changing governmental situations and political forces. In short, it is the will-o'-the-wisp of constitutional history.

Notwithstanding its protean nature, the rich history of the Rule of Law has been loosely connected by a strong thread of liberal legalism: it has been used as a seductive slogan in the struggle to establish or preserve individual autonomy and private action. On many occasions, this appeal to liberty has amounted to nothing more than moralistic window-dressing for otherwise naked attempts to seize political power, a rhetorical gambit in a continuing power play. But to reduce the Rule of Law's appeal to simply and always an exercise in mystification is to distort the historical record; it impugns the honourable motives of many and overestimates the credulity of even more.[9] Over the last millennium, the Rule of Law has occasionally proved to be an effective principle to check the indulgent abuse of power by the few over the many. However, over the long haul, rights-talk has been activated as a 'principled' counter in the shuffling of power among elite groups; it has served to inhibit as much as increase the flourishing of any governmental system of direct democracy. The historical development of any kind of democracy has been the by-product of a preoccupation with private autonomy. The Rule of Law is premised on the ideal of limited government; it has stood as a constitutional barrier between the governors and the governed, between power and people. The existence and extent of democratic governance are only justified insofar as they better serve the enhanced liberty of individuals. Democracy is a recent recruit on the proclaimed march to the truly liberal state. Indeed, universal suffrage is a decidedly twentieth-century phenomenon. Even today, representative democracy extends only to about twenty per cent of the world's nations (not population), and in many of these states the arrangements are extremely fragile and incomplete. In Canada, universal adult suffrage did not occur until 1960 with the enfranchisement of the First Nations.

The compulsion to reason within a closed system of premises is said to guarantee the enduring integrity and efficacy of the constitutional compact and to insulate the judges from ideological controversy. Within this constitutional scenario, adherence to the Rule of Law has come to be synonymous with compliance with a liberal scheme of constitutional governance. Although some form of representative democracy has become a modern component of this model, the history of the Rule of

Law's theory and practice reveals that it is more an optional extra than an essential condition. Indeed, the opposite often seems to be true: the Rule of Law has functioned as a clear check on the actual impact and expansion of a rigorous democracy. If not non-democratic in aspiration and orientation, rights-talk is democratically indifferent in character and scope. The enduring concerns of the Rule of Law are the limitation of state power, the maintenance of a broad sphere of private liberty, and the preservation of a market-exchange economy. In its many academic manifestations, it has been connected, to greater and lesser extents, to an individualistic theory of political justice and jurisprudence. Ostensibly, there have been two versions of the Rule of Law, but they both represent a commitment to liberalism; it is simply that one tends to be more explicit and marked than the other.

The *thin* version of the Rule of Law amounts to a constitutional principle of legality. It demands that government be conducted in accordance with established and performable norms; its voice remains silent or, at best, whispered on the issue of substantive policies. Rule must be by law and not discretion. Also, and especially, the lawmaker itself must be under the law, at least until it changes the law. In this attenuated form, the Rule of Law is targeted against arbitrary government and palm-tree justice. Its critical logo is 'a government of laws, not men'; its operative axioms are the generality of official rules and the faithful adherence by government to those declared standards of conduct. Its modern defence is that the preferred system of governance is that in which 'the law furnishes a base-line for self-directed action, not a detailed set of instructions for accomplishing specific objectives.'[10] Although far from explicit or inevitable, its substantive tendency is clearly toward a liberal society in which the best government is the one that governs least. However, unless such a constitutional requirement of official legality is supplemented by a 'thicker' theory of political justice, the Rule of Law will be a weak restraint on an ambitiously unjust regime. It might even tend to legitimate its substantive excesses under a patina of formal justice. Unrepresentative government and the Rule of Law are not mutually exclusive; democracy is an entirely dispensable feature of this form of the Rule of Law. As Herbert Hart has observed, 'however great the aura of majesty or authority which the official system may have, its demands in the end must be submitted to moral scrutiny.'[11] Accordingly, a full defence of the Rule of Law must be based on its foundational and substantive political connections.

The *thick* version of the Rule of Law incorporates the thinner one as merely one dimension of a liberal theory of justice; its major addition is a constitutional entrenchment of rights-talk. This conception of the Rule of Law goes back to the Greeks and Romans, but finds its modern roots in the Enlightment.[12] Indeed, there is an almost direct line of descent from the theory and practice of seventeenth-century England to that of late-twentieth-century Anglo-America. The intellectual lineage runs almost unbroken from John Locke and Thomas Hobbes to John Rawls and Ronald Dworkin, through Thomas Paine, John Stuart Mill, A.V. Dicey, and Friedrich Hayek. With some indigenously Canadian twists and turns, the contributions of contemporary Charter scholars follow this broadly liberal tradition; a communitarian limb or two have been grafted on to the individualist torso of traditional liberalism.[13] The modern defence of this thick version posits the necessary connection between procedural and substantive justice. The Rule of Law demands that positive law embody a particular vision of social justice that gains its constitutional justification and political appeal from the judicial enforcement of rights-talk in the institutional exchanges between the state and its citizens.

The Anglo-American tradition can be traced back to the Glorious Revolution of 1641 and, even beyond that, to the Magna Carta of 1215. In the early battle between the royalty and aristocracy, the idea and establishment of some democratic check on political governance was of little consequence or concern. Moreover, the progressive tenor of the seventeenth century was more libertarian than democratic. A major achievement and statement of political intent was the Bill of Rights. While this is the closest England has ever come to adopting a written constitution, it was never more than another piece of legislation, repealable by any later Parliament. The central thrust of the legislation was to force the Crown to rule through Parliament. Its constitutional ambition was not to popularize government, but to restore and conserve 'the true ancient and indubitable rights and liberties of the people.' The undisputed apologist for these constitutional developments was John Locke, the father of modern liberalism. In his *Second Treatise on Government,* he provided the enduring account of how people created civil society to protect better their individual rights enjoyed in a state of nature. Within such a constitutional scheme, the limited role of government was to enact law 'as guards and fences to the properties of all the members of society.' The Rule of Law was a pivotal principle. Laws were to be general in scope and operation; 'freedom of men under government is ... not to be subject to the inconstant, unknown, arbitrary will of another man.' While Locke justified the initial success, it was eighteenth-century writers like David Hume, Edmund Burke, and William Paley who consolidated the constitutional position of the Rule of Law. Yet it was the Americans who were to embrace and implement most directly the Lockean teachings.

Although England had proceeded on the path to parliamentary supremacy, the American colonists were more inclined to resuscitate the Magna Carta and its libertarian underpinnings against a recalcitrant English Parliament. While America was more representative in governance than most nations, the founders' rabid libertarianism was only matched by its faint-hearted commitment to popular rule: 'The evils we experience flow from the excess of democracy.'[14] People's supposed natural rights were to be put beyond the imagined vicissitudes of majoritarian politics. In particular, private property was not to be open to governmental interference: democracy had to prove itself to be of instrumental value to the security of liberty. In effect, the American Revolution only managed to replace the dominion of a foreign power with that of a domestic document. Entrenched individual rights would always trump any collective concerns of the democratic process. Enforcing this social compact, the courts were to function as the guardians of the Rule of Law. But, in the process, they were not to turn themselves into an independent centre of constitutional power. As John Marshall announced, 'judicial power, as contradistinguished from the power of laws, has no existence. Courts are the mere instruments of the law, and can will nothing.'[15] The Rule of Law demanded a scrupulously objective and formalistic judiciary.

While the upholding of the Rule of Law in the United States was being increasingly entrusted to the judicial interpreters of the written constitution, the English constitution remained proudly and defiantly unwritten; rights-talk was a matter for legislation and the common law. Mindful of the decades of constitutional pandemonium prompted by the French Declaration of the Rights of Man and of the Citizen in 1789, the English establishment and its more democratic critics saw little progressive merit in following the American or French exemplar. Jeremy Bentham went so far as to decry talk of natural rights as 'nonsense on stilts.'[16] Indeed, almost a century later, A.V. Dicey maintained that the constitution is not 'the source, but the consequence of the rights of individuals.'[17] The combined force and design of Dicey's principles was to make the Rule of Law into a bridle for a supposedly rampant administrative arm of government. This sceptism toward the benefits of an entrenched charter of rights has continued. It is only in the last few years, as much in the name of individual liberty as social democracy, that there has been a British resurgence of intellectual and political interest in such constitutional reform.

This Diceyian tradition of Lockean conservatism has been continued by Friedrich Hayek in the contemporary debate over the Rule of Law. For him, the Rule of Law as an embodiment of an unflinching commitment to individual rights stands in unequivocal opposition to state redistribution and planning; it is the essential and most important condition of individual freedom. It is not simply a constitutional principle of 'legality,' but comprises a substantive vision of the correct and just relations between individuals and society.[18] This tradition of liberal legalism has been continued by contemporary American writers and, in recent years, has come to insinuate itself into the mainstream of Canadian law and politics. Although the emphasis has become more liberal than libertarian, democracy remains very much a secondary feature of the constitutional order. Most jurists and judges agree that the Rule of Law is a vital protective and facilitative constitutional device for a fundamental scheme of individual rights; disagreement is over the scope and character of rights-talk. As such, Canadian lawyers look to the expected presence of Coraf – as the Canadian embodiment of liberal legalism – to guide their professional endeavours and to justify their constitutional calling.

LIBERAL EMPIRES

Liberalism remains the ruling theory of contemporary political and legal theory. Its central organizing principle is that the individual is the measure of values and that individual interests are the only real interests of social value. Within the liberal vision of society, people are portrayed as rational maximizers and self-interested consumers of utilities. There is no available metewand to make interpersonal comparisons of utility and thereby to generate a plausible account of the public good. While individuals seek to obtain the maximum freedom to pursue their own freely authored self-interest, their efforts to do so require some security from the subjective and selfish interference of others engaged in the same project. The central contradiction and paradox is that the more freedom that is allowed to pursue such ends, the less security is available against the intrusion of others. In short, individual freedom seems possible only through its collective limitation and negation: one person's freedom can only be obtained by curbing another's freedom and vice versa. Consequently, the acute challenge for contemporary liberal theorists has been to identify those regulative principles that can provide the necessary degree of social order and, at the same time, ensure that it comes 'as close as a society can to being a voluntary scheme.'[19]

Over the years, there have been almost as many different versions of liberalism as there have been liberal theorists. But the modern manifestations of the liberal weave can be divided into two main camps. Whereas as a 'teleological' strand insists that the individual *right* must be subordinated to the utilitarian *good*, a 'deontological' thread argues that the *right* must take priority over the *good*. It is essentially a moral debate over two principal issues: whether the source of an action is more important in the overall ethical scheme of things than its consequences and whether people must always be treated as ends in themselves. Of course, no credible theory can ignore consequences entirely or deny the intrinsic worth of certain actions absolutely. Accordingly, the difference between proffered answers is as much a matter of shading as anything else: both camps of theorists agree that the enhancement of individual freedom is the objective of social life and its organizational structure. Nevertheless, it is the deontological liberals who seem to hold the contemporary imagination and who have dominated the jurisprudential debate.[20] As such, liberal political and legal theory has become dominated by rights-talk.

Under a deontological mandate, the creation of a political state is posited to mediate the anarchic *bellum omnium omnes*. Yet, as liberals concede, the existence of a political state to limit individual freedom in the name of greater freedom does not resolve the dilemma of order and security. It merely serves to institutionalize the contradictory conundrum of the extent and manner in which certain freedoms can be limited in order to maintain sufficient social stability and peace to allow greater freedom in general. The theory of rights has been offered as the jurisprudential solution: a constitutional charter of rights is its institutional complement. In one neat move, the idea and practice of a judicially enforced set of legal rights is claimed to offer the possibility of resolving the perennial problem of liberalism and the chance of achieving its ambition. Guided more by the light of reason than by the pull of sectarian ideological interests, liberals contend that the courts are able to administer rights-talk in accordance with the political aspirations and institutional requirements of a liberal democracy. While it has received various renderings, liberal legalism is the academic faith of contemporary jurisprudence.

The work of Ronald Dworkin, temporarily at least, dominates the animated contemporary debate in the United States and Canada over the judicial role under the rights-based interpretation of the Rule of Law. Adjudication is claimed to satisfy the Rule of Law by meeting the democratic demand for judicial objectivity and the popular need for political justice. While some rail that an activist judiciary is antithetical to democratic governance,[21] Dworkin argues that if judges are to fulfil their democratic responsibilities under the Rule of Law, they must make political decisions, albeit not personal or partisan ones. His claim is bold and brilliant. The traditional formalistic, rule-book conception of the Rule of Law requires judges in hard cases to be unconstrainedly creative or to dissemble. Dworkin's rights conception of the Rule of Law incorporates a dimension of substantive fairness and thereby appropriately constrains and guides the judge in the resolution of hard cases. In defending such a version of the Rule of Law, Dworkin keeps himself firmly within the tradition of Locke and the constitutional priority of liberty: 'The idea of individual rights ... is the zodiac sign under which America was born.'[22]

For Dworkin, judges are political actors whose power is limited by a legal system's history and its liberal character. The state does not give them a blank cheque on which to write in the political currency of their choice; they must interpret the regnant legal materials in their best light as a theory of political morality. The judge breathes political vitality into the lifeless words of legal texts by applying the twin tests of 'formal fit' and 'substantive justice.' Any interpretation must be able to demonstrate some plausible connection with society's legal history. However, the better theory is not necessarily the one that accounts for the most decisions or statutes; 'formal fit' is only a heuristic device or rule of thumb. This requirement acts as a threshold and combines with the test of 'substantive justice.' This obliges the judge to develop a scheme of rights that a just state would establish and enforce. While this task can only be provisionally and partially performed, the conscious striving for such a perfected theory is the hallmark of adjudication under the Dworkinian conception of the Rule of Law. Accordingly, judicial power is legitimated by this commitment to uphold the existing political order of rights and only to extend it in a consistent and principled manner. In this way, law is and remains rational, determinate, just, and objective.

It is to Dworkin's credit that he does not disguise his individualistic revitalization of the Rule of Law. He openly concedes that his conception of law might well exact a price in the development of a communitarian spirit, but insists that members of a genuine political community are governed by a common set of principles that are constitutive of social justice. Yet, anxious to deflect charges of being insufficiently democratic, he reminds citizens that the Rule of Law 'is the parent and guardian of democracy'[23] and 'enriches democracy by adding an independent forum of principle ... [where] justice is in the end a matter of individual right, and not independently a matter of the public good.'[24] He casts the courts as the central constitutional institutions through which the citizenry can debate, articulate, and implement its collective standards for social justice. In elevating legal conversation to a privileged form of democratic discourse, Dworkin is not alone. Joined by other contemporary American writers, like Owen Fiss and Laurence Tribe, Bruce Ackerman has gone so far as to suggest that

> not that a vigorous and constructive legal dialogue can ever hope to compensate for an apathetic and muddled political debate. Yet the reverse is also true: political commitment is no substitute for legal deliberation. While the future of America depends on the American people, the future of American law depends, in a special way, on the way American lawyers interpret their calling.[25]

THE PEOPLE'S PACKAGE

Less than twenty years ago, any claim that Canadian lawyers and judges might hold such a pre-eminent role in Canadian society would have been met with bemusement – it would have been too far from the truth to warrant anything more adamant by way of agreement or dissent. Today, the response would be a little harder to gauge. In a nation obsessed with defining a distinctive identity for itself, Canada is caught within a constitutional matrix of contending ideological forces. Although Canada's historical traditions of government are very much part of British culture, modern constitutional developments suggest that the United States is beginning to have a dominant effect on Canada's constitutional self-image and structures. Whatever the accuracy of the conclusion in 1955 that 'Canadians are more aware of the difference in their attitudes toward the law than anything else distinguishing them from Americans,'[26] the enactment of the Charter of Rights of Freedoms in 1982 was a unilateral Canadian confirmation of a free-trade agreement in constitutional arrangements and liberal aspirations.

In the past, Canada took its constitutional cues from its colonial ancestors, the British. Independently self-governing by 1867, Canada did not acquire the status of international nationhood until 1930 and, even today, the Queen of England remains the titular head of state. Divided by a common law culture, Canada is drawn to British customs and conventions, but remains separate from them. There is a vigorous commitment to a federal system of democratic governance that introduces an alien dynamic to the British model. Nonetheless, the idea and practice of parliamentary sovereignty has always loomed large in Canada, along with its constitutional corollaries of cabinet government and ministerial responsibility. Within this governmental scenario, courts have cast themselves as decidedly subservient institutions whose task in constitutional matters is to decide discrete and formal issues of federal–provincial competence and to refrain from excursions into sweeping and substantive questions of constitutional politics. Notwithstanding the European ties of Quebec, Canadian law and politics were beholden to Westminster for both their general framework and animating temperament until the patriation of the Constitution in 1982.

The enactment of the Charter as part of the 1982 patriation deal put a change to all that. While a benign anti-Americanism has always been a significant component of the Canadian psyche, the American way of government and living has had a less obvious, but more insidious effect on Canadian constitutional law and politics. Although Canada is less like the United States than most Americans assume, Canada is more like the United States than many Canadians care to admit. From the earliest times, the friendly aggression of the United States has been a powerful formative influence. Commencing with the Quebec Act of 1774 and resonating today with the North American Free Trade Agreement of 1993, Canadians are painfully aware that they share North America with a sleeping elephant who might roll over at any time. Whereas Canadians placed democratic faith in parliamentary sovereignty, Americans were always less sanguine about the virtues of unchecked government authority. Instead, they opted for a constitutional ideology of republican government that provided citizens with a written guarantee of rights against the state. Judicial review became the heartbeat of American democracy.

In 1982, Canada brought home the Constitution and became a truly sovereign nation. While retaining much of its British constitutional heritage, the Constitution Act of 1982 also heralded a formal transfer of democratic allegiance from parliamentary sovereignty to constitutional rights. The American tradition of liberal law and politics was embraced and given pride of place in Canada's new constitutional scheme.[27] Canadians were endowed with a broad series of justiciable claims that were to be enforced against the state by the courts. However, while the model and inspiration for such changes were clearly American, the Canadian approach to an entrenched bill of rights had sufficient differences to convince many critics that although Canada was becoming more American, it remained sufficiently different and, therefore, distinctly Canadian to appease the national anxiety over a looming American take-over. Indeed, many of the conceptual innovations and textual nuances of the Charter seem to be directly intended to avoid or diminish the excesses of the United States' attachment to judicial constitutionalism in recent times. Of course, Canadian constitutional law's involvement with rights-talk did not begin with the advent of the Charter in 1982. The common law has always protected civil liberties, and courts have traditionally acted to bridle arbitrary government acts.[28] However, such rights were not entrenched or guaranteed against legislative encroachment; they were the presumptions to be rebutted rather than the parameters to be respected. Despite the courts' efforts to locate an 'implied bill of rights' within the interstices of the Constitution Act 1867,[29] these rights were often selectively applied and intermittently withheld by judges who were not beyond their own brand of official high-handedness. As such, although the constitutional review of legislative and government acts is not foreign to Canadian judicial practice, the historical record of courts in protecting people's freedoms is more than desultory, but less than encouraging: judicial interventions have been sporadic and spotty.[30]

In 1960, the Progressive Conservative government of John Diefenbaker introduced the Bill of Rights. While the institutional result of many forces' confluence, its enactment was intended to respond to an increasing popular awareness of individual entitlements against the state and a growing professional dissatisfaction with the courts' ability to deal effectively with the spreading reach of the Canadian state. It was an early and largely ill-fated attempt to capitalize on the apparent contribution of American courts to enhanced social justice in the *Brown* era of the 1950s and '60s. The general consensus is that any potential that the Bill of Rights might have had for improved democratic governance was effectively stymied by the usually indecisive and occasionally perverse interpretations of its provisions by the courts.[31] Introduced by way of legislative enactment rather than institutional amendment, its political edge was blunted because of continuing debates over the constitutional status of the Bill of Rights and whether it took precedence over later federal acts that offended its provisions: the doctrine of parliamentary sovereignty was the constitutional fly in the democratic ointment. Consequently, the Bill of Rights was not the auspicious innovation that many liberals had hoped that it would be. However, with a characteristic combination of undaunted resolve and critical naïvety, lawyers and politicians maintained that the problem was not with the very idea of rights or the flawed practice of its judicial enforcement. For them, the solution was to be found in more, not less, rights and in more, not less, judicial power.

Liberals got their wish in 1982. After bitter talks, and with Quebec still outside any constitutional compact, the Charter of Rights and Freedoms was signed into law by the Queen under a grey Ottawa sky on 17 April. Promised as a 'People's Package,' it was celebrated as the harbinger of a new dawn in the Canadian democratic politics. Energized and guided by the Charter's beam of justice, Canadians could continue along the path to becoming a modern democratic polity in which each citizen could be proud to play a leading part. As prime minister Brian Mulroney would later put it in 1985, the advent of the Charter and the constitutional changes that it brought ensured that Canadians 'live in the kind of democracy for which we are all grateful.'[32] The provisions of the Charter combined to establish the constitutional entrenchment of rights-talk through judicial review as the primary institution for distributing and controlling political power. As the British constitutional tradition waned, the American tradition waxed strongly in Canadian discourse. No longer would the courts be entrusted only with the task of determining whether it was the federal or provincial government that had the constitutional authority to take particular action, but also of determining whether any government action of that kind could be taken at all; the substance of legislative actions became as constitutionally pertinent as their institutional source. To much rejoicing in academic and professional quarters, liberal legalism had finally come to Canada in all its political amplitude and jurisprudential glory. All that was left to do was to wait for Coraf and set the Canadian state to rights.

While these Corafians acknowledged the influence that the liberal empire of the United States had upon the style and direction of constitutional change, they were quick to point out Canada's new Charter contained crucial modifications to the American model. Apart from adopting a slightly different slate of rights, the Charter gave no explicit protection to property. Moreover, mindful of American experience, it expressly conferred power on the courts to override federal and provincial statutes. However, from the troublesome perspective of democratic legitimacy, the Charter included two seemingly fundamental caveats to the constitutional primacy of individual rights. First, its opening section both guaranteed the availability of all individual rights and, at the same time, directed that they were to be balanced against larger social values: 'The Charter of Rights and Freedoms guarantees the rights and freedoms set out in it subject only to such reasonable limits prescribed by law as can be demonstrably justified in a free and democratic society.' Section 1 has come to represent the importance of communitarian considerations in the institutional articulation of rights-talk.[33] Second, section 33 permits Parliament or a provincial legislature to override certain rights and, unlike in the United States, removes the courts' conclusive veto over legislative authority: judicial decisions over constitutionality can be reversed by something much less than a constitutional amendment.

Emboldened by the constitutional entrenchment of the Charter and reassured by its significant differences from the American Bill of Rights, judges and jurists could begin to usher in a new era of liberal legalism in the service of political democracy. After some initial hesitancy and understandable anxiety, the legal community soon warmed to its constitutional calling and began to fulfil its democratic destiny as guardians of liberal rights-talk. One Supreme Court judge went so far as to state that 'adjudication under the Charter must be approached free of any lingering doubts as to its legitimacy.'[34] In the first few years of the Charter, the court upheld many more claims than it rejected and struck down laws with relative abandon. More recently, the Supreme Court has settled into a more measured pace and has begun to worry about the legitimate scope and thrust of its mandate; the weight of democratic propriety has begun to rest a little heavier on the courts' constitutional shoulders. While there is clearly no doubt that the courts have the political responsibility and institutional authority to adjudicate under the Charter, there are 'lingering doubts' as to how they can do that in a way that is legitimate in a constitutional democracy. Indeed, such doubts do not so much linger as pervade the whole enterprise. Throughout the legal community, the mien of cautious optimism masks a serious anxiety about the validity and worth of the overall enterprise of liberal legalism; the chilling spectre of Vladimir and Estragon haunts lawyers, judges and academics in their collective expectation of Coraf's imminent arrival.

CRITICAL RESISTANCE

As strong a grip as the dream of liberal legalism and rights-talk has on the Canadian constitutional and legal mind, there exists a critical strain in political and jurisprudential thought that refuses to lie down and succumb to the soporific blandishments of the academic and judicial establishment. Such critics do not merely quibble over the present performance of the constitutional project and its personnel, but challenge its whole raison d'être. Resonant with echoes of the celebrated dispute between Galileo and the Italian establishment, it is not merely the legal truth of constitutional nature that is at stake, but the nature of Truth itself. The critics challenge the whole basis for legal theorizing and seek to revise the criteria for distinguishing good knowledge from bad. Although traditional scholars purport to be engaged in a continuing exchange with reality, the critical challenge rejects the basis of that exchange and the nature of that reality. While this confrontation is located on the Canadian terrain of constitutional law and adjudication, it is framed in the larger contest of the struggle over the establishment and enforcement of 'the entrenched clauses of the constitution of the republic of knowledge.'[35]

Such critics are not the kind who attribute the failure of the constitutional project to the personal shortcomings of particular practioners and, in so doing, insulate the project itself from systematic assessment and abandonment. Nor are they the kind who throw up their hands in despair and preach the virtues of a complete retreat from engagement with prevailing institutions and systems of thought. The reformist and the revolutionary both evade critical responsibility: the former tends to apology and the latter to apocalypse. Instead, the responsible critic attempts to cultivate 'a touch of the apostolic.'[36] Although critics can never stand apart from their society, they need not abandon their critical calling to enlist in the ranks of prevailing orthodoxy; they see themselves more as agents provocateurs than as terrorists. More distanced than distant, they measure critical distance in inches and, although they cannot divine Truth or presume to speak in the name of Reason, they can tell hard truths and offer useful reasons. Critics can and should resist oppression on behalf of ordinary people by fostering an antagonism toward privilege rather than an attitude of alienated cynicism or resigned despair. While courts and revolutionaries might feel obliged to trade in certainties and feign an answer for everything, academics must resist such expedient hubris and cultivate a tolerant humility that forever struggles 'to comprehend the world as a question.'[37]

Not surprisingly, such a critical tendency disavows any belief in the existence or arrival of Coraf. It maintains that the actors in the constitutional drama are, at best, naïve ingénues whose desultory efforts betray their noble aspirations and, at worst, duplicitous schemers whose public-spirited manoeuvrings belie their private aspirations for personal power. In both instances, the drama is a dangerous and regrettable diversion from the serious business of organizing and living in a democratic society. At their most cynical, critics contend that if there is anything that gives meaning and purpose to legal life, it is not a beneficent, Godot-like Coraf, but a constitutional incarnation of the bullying and ignoble Pozzo – 'made in God's image!' – which is mistaken for Coraf by the feckless Vladimirs and Estragons. Moreover, in their misguided charade of Charter paternalism, constitutional protagonists engage in a cheery banter of fragile reassurance and false optimism. In sum, the critics contend that the idea of Coraf is so much 'wind in the reeds.'[38]

While they are waiting for Coraf to come, the butt of the pitiful duo's anxious diversions is the hapless and abused Lucky. As he is someone who is in even more straitened misery than their own, Vladimir and Estragon's instinctive sympathy for Lucky soon turns to a vicious contempt: they see him as a convenient foil for their own frustrations and join Pozzo in his uncaring treatment of his slave. Like a disenfranchised citizenry, Lucky's abject servitude is justified on the basis that he is relieved of the onerous responsibility of thinking or acting for himself – 'Leave him in peace! Can't you see he wants to rest?' At the same time that they attribute the civic Lucky's inferiority to 'the natural order,' they also chastise him for his own lack of ambition and deplore his ingratitude for Pozzo's sacrifices as his burdened master. However, like their constitutional counterparts, they are also driven by the fear that a liberated Lucky 'might run amuck at any minute' and turn the tables on his captors – 'Lucky might get going all of a sudden. Then we'd be ballocksed.' As such, judicial Vladimirs and juristic Estragons are inhibited by a potent combination of self-interest, fear, and habit – 'the great deadener' – from accepting that the existence of Coraf is a sad figment of their own fevered imaginations and that any continued belief in its arrival is a cruel denial of people's entitlement to govern themselves.[39]

As the metaphorical comparison with Beckett's *Waiting For Godot* seeks to show, the jurisprudential effort of both judges and jurists to wrap lawyers in the security blanket of abstract philosophy has very definite ideological motivations. Trading off the traditional understanding of philosophy as a meditation on human thought that is separate from the vicissitudes of politics and history, the aim is to underwrite the democratic legitimacy of law and rights through resort to the blue-chip credentials of rationality as the neutral and universal solvent of social conflict.[40] Although contemporary judges and jurists acknowledge that law is political in so many ways, they insist that it remains distinguishable in a few important ways from the more open-ended ideological debates that are the stuff of political struggle. When litigating and adjudicating disputes over the application of rights, lawyers and judges do not indulge their own ideological preferences. While they act as moral agents and political brokers, they do so in a way that is impartial and objective; their interventions and interpretations are sanctioned by the political morality that underpins the law itself. In their Canadian incarnation, they are devoted Corafians, guided and constrained by the moral values and political visions that constitute Coraf.

This hope or aspiration has neither convinced nor persuaded all lawyers or theorists. Others see it more as a nightmare from which people must be awakened. The problem is that the more law is seen as an instrumentality, the less it is able to retain its claims to immanence: the more embedded it becomes, the less transcendental it appears. This leads to a crisis of normative authority and democratic legitimacy. The charge is that philosophical revelation is a poorly disguised style of political advocacy and that the law's immanence is the reflection of lawyers' instrumentalities. Rational discourse does not exist in any pure form, but is thoroughly beholden to its ideological context. As such, law and rights-talk are not so much a rational enterprise as a vast exercise in rationalization. As psychiatrists create 'a monologue of reason about madness,'[41] lawyers tend to establish a sham discourse of reason about the contingent confusion of political and social life. The supposed existence of Coraf is denied and its sovereignty is challenged as being the well-intentioned but self-righteous opinions of a professional elite that can have no claim to constitutional priority over democratic deliberation. In short, law is politics.[42]

For instance, according to conventional wisdom, a constitution is a power map that charts the distribution and diffusion of political authority in society.[43] Within such an understanding, the role of traditional scholars has been to work as official cartographers. Operating in that precarious terrain between rhetoric and reality, they map the evolving contours of political authority and record its historical progress. Yet this is a limited and limiting understanding of a much broader and richer concept. A constitution is an organic process through which states determine the kind of society and citizens that they are and can become. It embraces the dynamic efforts of people to negotiate and establish the institutional and substantive terms of their collective existence; the process, the product, and their dialectical relation are all within its conceptual provenance. It is not a one-time event or a purely practical act of political will. It is an enduring moment and continuing occasion through which societies, sometimes as much by default as design, constitute themselves and define the temporary circumstances and transitory possibilities of their existence. While the formal documents and conventions of nationhood represent a privileged resolution of constitutional debate, each attempt to interpret and reinterpret that compromise gives fresh meaning and effect to it. At the same time, the efforts of workers and the poor to achieve better social programs and a fairer distribution of wealth should also be counted as constitutional expressions. Thus constitutionalism embraces the practical and the utopian, the institutional and the ideological, the real and the imagined, the past and the future. It is the heart of politics; the formal documents of legal statehood no more contain a nation's constitution than an electrocardiogram's chart captures the life of the patient under observation.

The immediate events that led to the constitutional entrenchment of the Charter give the lie to the romantic version that has come to prevail in Corafian quarters. It was not a cathartic moment of constitution-building when politicians set aside their ideological agendas and acted for the national good. The Charter was not so much 'an antidote to the frustration and alienation' of politics,[44] but its grubby and typical continuation by other means. As part of the larger patriation process, the entrenchment of individual rights was one legal tactic in an overall political strategy for constitutional reform that was utilized by Pierre Trudeau's Liberal government. Just as patriation was as much about reshuffling the deck of dominant powers in Canadian politics as it was about effecting national independence from the United Kingdom, so the enactment of the Charter was as much about establishing a centralizing counter-balance to Quebec's demands for a measure of constitutional sovereignty as it was about entrenching the program of liberal legalism. Promoted as a 'People's Package,'[45] the Charter's conception and gestation was a profoundly undemocratic affair in that it was the product of executive deal-making rather than popular consensus; it was as much about federal–provincial relations as anything else.

The political realities of constitutional reform were wrapped in the placating rhetoric of democratic principle. For example, in a Dworkinian accent, Justice minister Jean Chrétien informed a sceptical public that the Charter rendered 'a great service to Canada by taking [controversial] problems away from political debate and allowing the matter to be debated, argued, coolly before the courts with precedent and so on.'[46] Whatever its intentions, however, the government brought into being an ideological entity – Coraf – whose impact would be so deep and broad that it would transform the whole direction and discourse of Canadian constitutionalism. The theory of constitutional supremacy has facilitated the practice of judicial supremacy because what the Constitution means is ultimately what the judges say it means: the saving grace of section 33 has proved to be more honoured in its incantation than in its utilization.[47] Moreover, not only has the Charter taken discrete issues out of the political forums of democratic debate and into the legal arenas of judical pronouncement, but the whole ethos of rights-talk has saturated Canadian politics and society. As well as enumerating specific checks on collective action, the Charter has established a way of talking that frames who people, both individually and socially, can be and who they can become. The expansive possibilities of popular government have been cramped and confined by the restrictive parameters of judicial review. It is the triumph of liberal legalism over the promise of social democracy.

TAKING DEMOCRACY SERIOUSLY

In this book, I want to build on these critical insights and push them further than they have been taken to date in Canadian law and jurisprudence. Heightening a condition that has existed throughout the history of the common law, the advent of the Charter has poignantly demonstrated the indeterminacy of rights-talk; any predictability that it has flows from the general political presuppositions that it rests upon and is framed by. These liberal assumptions offer an account of social life that is neither descriptively accurate nor prescriptively desirable. In short, rights-talk is premised on an impoverished and partial notion of social life: it provides the institutional means to express and entrench a pseudo-tolerant morality of liberal legalism. Despite its recent communal trappings, it depicts individuals as separate and egoistic, striving for a liberty that is self-regarding and a sociability that is hollow. As such, it provides an inherently false account of human community both in its present practice and future possibilities. Rights-talk is not a direction for contemporary Canadian society, but a distraction from its democratic mandate.

Accordingly, this book intends to offer a more satisfying critique of civic life that can better inform the deconstructive and reconstructive dimensions of an uncompromising commitment to the radical cause of unmodified democracy. In particular, I will concentrate most of my efforts on demonstrating the structural and ideological failings of a rights-based resort to courts as a forum for social transformation. A corollary of this will be the occasion to chastise academics for their complicity in the misguided efforts to justify and encourage the increasing tendency to litigate lasting and effective social change. In light of recent interventions in the academic literature and legal practice, the role that rights litigation might play in a revised vision and practice of egalitarian politics is explored. While rights-talk is not always inimical to social transformation, I contend that it is always limited and limiting. At best, I can tolerate, but have little faith in, the possibility of progressive intervention through rights litigation.

In carrying off this stated objective, I will draw on a whole range of eclectic material to make the case against the Canadian political and legal establishment's romance with rights-talk and its judicial enforcement through the Charter. In a sense, the book will follow through on the work of the Realists and put it to more radical use than its practitioners were prepared to do. As the arch-iconoclast Fred Rodell put it, when writing of the formalistic tendency to regard the American Constitution as a source of explicit commands capable of direct implementation by a professional judiciary, 'the alleged logic of constitutional law is equally amorphous, equally unconvincing, equally silly whether the decisions the court is handing down are "good" or "bad", "progressive" or "reactionary", "liberal" or "unliberal".'[48] Moreover, the evidence of the Charter's first decade is that such Canadian decisions are more bad than good and more reactionary than progressive. As such, I will take seriously the quip that there are only two things wrong with the work of Canada's constitutional courts and commentators: its form and substance.

It is the considerable burden of the following chapters to develop and defend the admittedly extravagant claims that have been made in this opening chapter. To this end, I began in this opening chapter to make a serious effort to understand the liberal tradition that Canadian constitutional law and scholarship continues and customizes. However, throughout the book, there are frequent and full references to specific Canadian instances of the judicial exposition and scholarly elaboration of liberal legalism. If I am to succeed in my jurisprudential ambitions, I must offer a convincing and fair account of the contemporary constitutional project from the point of view of its liberal advocates as well as support the critical allegations that I make about that project. In pursuing my critique, I hope to operate at a level that will engage both the jurisprudes and the non-jurisprudes in equal measure: the risk of falling between the stools of the legal theoretician and the practical lawyer is not enough to discourage me from trying to construct a welcoming couch for their joint occupation.

The second and third chapters take issue with claims about the alleged virtues of determinacy and objectivity in the Charter adjudication of rights. In explicating this critique, I intend to clarify the epistemological and political nature of my own critical stance and, in particular, to put to rest the idea that under a postmodern analysis, decision-making is a purely subjective and capricious exercise in judgment. The fourth and fifth chapters address the contested political assumptions and ideological values that underpin and energize the constitutional resolution of disputes over rights. In my attempts to expose the ideological roots and results of such a liberal understanding of society, the aim is to disabuse lawyers and theorists of the idea that the Charter and its judicial enforcement is progressive in any general or lasting way. The last three chapters are more constructive in focus and ambition. Chapter 6 looks at the topical and spirited responses that have been made to the critical assault on rights-talk. Although there are different reasons to revisit and revitalize rights-talk, each contribution attempts to tap into the contemporary pervasiveness of rights-talk and harness it to a more egalitarian vision of social justice. In explaining the danger of such a reworking, I accept that, unlike in some countries, Canada already has an entrenched constitution of rights-talk that narrows and pervades the available means of social change. Accordingly, I introduce and defend a postmodern mode of strategic lawyering that better avoids the traditional pitfalls of liberal legalism and better meets the institutional responsibilities of progressive activism. From there, in the seventh chapter, it is a short step to the adumbration of a critical theory and transformative program that can effect a shift from the reneged promise of liberal rights-talk to the untried possibilities of dialogic democracy. In place of the new liberals' half-hearted appeal to communitarian rhetoric, I propose an expanded account of the modern state and a revised version of involved citizenship that places indeterminacy and personal empowerment at the heart of its progressive practice.

The eighth and final chapter returns to some of the larger themes of this introductory chapter. An ennervating sense of hopelessness saturates Beckett's tragicomedy and issues in a profoundly nihilistic view of life – 'They give birth astride of a grave, the light gleams an instant, then it's night once more.' However, notwithstanding *Waiting For Godot*'s endemic pessimism, it need not only amount to a counsel of despair. Read as a diagnosis of law's present plight rather than as a universal prognosis of the human condition, it can be interpreted as a stirring call to democratic action. Lawyers might hear it as an urgent appeal to their better selves that asks them to forgo the ingrained habits of aristocratic privilege in the name of popular emancipation and democratic governance. Unlike Vladimir and Estragon, it is not enough for lawyers to 'boast' that they have 'kept their appointment' and to find professional solace in 'waiting for Coraf to come.' They must turn their backs on the constitutional farce that they have helped to produce and sustain. Leaving the political stage and handing back directorial authority to citizens is the most noble course to follow. In that way, democracy can become the kind of constitutional dialogue that reunites political vision with civic performance. The result would be a popular drama of heroic proportions.

2

Indeterminately Speaking: From Axiom to Action

Rights-talk is the institutional métier of liberal society. In one neat move, the idea of a legally enforced set of legal rights is claimed to offer the possibility of resolving liberalism's perennial conundrum of how to balance the need for public security with the desire for personal liberty. It endows individuals with certain 'rights' that can be used against state interference so that individual freedom is maintained and a rampant government is checked within certain limits. However, for such a theory to become operative, rights-talk must be capable of moving from abstract statements of good intent to practical instances of proven performance: it must be able to generate concrete responses to particular situations of conflict. Without such a full quality of definitional determinacy, liberals' exhortation to trust in the dispositive force of rights will ring particularly hollow: belief in rights-talk will be revealed as at 'one with belief in witches and unicorns.'[1] The history of liberal political theory and legal practice provides cogent evidence of its failure to achieve that measure of operational efficacy. Contrary to democratic expectations and liberal assumptions, rights-talk is more debilitating than therapeutic.

In countless examples, the short experience of Charter adjudication has richly illustrated and sharply reinforced the common law's long history of futility in rendering legal rights sufficiently determinate to be workable on their own terms. For example, the enumeration of a right to free speech in itself provides no precise answer to how society should deal with thorny problems such as pornography, hate literature, picketing, advertising, soliciting, and the like. Between theoretical axiom and practical application, there always exists in law the surreptitious infiltration and exercise of power to convert general rights into particular results. As such, lawyers and judges must always look beyond rights-talk to give discrete rights any purchase or precision. Touted as a solution in itself, rights-talk is more effectively understood as a convenient screen of institutional propriety behind which competing interests can be accommodated and the ideological choices required to affect such an accommodation can be hidden. Rights-talk is one kind of ideology, not an escape from one: there is no relief from the heavy burden of political choice and institutional responsibility.

In at least five instances, rights-talk fails to provide the determinate guidance and operational efficacy necessary to resolve the self-defined dilemma of a liberal society:

- *There is no neutral standpoint from which to identify who are to be the recipients of such rights* – are corporations, animals, or fetuses covered or are they beyond the purview of rights?
- *There is no non-political way of arriving at what particular group of rights are to be recognized and enforced* – are socioeconomic rights to be included and are collective rights welcome in the family of rights?
- *There is no uncontroversial means of determining the scope and nature of each particular right* – does speech include advertising and can flag-burning and swearing be part of rights-talk?
- *There is no method internal to the theory of rights that can be used to adjudicate upon the clash of competing rights* – does liberty take priority over equality?
- *The recognition that rights are fundamental, but not absolute, gives rise to the difficulty of balancing the public interest against the individuals' claims* – can speech rights be exercised anywhere at any time and are all claims to equal treatment of similar merit?

This chapter will defend the contention that, in all cases, rights-talk fails to ensure the operational efficacy that it promises and requires in order to become a safe methodological haven for advocates and judges in a dangerously ideological world.

THE IDENTITY OF RIGHTS-HOLDERS

The first challenge to be met by the supporters of rights-talk is to identify who can be the holders or recipients of any particular set of rights. Much of the legal debate over the identity of rights-holders is centred upon the definition of who or what a 'person' is. In Canadian discourse, this controversial project has been made more urgent by the constitutional need to resolve the meaning to be given to the Charter's guarantees of different rights to different entities – 'everyone,' 'citizens,' 'persons,' 'members of the public,' and 'individuals.' However, the need to decide the ambit of legal personality has long occupied the legal intellect and political imagination.[2] Indeed, the traditional attributions of legal personality have influenced strongly the task of picking the constitutional cast of rights-holders.

While the popular connotation of 'persons,' 'individuals,' and 'everyone' is to human beings, the legal community has always taken the view that a legal 'person,' 'individual,' or 'everyone' is an abstraction and that such descriptions could be legitimately conferred on both human and non-human entities. For instance, certain rights, such as voting and mobility, are limited to 'citizens' of the state. This is clearly a legal creation. While it evokes strong and resonant images in the democratic mind, it has no precise definition or obvious reference. Although it has constitutional significance in the conferral of rights, citizenship is a status that will have the reach and identity that is legislated for it from time to time by Parliament.[3] Moreover, as a theoretical contrivance, legal history shows that certain humans have not been designated as persons or have been deprived of that ascription. For centuries, Africans were captured and forced into slavery, considered to be non-persons, and treated as chattels to be bought and sold. Also, people who became outlaws had no legal status and could not be murdered. Of course, the status of women has gone through many legal incarnations, and their ability to hold and exercise rights has been severely constrained. It took until as late as 1929 for it to be decided that a 'qualified person' for Senate membership included a woman.[4] Thus, these people were not considered legal citizens by the state and could have no legal rights.

Even accepting that 'persons,' 'individuals,' and 'everyone' include all human beings, there remains the infinitely perplexing and politically controversial question of when human life begins and ends; the determination of these temporal boundaries is crucial in the provenance of rights-talk. While the most obvious and pressing question is whether a fetus is a 'person,' 'individual,' or 'everyone' for the purposes of the debate over abortion,[5] the law has always refused to take a firm or fixed stand on the rights of the unborn. The general rule is that jural rights only vest or arise when the child is born, but there are many exceptions. In criminal law, although homicide cannot be committed against a fetus, the infliction of prenatal injury that prevents birth is criminally actionable.[6] The civil law tends to confer legal benefits on unborn children by way of property entitlement or tort claims as long as they are eventually born alive; they can sue for bequests under will and for injuries sustained in accidents. Not only is the definition of death imprecise and dependent on changing scientific innovation, but the impact of death on the continuing existence of legal rights is variable. Civil actions could be commenced against or by a deceased person's estate, and the body of a deceased person is entitled to certain legal protections.

Nonetheless, whether or not there is some general but indeterminate consensus on the designation of human beings as qualified rights-holders, the question of what non-human entities can claim legal status as rights-holders is almost open-ended in the answers it invites and receives. For instance, in 1925, the Privy Council decided, in an appeal from India, that a Hindu idol was not a movable chattel, but a distinct juridical entity and was 'as clearly a legal person as a man or corporation.'[7] Of course, this decision was made before the same court had bestowed that status on women. As this ridiculous state of affairs reveals, the recognition of legal status is a significant political act and has profound consequences for those affected. Unless persons can cross the threshold of legal personality, they neither have nor can they achieve any existence in the legal scheme of rights. In this way, law and rights-talk have managed successfully to render all manner of people invisible and erase them from social consideration and respect. In the process, the identity of legal non-persons has been determined in accordance with dominant views and political forces. This process continues today as gay men and lesbians have no separate legal identity from heterosexuals and, therefore, no rights in the eyes of the law. In the law's tortured logic, gay men and lesbians are not discriminated against when their relationships are not recognized because the law does not prevent them from being married to someone of the opposite sex.[8]

In giving content and substance to the indeterminate idea of legal personality, the law has not hesitated to extend the status of rights-holders to certain non-human entities. The most celebrated and significant example is the recognition of corporations as legal persons. A clear-cut and important separation is made between the individuals who form and control the corporation and the corporation itself.[9] It is only in the most limited and rare circumstances that the law is prepared to throw back the corporate veil and implicate the individuals who make up the corporation. Indeed, this abstract manoeuvre has had some perverse effects. In *People's*

Pleasure Park Co., a corporation was allowed to purchase land with a restrictive covenant on it against the sale of the property to black owners. The shareholders of the corporation were black. The court held that the corporation was separate from its shareholders and, therefore, the transfer was valid. Accordingly, the shareholders were afforded a legal status through a corporate façade that they were denied as individual human beings.[10] The hold that the corporate legal identity has on the legal intelligence is very powerful and often perverse.

While there are many explanations as to why the law treats economic organizations as legal persons, the fact is that corporations have always enjoyed a special status among non-human entities in matters of legal personality.[11] In Charter matters, the courts have had little hesitation in interpreting 'any person' or 'everyone' to include corporations so that they could benefit from the protection of various rights.[12] The potent social impact of extending rights to corporations and the patent absurdity of treating them as persons is demonstrated by the constitutional protection of commercial speech. The fact is that people speak, corporations do not; they are the artificial mouthpieces of accumulated power. As Wallace Stevens put it, 'To say more than humans with a human voice. / That cannot be: to say human things with more than human voice, that also cannot be; / To speak humanly from the height or depth of human things, that is acutest speech.'[13] The general recognition of corporate rights underscores the constitutive relation between political discourse and social power; corporations acquire a meaningful existence and political influence through the language of legal rights. By insisting that economic fictions are rights-carrying entities at least as deserving of protection and concern as human beings, law and rights-talk combine to constitute a particular social and normative reality.

Relying heavily on its earlier decision in *Ford*, the Supreme Court in *Irwin Toy* emphasized its staunch commitment to the protection of expression as an indispensable pillar in a democratic and pluralistic society.[14] As a fundamental value to the community and the individual, the Court stated that free expression is 'little less vital to man's mind and spirit than breathing is to his physical existence.'[15] Repeating at length that the law's solicitude for free speech centres upon 'individual self-fulfillment and human flourishing,'[16] whether as an end in itself or as a means to truth-finding and democratic participation, the Court managed to overlook the fact that the Irwin Toy company is not human, but only a human creation. It is a corporation and no more human than the teddy bears and toys it makes: the only 'flourishing' and 'fulfillment' it is concerned with are its own economic flourishing and financial fulfilment. The ludicrous logic of such a fictitious argument is that if IBM or Domtar can be presumed to speak, perhaps they should be able to vote and be candidates for political office (or is that the idea?).

The injustice of treating an economic unit such as a corporation as a human being and conferring constitutional rights upon it was fully revealed, but not openly recognized, by the Supreme Court itself. At the end of the majority's judgment, there was a short digression on whether a corporation can invoke the Charter's section 7 'right to life, liberty and security of the person.' This was occasioned by the fact that the challenged legislation imposed imprisonment and fines on violators. The Court held that while officers of the corporation would be able to explore the possible protective implications of such rights, the corporation itself would not. As the Court said, 'it is *nonsensical* to speak of a corporation being put in jail.'[17] It most certainly is nonsensical. But it is no less nonsensical to speak of a corporation speaking. Indeed, the courts have effectively gone so far as to say that although the right to freedom of conscience and religion does not apply to corporations because they cannot hold religious beliefs, they can invoke the right as a defence to a criminal charge; no personal corporation can be convicted under a law that is constitutionally flawed.[18] Accordingly, not only do corporations receive the direct benefits of certain rights, such as freedom of speech, they can also indirectly rely on rights, such as freedom of conscience, that do not directly extend to them.

The organizational analogue on the labour side of business is the union, but its traditional identity in Anglo-Canadian law has always been very different from that of corporations. The language of rights-talk suggests a functional equality between labour and corporations that is clearly not the case. While a union can enter into contracts and sue in its own name, it has not been granted the privileges of a separate legal personality. As separate legal entities, corporations have more 'rights' than the individuals that make up the corporation because, although corporations are attributed personal characteristics, they are free from personal punishment, such as imprisonment. Unions and their members have no such protection. Indeed, in constitutional matters, the union can initiate litigation but it cannot claim any constitutional rights for itself. Unlike a corporation, a union can only benefit indirectly from those rights that are held directly by others. For instance, the courts have insisted that the rights of assembly and association are individual, not collective rights and cannot be exercised by associations. The judicial interpretation of the Charter goes so far as to say that freedom of association does not include the right to strike or bargain collectively because this would confer rights on associations that are more extensive than those possessed by individuals.[19] But this line of argument only operates by doctrinal sleight of hand; the courts could easily treat labour organizations as individuals and endorse such rights for them. The fact that they have effectively done this for corporations serves to underline the courts' inconsistency and partiality.

Once it is decided to bring artificial economic entities within the discursive provenance of rights-talk, it is extremely difficult to resist, as a matter of logic or consistency, the claim to rights made on behalf of other non-human, but less artificial entities. There is a vigorous philosophical and ethical lobby to recognize animal rights. The contention is that the arguments that support human rights are over-inclusive and actually encompass animals. As they have the capacity to reason and experience pain, animals deserve basic protection from others in the same way that vulnerable humans do: every living creature has an interest in its own survival and that of the species. Moreover, as the atrophy of the capacity to think or suffer does not deprive humans of their rights, the fact of life itself ought to be sufficient to justify the availability of protectable rights among non-human beings.[20] Of course, the recognition of animals as the bearers of rights raises the correlative problems of the nature and limits of such rights and the criteria of sufficient and proportional justification for their infringement.

Similarly, when it is conceded that there might well be a case for extending rights to animals, the corollary is not far behind that all living creatures or natural objects are entitled to some rudimentary rights. For instance, Christopher Stone has 'quite seriously propos[ed] that we give legal rights to forests, oceans, rivers and other so-called "natural objects" in the environment – indeed to the natural environment as a whole.'[21] The central claim is that natural objects, both animate and inanimate, possess moral worth and deserve to be valued *for themselves*, not merely as resources for social exploitation and environmental degradation. By recognizing rights in such entities, advocates insist that it might be possible to provide operational protection to the environment. Furthermore, in a world in which rights-talk has special salience and priority, this might encourage a symbolic affirmation of the intrinsic value of nature. While this gambit may seem instinctively silly, it gains a semblance of plausibility when it is remembered that the law has afforded legal personality and rights to idols and corporations. Mindful of rights' incorrigible indeterminacy, it is not surprising that the threshold question of who or what can be a rights-holder resists final resolution and any answers must be tentative and provisional. Rights-talk does not stand outside the dynamic play of politics, but is inescapably inside its contingent contestation. The point is not that animals or trees should not be protected or considered in social living, but that rights-talk is a singularly unhelpful and inappropriate medium through which to tackle environmental concerns. It lacks the necessary nuance and subtlety to make sense of a complex world.

THE CONTENTS OF RIGHTS-TALK

While there is an almost universal appeal to rights, there is little or no agreement on the content of rights-talk. At different times and in different places, the idea of rights has been given varied substance and form. The history of rights-talk has been a discursive site for shifting claims over the need to place certain claims and values beyond the cavil of political expediency and government authority. In order to preserve rights-talk's dominant position in ideological debate, the pressing concern has been to distinguish certain fundamental or minimal rights that go to the core of rights-talk; mere wants or preferences are to be excluded from its privileged métier. However, engagements over the identities of these fundamental rights have been particularly divisive. More than any other item on the political agenda, the divergence of opinion and its heated articulation work to emphasize that rights are part of partisan politics, not a precondition or boundary to the legitimate realm of contested politics. In its traditional performance, debate manages both to devalue rights-talk by excluding some values that are clearly fundamental and to trivialize rights-talk by including some claims that are clearly not fundamental.

The basic tension is between the orientation of rights around the notions of civil claims and social entitlements. Civil rights are traditionally thought to encompass life, liberty, and security of the person; freedom from cruel and unusual punishment, and arbitrary arrest; fair trial; and freedom of movement, speech, conscience, religion, peaceful assembly, and voting. In contrast, social rights are most often used to include work, social security, leisure, adequate standard of living, health, education, and housing. Interestingly, the right to the enjoyment of one's own property and not to be deprived of it arbitrarily has historically been associated with civil rights, even though it clearly speaks to questions of economic rather than political entitlement. This competing allegiance to civil or social rights is, of course, traceable to the different political traditions of liberalism and socialism that energize the contending forces in the rights debate. In contrast to the civil rights advocates who concentrate on the political liberty of individuals from government abuse, the social rights proponents rely on a notion of collective responsibility that expects the state to intervene actively to ensure an equitable distribution of opportunities and resources. While these disparate ideologies often overlap in their concerns, they suggest a very different approach to the interpretation and ambit of their shared rights. This is particularly so in regard to the meaning of equality.[22]

In North America, liberal individualism still remains the predominant ideology. Although a progressive form of welfare individualism is sensitive to the dangers of too doctrinaire a reliance upon an individualistic vision of social justice and seeks to combine 'the pursuit of individuality with sociality and membership in a community,'[23] there remains a liberal preference for the priority of civil rights over social rights. For instance, in his elaborate and influential philosophy, John Rawls sanctions two basic principles of liberty: the equal right to the most extensive total system of equal basic liberties compatible with a similar system of liberty for all and the diminution of economic inequalities. However, he makes it clear that the former takes precedence over the latter and that it is never justifiable to restrict individual liberty in the name of social equality.[24] In this, Rawls is the latest progeny in a long line of liberal individualists that includes Thomas Hobbes, John Locke, and John Stuart Mill.

The abiding problem with this tradition is, quite simply, that such reasoning plays fast and loose with the idea of basic or fundamental rights. As John Hart Ely so tellingly observes, 'watch most fundamental rights theorists start edging towards the door when someone mentions jobs, food or housing; those are important, sure, but they aren't *fundamental*.'[25] However, without food or shelter, the so-called basic rights of speech, association, and conscience seem hollow and beside the point. To be blunt, starving, poor, or dead people have no need of civil rights. If constitutions are supposed to be documents that articulate those fundamental values and beliefs to which a society aspires and to establish the institutional and substantive terms of its existence, the failure to guarantee the basic means for survival or subsistence is a colossal arrogance or crass oversight. In a Canadian society in which hunger and homelessness are still a fact of social life, such an omission reflects the political dominance of a middle class whose preoccupation and indifference underpin the constitutional conversation of fundamental rights.[26]

In the twentieth century, the constitutions of many countries, as well as a variety of regional and international treaties, promulgate the protection of social rights. Of over half of the written constitutions in the world that contain social rights, about 60 constitutions refer to the right to work and more than 55 refer to the right to health care and social assistance or security. In addition, many countries, including Canada, are signatories to the International Covenant on Economic, Social and Cultural Rights, which protects the right to work, leisure, adequate standard of living, social services, social security, health care, and education. However, the formal acknowledgment of rights has always been doggedly civil in substance and effect. In the debate in the late 1950s around the Canadian Bill of Rights, the traditional and limited understanding of rights-talk was successfully invoked. Stressing the negative thrust of rights and their purported apolitical character, Bora Laskin argued that civil liberties were more fundamental than social rights and stood on a more 'exalted plane' that implicated no particular pattern of economic planning.[27]

This general orientation toward a civil libertarian rather than socio-economic vision of rights was entrenched in 1982 in the Charter of Rights and Freedoms. The vast bulk of its rights are civil and political in their focus and consequence. While there are provisions that relate to language and public services that make concessions to a more socialistic imagination, the overall ambience of the Constitution is distinctly liberal and individualist. The most significant impact of a non-liberal conception of rights is the equality section. Not only has there been an explicit expansion of the prohibited grounds of discrimination to include age and disability as well as race, national origin, religion, and gender, but there has been an improved guarantee of equal benefits of the law as well as equal protection of the law. Influenced by a more substantive sense of equality, section 15(2) of the Charter expressly permits an affirmative-action initiative 'that has as its object the amelioration of conditions of disadvantaged individuals or groups.' Nonetheless, despite (or, perhaps, because of) these progressive reforms, the question of what rights are fundamental and essential features of rights-talk is more open and less determinate than it ever has been. Contingency permeates the whole debate in and around rights-talk.

The danger of this almost limitless proliferation of rights is that as people try to express all their claims and aspirations within its one-dimensional vocabulary, rights-talk becomes almost infinite in its scope. As such, it begins to trivialize its original motivation to protect fundamental values and personal integrity. By embracing any and all interests, rights-talk loses its special cadence and becomes a vacuous mode of political discourse. The sweep of rights-talk is becoming so broad that people are beginning to frame life-style preferences in its inviting rhetoric. For example, in consequence of recent efforts to abate smoking, some people have claimed a particular right to smoke as part of their more general right to pursue a personal life-style and be free of social persecution. As one pundit put it:

> The most interesting phenomenon of the 90's has got to be the persecution of smokers. There seems to be a form of persecution beyond reproach these days and it's consequently becoming ubiquitous and, quite frankly, obnoxious. No one will deny that smoking is a health risk and that second hand smoke poses a risk to others. But isn't smoking like choosing to drink or eat fatty foods, a personal life-style choice? It's surprising that these days when everyone is generally so careful not to interfere with anybody's rights or freedoms, it's not objectionable to interfere with the right to smoke. What's going on here? Since when is it permissible to allow a minority to be so systematically harassed?[28]

The problem with this exaggerated plea for tolerance is not so much that it is wrong-headed: plenty of people were quick to assert their own prior right to breathe clean air and enjoy a smoke-free environment. The difficulty is that there is no viable way *within* the rights tradition to reject conclusively the possibility of a right to smoke. Rights-talk cannot determine its own jurisdictional reach and substantive content. To fix the limits and contents of rights, resort must be made to its informing context of normative values and ideological assumptions. Far from providing a non-political vocabulary through which to engage in and resolve disputed issues of social living, rights-talk can only function if there already exists agreement on those very contested values. As such, rights-talk is constitutionally incapable of fulfilling the ameliorative task that its champions set for it. Thus, the decision to include or not include shelter, speech, or smoking in the canon of rights is an ideological one that colours every utterance and application of rights-talk.

THE SCOPE OF RIGHTS

The ringing affirmation of the right to liberty or equality is a powerful force in political debate. Rights-talk has been a popular rallying call for the disadvantaged and oppressed in the historical struggle for human dignity and social justice. The problem is that even when there is some agreement on which rights are fundamental, their meaning is far from clear. As in the Charter, the enumerated rights are characterized by their indeterminacy: they can mean different things to different people at different times. Indeed, their malleability is one of the reasons why they enjoy such widespread public support. While the rights' plasticity is an inconvenience in specific disputes, it is an attraction in general terms. Rights, such as equality, liberty, and freedom of association, are central to the Charter and its political appeal. Yet these rights have no definite or uncontroversial meaning. They are contested concepts; the struggle to fix them with determinate meaning has been a major and elusive preoccupation of continuing political debate. In an important sense, rights are like empty that will not stand up on their own without being filled with some political content. 'Who fills them?' and 'with what?' are the key questions for Canadian law and politics.

The best example of rights' indeterminacy is the popular principle of equality. Although this principle receives almost universal approval, there is very little agreement on its precise scope and meaning or on its relation to other fundamental rights. There are many competing conceptions of equality. Two related illustrations will suffice to make the point. One travels the axis of formal and substantive values. Some commentators espouse a formal vision of equality that simply demands that all individuals be *treated* equally. Others urge the embrace of a more substantive vision of equality that looks to ensure that all individuals are *made* equal in their condition. The other related and contradictory understanding of equality concerns its attachment to an idea of sameness or difference. Some maintain that the aspiration to an equal society is to guarantee that everyone is treated the same. Others insist that an equality ethic is only satisfied when those who are similarly situated are dealt with in the same way and those who are differently situated are dealt with differently. On both axes, for instance, it is obvious that it will not be possible to make the poor equal in condition to the rich by simply treating them the same. Thus, while women's rights groups invoke equality to support special programs for women, men's rights groups invoke equality to attack special programs for women.[29]

The enduring attraction of equality is its lack of content or, more accurately, its almost inexhaustable capacity to accommodate all manner of different aspirations and standards. At its most beguiling, the norm of equality has been interpreted by some courts as being met by providing nothing to everyone.[30] To be intelligible, a principle of equality must incorporate some external values to decide which categories are to be employed in marking out those persons and treatments that are alike and unalike. Of course, once these external values are identified, equality becomes a secondary and derivative principle; it amounts to a subsidiary check on a prior commitment to particular values. The one independent and important function of an equality provision is to ensure that those substantial and substantive entitlements that are decided upon are available to the community at large.[31] These substantive entitlements, of course, are themselves the subject of fierce ideological confrontation. While there is some consensus over discriminating treatment based on gender or race, there is no agreement over the number of prohibited categories. This is clearly revealed in the litigation over sexual orientation as a form of unconstitutional discrimination. Indeed, the Charter leaves the list of grounds partially open. For example, the relevance and centrality of 'wealth' (or lack thereof) as a standard to be used in the resort to the equality norm go to the heart of ideological controversy. Not surprisingly, considering its massive implications for social arrangements, the courts have not taken this possibility seriously.[32]

An example of equality's indeterminacy is the challenge to certain forms of regulation that allegedly discriminate on the basis of age. Although some seem to counsel a crude approach in which the use of age as a criterion for distributing benefits and costs is considered illegitimate, the question of age discrimination raises much more subtle issues. Legislation that stipulates a minimum age for being able to drink alcohol or drive a car is considered uncontroversial and approved by large sectors of society. However, the validity of legislation that requires mandatory retirement at a specified age has provoked considerable division of opinion, even among those who usually share similar visions of social justice. In such disputes, an invocation of equality will do nothing to resolve the underlying issue. It will require the practitioners of rights-talk to choose one conception of equality over another. In so doing, they will have gone outside rights-talk and resorted to competing political or moral theories. Accordingly, rights-talk will not have resolved ideological conflict, but will have provided a partial context for its continuing performance.

In *Andrews*, the Supreme Court of Canada tackled the issue of delineating the nature and scope of equality.[33] A majority of the Court held that the Charter gave non-citizens the right to practise law in British Columbia. The importance of the decision lies in the Court's being resigned to the open-ended nature of equality rights and taking steps to limit the use of those rights by corporations and other powerful interests. However, in matters of rights-talk, it remains the case that inside every silver lining there lurks a cloud. Speaking for the Court, Justice McIntyre set out a three-step approach to equality claims:

- First, complainants must show that legislation treats them differently or affects them adversely. Yet not every difference in treatment qualifies for Charter protection. Protection is limited to differences relating to an enumerated Charter ground – 'race, national or ethnic origin, colour, religion, sex, age or mental or physical disability' – or to analogous grounds, like citizenship, 'which involve prejudice or disadvantage.'[34]
- Second, complainants must show that the distinction or adverse effect is 'discriminatory' – that it imposes burdens or withholds benefits based on grounds relating to personal characteristics of an individual or group. 'Distinctions based upon personal characteristics attributed to an individual solely on the basis of association with a group will rarely escape the charge of discrimination, while those based on an individual's merits and capacities will rarely be so classed.'[35]
- Third, a discriminatory law will survive Charter scrutiny if it represents a 'reasonable limit' on equality rights within the meaning of section 1. The onus for satisfying this standard rests with those seeking to uphold the law, usually governments.

What does all of this amount to? In particular, what does it mean for the disadvantaged? The restriction of equality rights to enumerated and analogous grounds of discrimination is undoubtedly a positive development. Corporations and others are unlikely to be able to bring equality claims attacking all manner of regulatory distinctions. But the remainder of the decision is so strewn with uncertainties and contradictions that, like the conceptual sack of equality itself, it can be made to stand for virtually any proposition that its users wish. For example, some have interpreted the second requirement as restricting the benefit of equality rights to members of socially disadvantaged groups. According to this interpretation, men would be unable to invoke gender equality to challenge special programs for women; whites would be unable to rely upon racial equality to attack legislation favouring Natives. Yet it is not clear that this is what the Court is saying. To be sure, there is plenty of rhetoric about 'disadvantage.' However, the actual definition of discrimination adopted by McIntyre J. suggests that real disadvantage need not be shown in order to bring an equality rights claim. A formal disadvantage flowing from a legislative distinction may be enough.

Underlying this ambiguity is the fact that while McIntyre J. purports to reject an Aristotelian conception of equality (one that requires that likes be treated alike and unalikes be treated differently), the division he embraces between distinctions based upon 'personal characteristics' and those based upon 'merits and capacities' is little more than a vacuous restatement of Aristotle's formula. Indeed, it was Aristotle who argued that equality requires 'that awards should be "according to merit".'[36] The confusion is further heightened by a disagreement within the Court concerning the application of section 1. While Justice McIntyre was prepared to uphold the citizenship requirement as a 'reasonable limit' on equality rights, the majority of judges were not. They struck the requirement down. In short, while the case is helpful in limiting the scope of equality rights, it is singularly unhelpful in defining what those rights mean. On this key issue, the decision is a masterpiece of obfuscation. Equality means whatever future judges want it to mean.

On at least one point, however, the Court is all too clear. Although ignored or overlooked by most commentators, it is a point whose painful effects the disadvantaged and underprivileged will recognize and continue to experience. The Court's decision is premised on the assumption that the Charter is concerned only with inequalities that can be linked to some legislative source. Justice McIntyre insists that 'discriminatory measures having the force of law' constitute the 'evil' against which the Charter's equality guarantee is directed. The Charter 'does not provide for equality between individuals or groups within society in a general or abstract sense, nor does it impose on individuals or groups an obligation to accord equal treatment of others.'[37] In other words, oppression and inequality that flow from private conduct or from the seemingly natural operation of the market economy lie beyond the scope of the Charter's remedies. By implication, the Charter places no obligation on governments to take positive measures to redress such inequalities. The underlying disparities in wealth and power that are the root cause of social inequality and the systemic practices that reinforce them remain safely hidden from Charter scrutiny. Indeed, this is precisely the issue that was dealt with in *Symes*.[38] Although the case raises complex matters of tax and business policy, the focus of Charter debate around *Symes* fails to grasp that the provision of affordable day care will not be improved by subsidizing the more financially advantaged in society through tax relief; such remedies are inadequate and entrench, not reduce, the vast disparities in private wealth distribution.

The right to liberty is similarly indeterminate in scope and regressive in application. For instance, some subscribe to a negative vision of liberty and conceive of it as a right not to be interfered with by others. Others subscribe to a positive vision of liberty and prefer to represent it as the right to demand from others a greater share of social resources. Again, these visions are not only distinct, but are mutually contradictory. For instance, while property owners claim the liberty to exclude other people from their land, those without property claim the liberty to enter that land: the farmer of grazing sheep and the owner of a marauding dog both can frame their claims in the rhetoric of liberty. The validity of their competing assertions depends not upon the right to liberty, but upon the background conditions and sense of priorities that are seen to support and inform its operation. As with equality, competing liberty claims can only be resolved by reference to a set of normative values and ideological commitments that are extraneous to rights-talk.

Freedom of association is another Charter right that is susceptible to contradictory interpretations. Those who subscribe to a more individualistic conception of freedom of association consider that freedom to comprise a guarantee to individuals of the privilege to associate (or dissociate) as they see fit; the associated individuals can never do more as a group than they could do as individuals acting on their own account. Others subscribe to a more collectivist conception of freedom of association that understands freedom as being a guarantee of the right to act in concert to protect and promote associational activities. Again, both these positions can be invoked to support contradictory conclusions. For instance, while trade unionists look to freedom of association to support the power of unions to act on behalf of all employees at a workplace,[39] those who oppose trade unions point to the freedom of individual employees to dissociate themselves from unionized activity.[40] Rights are like tools; what they do will depend on the intentions and dexterity of those who have their hands upon them.

Accordingly, any consensus on the existence and desirability of certain rights is fragile and masks a deeper lack of consensus on the meaning and application of those rights. This disagreement represents a profound taking of sides on the operative assumptions and underlying visions that inform the activities and allegiances of political antagonists. At bottom, they are a matter of 'deep-seated preferences.'[41] The appearance of any consensus is illusory *even at the point of definition*. Nevertheless, the fact that rights are indeterminate in theory does not mean that their interpretation by the courts in practice cannot be predicted with some degree of confidence or certainty. The interpretation given to the different rights is informed and reinforced by the values of the legal system. In turn, these norms reflect the attitudes and assumptions of the legal and political elites.[42] These values point in the direction of formal equality, negative liberty, and an individualistic conception of associational rights. This represents the hidden agenda of the Charter. So long as it remains hidden, people of all stations and political persuasions will see in the Charter something to placate or reassure them. It is only when groups, such as women and workers, experience that agenda openly and directly that the illusion of social consensus, which the abstract rights themselves engender, will be threatened. Like all illusions, the determinacy of rights-talk is suspended in the consciousness of citizens rather than embedded in the reality of political conditions.

COMPETING CLAIMS OF RIGHTS-TALK

Conflicts not only arise within Charter rights and the struggle to fix their scope and limits; there is also a distinct antagonism between these rights. These tensions between rights cannot be resolved by some vague and hopeful appeal to an elusive social consensus. The courts can only act as a venue for the ceaseless efforts to negotiate competing claims. Legal doctrine is not a reflected embodiment of one indwelling and sufficient vision of social justice, but is the formal site for the attempted, but elusive, blending and reconciliation of these competing visions. The temporary accommodations made are more a result of political expediency than ideological purity.[43] For instance, the tension between the rights of equality and liberty represents a classic conflict; it has energized a whole tradition of political theory and debate. Under the Charter, the courts are entrusted with the thankless task of providing an answer to this conceptually fraught and politically charged conundrum. The Charter itself offers no guidance at all on how claims framed in the competing rhetoric of 'liberty' and 'equality' are to be resolved. As such, the judges are on a sleeveless errand when it comes to resolving the competition between rights in a way that is intellectually consistent or compelling.

A prime example of this dilemma is provided by the pre-Charter case of *Gay Alliance*.[44] In that case, *Gay Alliance* relied on the British Columbia Human Rights Code to attack the *Vancouver Sun*'s policy of denying classified advertising to gay groups. A Board of Inquiry found for the Alliance, holding that the *Sun*'s policy denied citizens equal access to services customarily provided to the public at large. When the case went to the courts, the *Sun* argued that the Human Rights Code should not be applied to the present situation because doing so would violate its fundamental freedom of the press. In order to reach a decision, the courts were forced to choose between competing rights – whether the equality rights of gays and lesbians to services provided to the public were to take precedence over the liberty of newspaper owners to publish what they wanted. In the Supreme Court of Canada, the majority plumped for liberty over equality: there was not even a rudimentary attempt to explain the reasons for preferring one right over the other. In such circumstances, to talk of consensus is far-fetched; there was no agreement even among the members of the Court, let alone among the community at large.

Another telling example of the law's instinctive preference for liberty over equality in balancing rights is the English case of *Wheeler*.[45] A local council allowed the Leicester Football Club to use a recreation ground for matches and general training. Three of the Leicester players were selected by the English national team to tour South Africa. After much public uproar among Leicester's large ethnic community, the council decided that unless the club officials were prepared to condemn the tour and urge its players not to play, it would suspend the club's use of its recreation ground. Although the club joined with the council in condemning apartheid, it refused to comply with the council's request. After the tour had taken place, the council banned the club from using the recreation ground for twelve months. While framed in the doctrinal rhetoric of 'administrative reasonableness,' the decision of the House of Lords to invalidate the council's decision was based squarely on the understanding that the right to free speech is always prior to the need to promote good race relations. Indeed, opining that 'the laws of [England] are not like the laws of Nazi Germany,'[46] the law lords went so far as to declare that the council had acted in a way that was so absurd that no sensible person could ever dream that it lay within the powers of the council.

This itself is an absurd and offensive conclusion. Rather than think in terms of free speech, the council was more concerned to enhance racial equality. Unlike the courts, it considered the objectives of equality to be more important than those of free speech in the struggle for improved social justice. While there is no neutral or objective way to fix the relative ordering of equality and liberty, a different cluster and priority of considerations arise if *Wheeler* is treated as primarily a case about equality and race relations rather than about liberty and freedom of speech. Importantly, there is no longer any need to construe the council's action as an exercise of power that undermines the Rule of Law and exposes a few innocent individuals from the unbridled force of majoritarian rule. In fact, *Wheeler* is exactly the opposite case because a majority of local citizens, through the council's decision, made a firm commitment to the democratic value of promoting enhanced race relations and respecting the interests of ethnic minorities. In essence, *Wheeler* brought into sharp focus a deep and enduring disagreement between two competing conceptions of social justice: it pitted the council's espousal of an egalitarian justification against the courts' adherence to a libertarian ethic.[47]

The council's preference for an equality ethic is, of course, far from radical or novel. Concomitant with a commitment to freedom of speech, many countries have enacted proscriptions against incitement to racial hatred. By sanctioning such offences, the courts do not abandon people to majoritarian tyranny, but opt for an egalitarian vision of social justice over a libertarian one. By allowing for policies that encourage racial harmony, the courts do not forsake the Rule of Law, but support a more progressive rendering of the judicial role than a traditional one. In either case, the courts must take a political stand. It is not that they have strayed into the debate over equality and liberty; there is no way not to be part of that debate. The only choices available are those of candour or subterfuge. In *Wheeler*, the courts chose liberty over equality and subterfuge over candour; the council chose equality over liberty and candour over subterfuge. It is a question of ideological alignment, not an internal dispute within rights-talk.

In *Keegstra*, the Supreme Court of Canada upheld the constitutionality of criminal laws against the dissemination of hate literature, but it did so in a roundabout and less-than-convincing way.[48] Keegstra was charged with wilfully promoting hatred by teaching anti-Semitic lessons to his students; although his right to free speech under section 2(b) was held to have been infringed, the Criminal Code provisions were saved under section 1's 'reasonable limits' clause. The majority of the Court took it as a given that free speech was the dominant principle and indicated that the equality guarantee under section 15 should not be used to limit or interpret that right: recourse to the values of equality were only important as buttresses to the 'reasonable limits' analysis under section 1.[49] The dissent was even more dismissive of equality concerns and held that section 15's prohibition of racism was not applicable at all to speech matters. For all the members of the Court, free speech simply trumped any other competing rights claim because it had 'its own intrinsic value.'[50] Accordingly, the Court implicitly relied on a hierarchy of rights whose probity was based more on ideological predisposition than legal argument.

Another classic conflict that has riven debate in political theory is the conflict between individual and collective rights. Two cases testify to the enduring and pervasive irreconcilability of these rights. The first case concerns the dispute surrounding denominational school rights in Ontario. When the Ontario government extended public funding to Roman Catholic high schools, it sought to justify its action on the basis that such funding was required by the original constitutional compact that afforded protection to denominational schools. Other religious groups however took a different view. They contended that the funding amounted to discrimination on the grounds of religion and was a denial of their equality rights. As usual, it was left to the Supreme Court of Canada to make a choice between denominational rights and equality rights. The Court *chose*, for there is no other word for it, denominational rights over equality rights. The reasoning of the Court is more conclusory than explanatory.[51] It would take a particularly inspired or desperate imagination to argue that this choice was based upon a consensus that the courts were able to detect within the larger Canadian community.

The second example is the controversy concerning Quebec's language laws.[52] In this case, shopkeepers challenged the constitutional authority of the Quebec government to require that all signs be in the French language alone. The province defended its course of action by claiming to act on behalf of the Québécois collectivity in order to protect the precarious nature of its cultural heritage in light of its isolation within a predominantly English-speaking North America. The shopkeepers, on the other hand, resorted to the familiar arguments of individual freedom. They contended that the interests of the collectivity could never trump the rights of its individual members. Although the Supreme Court had decided on an earlier occasion that 'though couched in individualistic terms, language rights, by their nature, are intimately and profoundly social,'[53] it decided that the individual shopkeepers' freedom of expression took constitutional priority over the French collectivity's right to preserve its language and cultural heritage.

In each of these disputes, the Court is presented with an unenviable task. In order to meet the challenge, the courts and the apologists for rights-talk have fallen back increasingly on the interpretive practice of 'balancing' because 'no right can be regarded as absolute ... [and] the rights of one will inevitably come into conflict with the rights of others ... it is obvious that all rights must be limited in the interest of preserving a social structure in which each right may receive protection without undue interference with others.'[54] The major thrust of this rudimentary methodology is to identify different interests, attribute respective values to them, and weigh them on a constitutional scale. However, rather than amount to a solution to the judicial dilemma of constitutional legitimacy, balancing seems to concede the fundamental incommensurability of constitutional argument. Simply seeking to make the political best of a bad legal job, it is a weak metaphor for political haggling. For all its open-endedness, balancing seems to be a convenient screen behind which the thumb of individualism can be placed upon the illusory constitutional scales of social justice. In the conflict between competing claims, rights-talk itself is dumb and concedes dominion to deeper ideological forces.

RIGHTS AND THE PUBLIC INTEREST

As well as there being competition within and between the Charter's enumerated rights, there is a fifth and final category of conflict. This occurs between Charter rights and competing social interests. Indeed, this kind of conflict arises in virtually all Charter cases. While it most explicitly occurs in the application of section 1's injunction to place reasonable limits on the interpretation of the Charter's fundamental freedoms, it is an implicit component of the process of ascertaining the limit to the fundamental rights themselves. It is tempting to presume that where there is a conflict between a right and some other interest, a commitment to rights-talk would mean that the competing interest would have to give way; any other response would seem to reduce the importance of rights-talk to mere window-dressing. But even the strongest rights advocates recognize that there are cases in which rights claims should yield to competing social considerations.[55] While rights are considered to be fundamental, they are not defended as being absolute. For instance, the right to equality does not entitle a six-year-old to obtain a driver's licence or an alcoholic drink. The question, therefore, is not *whether* Charter rights should yield to competing social values, but *when* they should yield. Any answer to this puzzle will certainly not be found within the confines of rights-talk, but will have to be resolved by reference to some set of values that are outside and prior to rights-talk.

The Charter's section 1 stipulates that its guaranteed rights and freedoms are 'subject only to such reasonable limits prescribed by law as can be demonstrably justified in a free and democratic society.' The obvious implication is that 'a free and democratic society' is one in which rights-talk has an important role but not one that takes precedence over other important values. Indeed, the constitutional scheme seems to countenance and mandate that certain interests and concerns are *more* important and ought to trump rights-talk: the exercise of rights can and will be inimical to the realization of a free and democratic society. As Chief Justice Dickson put it, 'the underlying values of a free and democratic society both guarantee the rights in the Charter and, in appropriate circumstances, justify limitations on those rights.'[56] However, a pervasive and obvious problem for any resort to the values of 'a free and democratic society' is the task of giving some meaning and substance to its open-ended phrasing. Far from being a technical and legal endeavour, this goes to the heart of the historical struggle to confront the most profound issues on the ideological agenda. Moreover, the possibility that the conflict between rights and what might be called the greater public interest can be settled by resort to a prevailing social consensus is illusory and misleading. Such disputes speak to the fractures in community values, not to their availability as a source of normative instruction.

Two short examples suffice to make this general point. The first concerns provincial Sunday closing laws. These were attacked in *Edwards Books*.[57] The main thrust of the challenge was that such laws favoured the interests of the Christian community. In effect, Jews and other non-Christians were required by law to close on a Sunday and by their religions on their regular sabbath, whereas Christians were only obliged to close on one day of the week because the law confirmed to Christian religion. The Supreme Court of Canada agreed with this reasoning and held that the legislation was a denial of religious freedom. However, the majority of the Court went on to uphold the legislation on the basis that it was necessary to preserve a common day of rest; the selection of Sunday, while originally motivated by religious considerations, was now defensible as a secular and traditional choice. For present purposes, the important point is that the courts believed that the goal of preserving a common day of rest was sufficiently important to warrant an important Charter right being overridden. The court revealed no metric by which this decision could be guided or judged; personal intuition was passed off as impersonal judgment. The resort to some broader social consensus was unavailable because, as is so often the case, a breakdown in such consensus was at the root of the litigation.

A second example concerns laws banning secondary picketing. These were attacked in *Dolphin Delivery*.[58] The basis of the challenge was that the ban on secondary picketing violated the free speech of employees. The Supreme Court of Canada held that such laws were justifiable. Although the employees' freedom of speech was breached, the legislation was valid because it protected the economic interests of property owners and the community at large. Again, this was a goal that the Court judged to be sufficiently important to justify a violation of Charter rights. There is nothing in the Charter, in the judgments of the courts, or, especially, in any appeal to community consensus that provides a neutral justification for this decision about the priority of property rights over free-speech claims. Indeed, the Charter explicitly excluded the protection of constitutional rights-talk. In short, the appeal to community consensus is merely a convenient, if unintentional, ruse to hide the informing values and visions of social justice that drive and determine such difficult choices. While this element of choice can be hidden, it can never be expunged entirely.

In order to give some determinate shape and substance to section 1, the courts have developed certain doctrinal techniques and contrivances that are intended to limit and neutralize the open and political character of its constitutional task. While the primary responsibility for setting the details of this social agenda and their implementation is for Parliament, the courts have decided that they have a crucial role to play in ensuring that the legislative duty of social engineering is undertaken in a way that is least restrictive of individuals' freedom. The method for achieving this is the *Oakes* test.[59] Whereas there ought to be general deference to Parliament's choice of policy objectives, the courts must be vigilant and aggressive in policing the means employed to accomplish these ends. For the application of the *Oakes* test to pass jurisprudential muster, it must be shown that, unsupplemented by external values and policies, it can give clear and uncontestable guidance to the resolution of concrete disputes. As such, it must be sufficiently general to accommodate a diverse range of controversies and be sufficiently particular to deal with the details of individual disputes. In short, the *Oakes* test must be able to speak for itself and not have to be spoken for: legal ventriloquism is no more acceptable because it is performed with genuine craft and good conscience.[60]

The fact that *Oakes* does not and cannot apply itself is exposed by the decision in *Irwin Toy*, in which a ban on television advertising to persons under thirteen was upheld.[61] Having recognized an infringement of the corporation's speech rights and purporting to apply the same section 1 test, the judges divided over the weight and cogency of the social facts put in evidence before the Court. The majority felt that sufficient evidence was led by the Quebec government in support of justifiable intervention. It took the view that although there was a 'high standard of justification' on the government,[62] it had shown the existence of a pressing and substantial objective (protection of vulnerable children from commercial manipulation) and the proportionality of measures taken to attain that objective (a complete ban on television advertising). On the other hand, the minority was not convinced and insisted that freedom of expression should only be suppressed in urgent and compelling circumstances. It was not satisfied that the welfare of children was at risk or that the legislation was sufficiently proportionate to the perceived harm. The most troubling aspect of the decision is that after a thorough reading of both judgments, there is no obvious reason why this particular legislation was saved. Indeed, *Irwin Toy* offers no real guidance on how the Court might deal with future attempts at the legislative regulation of advertising. The test established by the Court under section 1 is woefully vague and indeterminate; it is more a conceptual curtain behind which the political dancing can take place than a choreographic script for the direction of such moves.[63] Nevertheless, the fact that the legal action must now take place around the section 1 venue does hold significant implications for future constitutional contretemps. In such argument, the burden is upon the government to justify that the law constitutes a reasonable limit. This doctrinal leaning not only insulates corporations from democratic regulation in the public interest, but enables them to set the terms for and dominate any debate over the public interest in such regulation. In an area where proof cannot be scientific and the issue is as much about values as empirical evidence, any doubts will be resolved in favour of the commercial interests. For instance, a challenge to the Tobacco Products

Control Act's ban on tobacco advertising and promotion is underway. It is anyone's guess – but only the Supreme Court judges' personal decision – what will be the fate of that enlightened legislation. The tobacco companies contend that such advertising is not intended to induce more smoking, but to facilitate brand selection. Under the *Irwin Toy* doctrine, the onus is upon government to show that smoking is dangerous to health and, more importantly, that the number of people smoking will be reduced by a decrease in advertising. Such matters are not easily susceptible to proof on a strictly cause-and-effect basis, especially in light of the information and relative financial resources available to government and tobacco corporations; the burden of non-persuasion in such matters can often be decisive.

Rather than proceed to criticize the *Oakes* test in an abstract and piece-meal fashion, I will take a more practical and sustained example. I will locate its assessment in a real issue that engaged the attention of lawyers and citizens alike: the constitutionality of the failed Bill C-43, which sought to recriminalize abortion.[64] The bill stated that it would be a criminal offence to perform an abortion unless a doctor was of the professional opinion that an abortion was required to protect the health of the pregnant woman. As one of the most controversial and compelling issues in political and constitutional debate, this will provide a telling and decisive testing of both rights-talkers and my own critical claims. In particular, I will argue that the *Oakes* test is so fluid and imprecise that it is incapable of providing determinate direction and constraining the exercise of judicial discretion. At all of its phases, the test is significantly manipulable: the ascertainment of whether a basic infringement of a guaranteed freedom has occurred, the articulation of the policy end in question, and the assessment of the appropriateness of legislative means are separately and cumulatively vague and indeterminate.

At the heart of this inquiry are both stated constitutional rules and judge-made precedents. The earlier decisions on abortion speak in many different voices and are difficult to synthesize into any meaningful or single message for future determinations.[65] Constitutional principles are neither unimportant nor irrelevant to any decision made, but they are never determinative in their own right and are never outside the play of political power. Accordingly, in the attempt to assess the constitutionality of any legislation or litigation about abortion, little is to be gained from examining the indeterminate directions of the Charter's language: all manner of interpretations are plausible under such a purely textual analysis. Nor is it advisable to always take the judgments of the Supreme Court at their word. It is as mistaken to presume that judges possess a self-conscious, fully coherent, and internally consistent theory of justice and judging as it is to believe that their general political inclinations do not influence their decisions. Understood as situated responses to expedient fact contexts, judicial pronouncements are simply data upon which to make informed calculations about the courts' reaction to future similar circumstances. 'Constitutionality,' therefore, is nothing more (nor less) than a present estimate of how judges will behave in the future in light of their past performances.

Also, in dealing with the determinacy issue, it is important to keep in mind the distinction between persuadability and plausibility. The challenge for the critic is to show that there are plausible alternative readings of *Oakes* that can meet general criteria of fit and justification. There is no need to demonstrate that an alternative reading is better or more compelling: this is the onus that those who insist on determinacy must carry and satisfy. Rights advocates must not only confirm that their reading is plausible, but they must persuade that it is the best reading possible. Most crucially, they must be able to do this without reference to some extrinsic value or intervening standard: this is the *sine qua non* of determinacy. To resort to such exogenous norms would be to concede that the *Oakes* test cannot determine in itself the resolution of particular instances. Accordingly, whereas rights-talk must show that an application of *Oakes* will provide a clear, compelling, and direct answer to Bill C-43's constitutionality, I have to demonstrate that there is at least one other application that leads to a different result and that can satisfy a rigorous standard of fit and plausibility.[66]

The first phase of *Oakes* requires that the challenged legislation be shown by a complainant to infringe an enumerated freedom. It has to be remembered that Bill C-43 would almost certainly have given rise to Charter actions by two diametrically opposed groups. On the pro-choice side, it will be contended that restrictions on access to abortion impair women's right under section 7 to 'life, liberty and security of the person': if women cannot control interference with their own bodily integrity, the constitutional guarantee is empty. While most commentators and judges agree with this claim, it is neither self-evident nor incontestable that this follows as a matter of linguistic logic or legal analysis: two judges of the Supreme Court thought otherwise.[67] It is incumbent on the defenders of rights-talk to demonstrate that a finding that no interest of women has been infringed not only is wrong as a matter of social justice, but is impossible as an issue of textual interpretation; this is a very problematic task and impliedly questions its judicial protagonists' bona fides. On the anti-abortion side, the claim will be that the rights of fetuses and fathers have been squarely denied. Protection is accorded to 'everyone' under section 7, and if courts are prepared to include corporations within its scope, they are also obliged by their own standards of doctrinal consistency to include fetuses.

Although the recognition of fetuses as 'persons' has been resisted by many judges, it has found favour with other judges.[68] Moreover, the judges of the Supreme Court are sharply divided over whether any form of balancing should take place in the definition of the scope of any particular right.[69] As such, the initial stage of *Oakes* is highly indeterminate. The courts must be prepared to come clean on the political values that inform and constrain the participants in rights-talk or they must refrain from making any threshold decisions on the boundaries of rights-talk. While picking and choosing is difficult to justify on a purely textual basis, the willingness to accept all and any claims of rights' infringements is to make the idea of a 'test' otiose. Accordingly, the only service that the first stage of the *Oakes* test performs for further analysis is to open the door wide to greater difficulties and ambiguities in the next stage of review.

The next step on the *Oakes* trail is for the government to identify the social objective to be advanced by the impugned law and to defend its pressing and substantial nature. Presumably, judges will not simply accept the government's assertions at face value, but will want to look behind the suggested objectives to ensure that these are the real intentions and effects of the regulation. To do otherwise would be to rob the test of any actual bite at all. Such a task is fraught with confusion and contestability: it is not amenable to resolution in an objective, precise, or apolitical manner that confines itself to the four corners of *Oakes* itself. For instance, as the troubled and public history of the abortion bill reveals, any attempt to isolate a collective intention of Parliament is even less achievable than usual.[70] Apart from the obvious hazards of statutory interpretation, the entire objective and rationale of the bill seems to be to effect a stark compromise: an effort to concede that each side has a legitimate claim and to fashion a position that reflects that understanding. Whether this is a pressing and substantial objective is doubly difficult to answer. Not only is it indeterminate on its own terms, but much will depend on the fate of the initial claims of the first phase of the *Oakes* test.

Provided the first two phases are successfully negotiated, the final stage will be to decide if the legislative strategy is the least drastic means to achieve the valid social policy. The problem here is that this again will depend upon which claim, the pro-choice or anti-abortion argument, is held to be prior in the constitutional scale of values. If the inquiry is carried out from the perspective of fetal rights, the availability of abortion throughout the pregnancy and the width of the exculpatory conditions would likely be construed as far from the least drastic concession to women's rights; a time limit on any availability and a more stringent set of exceptions to criminality *might* be considered more reasonable. From the perspective of women's rights, it will be forcefully contended that a blanket restriction on availability throughout the pregnancy and the need to obtain medical approval is not at all the least drastic acknowledgment of fetal interests; an extensive period of unrestricted access and less onerous exculpatory conditions *might* be considered more reasonable.

Even if the courts were to accept that each interest deserved some, albeit varying, weight in the constitutional balance and, therefore, that some compromise was constitutionally valid, the variety of possible compromise positions makes it impossible to alight on any particular scheme that would be uniquely recommended and sanctioned by advertence to *Oakes*. Consequently, it is submitted that the *Oakes* test cannot of itself give determinate assistance in resolving the controversial issue about the constitutionality of any abortion legislation and not simply Bill C-43. Of course, these kinds of problems are endemic to *Oakes* and will be present in any effort to apply it. Any apparent direction and substance that *Oakes* has comes from those who assume or are entrusted with its application. It is more of a rationalization than a reason for judicial dispositions of competing claims; it is a diverting smoke-screen rather than a productive tool. Between axiom and application, there always exists in law the exercise of power to convert general rights into particular results.

INDETERMINATE ENDINGS

A decade of Charter adjudication offers ample and cogent evidence of rights-talk's failure to provide the determinate guidance and operational efficacy necessary to its legitimacy as the constitututional métier of liberal legalism. It is not possible to think of rights-talk as an autonomous discourse. It is part of politics, not a precondition or boundary to the legitimate realm of contested politics. Lawyers and judges cannot exculpate themselves from the charge of exercising arbitrary power by expressing their decisions in the familiar rhetoric of rights-talk. Despite the best and voluminous efforts of jurists, there is no non-political way that is internal to rights-talk that can give it sufficient precision or clarity to meet its prescribed task. The judicial practice of rights-talk is an institutional site for political struggles, not a discursive resource for their resolution. Rights-talk is an indeterminate medium that only takes on any definite and determinate meaning within a particular form of social practice and ideological commitment. It is this set of preferred values and customary expectations that energize and inform rights-talk; it is not the other way round. Rights-talk is an empty vessel waiting to be filled with some political content.

Although some judges and commentators continue to insist that the performance of legal decision-making can be apolitical and value-free, the more sophisticated jurists of a liberal stripe accept that adjudication is an inescapably political and evaluative process. However, they insist that the resort to particular values and social practices can be effected in an objective way. Indeed, as proponents of a thick version of the Rule of Law,[71] they contend that if judges are to satisfy the institutional demands of democratic legitimacy, they are obliged to frame their decisions in terms of the political values and social visions that underlie and bind together the basic argumentative resources of rights-talk as a coherent and compelling account of social justice. In this way, judges can be both political and constrained in the fulfilment of their legal task in a democratic system of governance; they are not free to indulge ideological preference as legal reason. It is the burden of the next chapter to explain how a demonstration of objectivity cannot be made and that law is irredeemably indeterminate. In other words, I will argue that legal interpretation is thoroughly political because its performance and product can never be detached from the identities and interests of the interpreters. In short, the democratic prestige and authority of lawyers is unfounded in political practice and unfoundable in legal theory. The deficit in determinacy cannot be made up through a resort to objective values. Furthermore, while an explanation of the law's indeterminacy is fatal to the legitimacy of the adjudicative enterprise, it is not damaging to democracy itself. While indeterminacy jeopardizes any mode of objective decision-making, it does offer an understanding of how ordinary citizens can and must be entrusted with increased responsibility and authority in the name of democratic empowerment.

3

The Crisis of Legitimacy: Daydream Believing

O body swayed to music, O brightening glance,
How can we know the dancer from the dance?
– W.B. Yeats[1]

For an aristocrat, Lord Acton has had a profound influence on the popular development of modern democratic theory and practice. His famous apophthegm – 'power tends to corrupt and absolute power corrupts absolutely' – has become an entrenched piece of received wisdom. It has worked as a spur to the greater distribution and devolution of political power and has resulted in institutional checks to inhibit the concentration and centralization of such power. Some might consider that it has become a first principle of democratic government: society must be so organized that the corrupting influence of power is reduced to an operative minimum. Notwithstanding its popular appeal, this Actonian axiom of power is too limited in scope and too negative in character to warrant exclusive loyalty; it is a necessary, but not sufficient, condition of democratic governance. Power does not so much lead to corruption or ennoblement, but is a matrix of relations within which all action, good and bad, takes place.[2] Nevertheless, as a regulative ideal, Acton's principle does underscore the need to guard against the accumulation of power and emphasizes the attraction of democracy as a centrifugal process of government. In short, Lord Acton has provided an important, if rudimentary, benchmark against which to measure the organization of bureaucratic power and government authority.

DEMOCRACY AND ADJUDICATION

In the contemporary Canadian state, popular sovereignty is the primary device used to justify the power and legitimacy of government. Although government exercises vast power over people's lives, its authority is warranted by the fact that those with ultimate responsibility for governmental action are elected officials. While these representatives might not amount to the citizenry's alter egos, they are considered to owe a civic duty to the Canadian public and are accountable to them. In particular, it is their task to make contingent choices among competing values and to cut a reasonable clearing through politics' terrain of indeterminacy. Political representatives are entrusted with the liberty and burden of effecting closure in a world of incorrigible openness. Whatever the shortcomings of the actual practice,[3] the moral authority and political legitimacy of government rest largely on this principle of democratic representation.

However, the introduction of the Charter in 1982 presented a fresh challenge to the theoretical apologists of Canadian politics and democracy. Their task was to demonstrate that although the Charter withdrew large areas of social regulation from the legislative reach of elected bodies, it was more in fulfilment of the highest ideals of democratic governance than a renegation on the democratic compact between the rulers and the ruled. This apprehended crisis of legitimacy was heightened by the fact that the Charter was to be interpreted and enforced by a relatively small bureaucratic group of unelected government officials – the judiciary. Much conventional thinking manages to convince itself that although the judiciary are the third arm of government, they stand aside from government in disputes involving the deployment of official power and persuasion. Notwithstanding this unrealistic assumption, the challenge for supporters of the Charter was to explain the seeming paradox that democracy was best promoted by a reduction in popular sovereignty and a transfer of that power to a small coterie of unelected bureaucrats. As law seems to move to the centre of constitutional politics, the continued legitimacy of judicial review is more than ever dependent upon a successful demonstration of its essential objectivity and non-political character. In Actonian terms, why is it that while parliamentary powers tend to corrupt, absolute judicial power not only fails to corrupt absolutely, but actually guards against the corrupt exercise of power?

The business of judging has, of course, long engaged the attention of legal theorists. Such curiosity is understandable and desirable, for the judicial enterprise lies at the heart of the entire legal process and its commitment to rights. In almost all the literature, there is a deep conviction that something noble and fundamental is at stake when judges decide cases and enforce legal rights. It bears repeating that judges, unlike Rabelais' Judge Bridlegoose,[4] do not decide cases simply on the throw of the dice or through some other whimsical diversion. Instead, judges strive conscientiously to reach conclusions that are manifestly explicable and defensible in terms of legal principles and precedents. In so doing, judges seek to articulate their reasons and arguments for making particular decisions. Although most judges do not make explicit their method of reasoning, the existence of some method is necessarily implicit; 'in law, as in all other things, we shall find that the only difference between a person without a philosophy and someone with a philosophy is that the latter knows what his philosophy is.'[5] Although some judges have attempted to finesse the question,[6] the Charter gives a special urgency to the traditional need to explain the interpretive method of judges and to reassure citizens of their democratic legitimacy. The Charter bestows formal responsibility on the courts for its interpretation and enforcement, but it does not provide the judges with the hermeneutical tackle with which to perform this task. The problem is not about *who* should interpret, but about *how* judges should interpret the Charter.

The traditional response to this challenge is to claim that law and rights-adjudication are public and objective exercises whose performance does not depend on the personal values and subjective choices of judges. Despite common understandings about the political character of law, there remains a professional belief that law retains an essential degree of hermeneutical autonomy. Legal interpretation can and should be performed in a way that distinguishes it from the more open-ended ideological debates that are the stuff of political struggle. Although born in politics and practised in politics, law somehow manages to retain a distinct accent and idiom that speaks to politics, but is not entirely spoken for by that politics: '[judges'] authority and immunity depend upon the assumption that [they] speak with the mouth of others.'[7] Without such a distinction, lawyers and judges lose their claims to be the privileged and prestigious guardians of collective power: they become only its naked purveyors. Adjudication and rights talk is something more than simply what particular judges happen to say at any particular time. If it was only that, it would warrant no greater (or lesser) respect and deference than what ideologues, steelworkers, and accountants say or do.

To provide a convincing justification of the crucial distinction between law and lawyers, therefore, it must be shown that the doctrinal materials that comprise the law cannot offer determinate and objective guidance in the resolution of most legal cases. I maintain that such a demonstration of objectivity cannot be made and that law is irredeemably indeterminate; legal interpretation is thoroughly political because its performance and product can never be detached from the identities and interests of the interpreters. Because the deficit in determinacy cannot be made up through a resort to objective values, the traditional defence of Charter adjudication in the name of democracy as an exercise in objective reasoning is more an ineradicable contradiction than a seeming paradox. Furthermore, while an uncovering of law's lack of determinacy and objectivity does not hasten the demise of democracy (as many traditional writers seem to predict), it is fatal to the legitimacy of the adjudicative enterprise.

In this chapter, I will scrutinize the primary theories of adjudicative legitimacy put forth by commentators and courts in their attempt to account for this shift in Canadian democracy. The only real difference between the academic and judicial writings is that the former are more explicit and less superficial than the latter. Although there are many subtle shadings, the unifying theme of the academic literature is the reliance on a combination of a liberal theory of rights-talk and a conservative resort to conventional morality or communal values. By reference to the growing corpus of judicial decisions, I hope to demonstrate that as well as being inimical to democratic aspirations, a judicially enforced Charter is riven with conflicts that cannot be resolved in a principled or neutral manner. The recent interest in communitarianism is intended to smooth rights-talk's rough edges, not replace its central premises. In short, I offer an extended jurisprudential illustration of the 'moralized amoralism and rationalized unreason of rights-discourse.'[8]

THE FORMALIST FAITH

In any critique of rights-talk under the Charter, the structural framework within which judicial decisions are made is too often implicitly assumed rather than explicitly stated. The Charter is regarded as 'supreme law' because it is entrenched within the nation's Constitution. It is more difficult to amend than regularly enacted law and takes priority over those laws. As a broad-ranging document, it sets out certain general rights, such as equality, freedom, and liberty, which it guarantees to everyone. However, while these rights are fundamental, they are not absolute. They are almost always subject to limitations, whether specific or more general under the Charter's section 1 proviso. The interpretation of these rights and their limits is subject ultimately to determination by the courts, which are staffed by a relatively small group of appointed officials who hold office, hopefully, by virtue of their legal training and experience in the practice of law. In fulfilling their interpretive responsibilities, the judges do not have a roving commission. The agenda is set on a case-by-case basis in response to claims brought, for the most part, by private litigants at their own expense. To resolve these specific disputes, the courts have to develop an interpretive method that can fulfil its quotidian functions as well as reassure citizens of that method's democratic legitimacy.

The task of traditional jurists has been to give greater theoretical substance to these ideas and intuitions. Although given a definite boost with the advent of the Charter, this theoretical challenge to legitimate judicial interpretation has been the abiding preoccupation of common law jurisprudence. The claim that law is a distinct and objective social form that operates independently of politics and personnel is the essence of legal formalism. Legal formalism has had more lives than Shirley MacLaine. While it has taken many different identities and suffered many different fates, it remains the ruling theory of most lawyers. For formalists, reincarnation is a way of life. In the first half of the century, the dispute was over the possibility of establishing a mode of judicial activity or explanation that was fully separate from politics. However, in the past couple of decades, the jurisprudential focus has shifted subtly, but substantially.[9] The halcyon days of an (un)self-conscious formalism, characterized by an apparent reliance on a mechanical algorithm or logical pathogenesis, have gone. No self-respecting modern lawyer or legal theorist pretends that law is 'a brooding omnipresence in the sky'[10] that lends itself to formulaic application or provides robotic predictability.

Nevertheless, while it is acknowledged that legitimacy cannot be grounded in law as a sealed system of normative directives, there still remains a tenacious commitment and aspiration to 'bounded objectivity'[11] – the idea that there is a difference between law and the collective wisdom of its legal representatives at any particular time. Formalism's sustaining article of faith is that although law arises in and alters its sociopolitical context, it can best be understood and practised as distinct and independent from that constitutive milieu. Insisting that the form of law is inseparable from its substance, formalists of all stripes share the belief that whatever it is, legal reasoning is not only ideological wrangling in fancy dress. At their most forthright, formalists claim that legal reasoning is detached, determinative, and determinate: it can generate correct and predictable answers to social disputes in a way that marks it off, in a non-trivial and meaningful sense, from open-ended ideological debate. Lawyers can be immersed in politics without succumbing to that politics. Law is its own thing and is not reducible entirely to anything else: 'Law ... is deeply and thoroughly political ... but not a matter of personal or partisan politics.'[12]

Unsullied by ideological impurities, legal formalism is an intellectual attitude and analytical technique that demands institutional allegiance and universal obedience solely by dint of its inherent rationality and intellectual cogency.[13] Thus, formalists continue to believe that they can provide an account of law without having to take a stance on the major and controversial questions of what is the best way to live collectively and individually; the lasting demands of intellectual integrity can be satisfied without regard to the shifting dynamics of social experience. The burden of the formalistic judge and jurist is to show that even if legal doctrine does not compel definite results, it places sufficient constraints on judges to save them (and us) from themselves or, at least, to justify placing civic trust in them. How is it possible, in matters of normative judgment, to get beyond a discredited formalism, without turning law into an open forum of ideological debate?

Because efforts to justify constitutional adjudication as a purely apolitical and impersonal exercise in judgment were neither possible nor desirable, the project was to locate and explain the constraints that permitted judges to confront and resolve matters of political controversy as political issues, but to do so in a way that would distinguish such a practice from free-wheeling ideological debate. The challenge is to demonstrate that the law has sufficient flexibility to accommodate changing circumstances and particular facts, but has adequate fixity to be an enduring and general guide to judicial office-holders. In short, the legitimacy of constitutional law depends upon a showing that individual decisions are more than the aggregate opinions of sitting judges and less than the distant wisdom of a Natural Law. Adjudication is about interpretation rather than revealed truth on the one side and ideological prophecy on the other. Moreover, formalist scholars must demonstrate not only that constitutional law stands at some objective remove from its judicial interlocutors, but that it amounts to more or less than the scholar's own preferred scheme of social justice and institutional arrangements: scholarly distance is as essential as judicial detachment.

In a recent essay, Beverley McLachlin of the Supreme Court of Canada took up this challenge. She offered a spirited defence against the critical and 'fashionable' attacks on the democratic legitimacy of judicial power. Contending that it is wrong to characterize the judiciary as excessively powerful or political, she insists that 'a strong judiciary is essential to the maintenance of our democratic institutions.'[14] At the heart of her argument is the claim that at every turn, the potentially despotic power of judges is hedged and controlled by the traditions, conventions, and rules of the law: 'judges are guided by precedents which dictate particular results, quite apart from the judge's personal views' and 'the power of the courts is constrained by many factors, including their own rules, which forbid the exercise of power beyond their own statutory and constitutional mandate.'[15] It is because of, and not in spite of, this respect for the Rule of Law that Canada, according to McLachlin, manages to preserve the freedoms that are consonant with a democratic society.

An initial response to McLachlin's thesis is that its two main claims seem to be in flat contradiction of each other. If the judiciary are as cirumscribed and restricted in their power as she suggests, it is difficult to understand how they can carry out effectively their avowedly democratic 'role of protecting minorities.'[16] Similarly, she argues that, while the judiciary are subservient to the legislative arm of government, they are entrusted with the avowedly anti-majoritarian task of opposing the popular will in the name of individual rights. Contrary to what McLachlin asserts, it is surely the case that the unelected judiciary are powerful precisely because they can pass judgment on the actions of the elected legislators. The issue, therefore, is whether this exercise of anti-majoritarian authority can be put on a democratic footing by virtue of the modes of reasoning and methods used. Moreover, notwithstanding this, the central and enduring difficulty with McLachlin's argument is that it begs the question to be answered. She assumes the operative force of the supposed restraints – legal precedents and judicial conventions – whose very existence and efficacy are at stake and in contention.

In contrast to McLachlin's facile assertions, any adequate defence of judicial power in a democratic society must demonstrate that such alleged limitations exist independently and are capable of effecting the necessary control. However, the continuing efforts of traditional legal scholars to rescue formalism are as futile as they are fanciful. Although there are many theoretical interventions into the rights debate, there are two general trends and themes at large in the jurisprudential literature. One line of argument holds that Charter rights reflect a higher set of norms or values rooted in some transcendent system of justice, whether derived from Nature, God, or some lesser philosophical deity. Within this *naturalist* approach, the role of the courts is to identify and give interpretive effect to these higher norms and values. Another school of thought suggests that Charter rights reflect a broad social consensus comprising the shared aspirations and values of the Canadian community. For these *positivist* adherents, the role of the courts is to locate the changing social consensus and apply it critically to litigated cases. Within the Canadian oeuvre of Charter jurisprudence, the naturalist and positivist tendencies do not so much run in competing lines, but weave together in an attempt to overcome the failings of each and to emphasize the strengths of both. With characteristic Canadian genius for pragmatic compromise, contemporary writers have recognized that the invoking of a vision of natural rights – whether Preston Manning's, Brian Mulroney's, or REAL Women's – would not garner the necessary support unless there existed some social consensus about the identity of particular 'natural' rights. Accordingly, Canadian jurists combine in a Jovian search for an indigenous and evolutionary way of talking about entrenched rights.

In light of this jurisprudential alliance, theorists of Charter adjudication tend to differ more in emphasis than in kind. For instance, David Beatty gravitates more toward the naturalist pole. In his efforts to elaborate a constitutional labour code, he posits that the Charter entrenches the enduring principles of liberal politics that have developed and informed Anglo-Canadian law over the past century. He insists that the Charter has imposed this organic logic upon the future means and ends of legislators who must now engage in a 'conversation of justification' with the courts.[17] While Patrick Monahan pursues a similar idea of 'constitutional conversation,' he makes a more positivist presentation. Espousing a form of democratic communitarianism, he contends that a legitimate mode of judicial review must confine itself to nurturing and protecting active participation in public decision-making; this is a goal that is integral to the Canadian tradition of politics.[18] Whereas Beatty wants to hold the courts to the substantive dictates of an individualist ethic that is showcased by the traditional set of civil rights, Monahan seeks to enlist courts in the procedural ambition to maximize openness and revision in community relations by bringing the guarantees of multiculturalism, language rights, and equality into the

Charter foreground. Both intend their theories to check and legitimate the potentially limitless and undemocratic authority of judicial review.

This contemporary effort to downplay liberal legalism's traditional emphasis on individual autonomy and to emphasize its more egalitarian focus has received its most significant rendition in the work of Will Kymlicka. Influenced by the theoretical reflections of Charles Taylor,[19] Kymlicka has sought to re-jig liberalism so that it is better able to address and legitimate the claims of minority cultures. For Kymlicka, this involves a greater recognition of the social circumstances of choice in which individuals deliberate about and pursue their life plans. Moreover, mindful of the vast dissimilarities of people's communal context, it is necessary to facilitate membership in a healthy cultural structure as a primary social good if true individual autonomy is to be achieved. Accordingly, a right to cultural equality is at the heart of Kymlicka's revamped version of liberalism: 'Liberals should be concerned with the fate of cultural structures, not because they have some moral status of their own, but because it's only through having a rich and secure cultural structure that people can become aware, in a vivid way, of the options available to them, and intelligently examine their value.'[20]

The suggestion, elegantly expressed and sophisticatedly packaged, that the values expressed in the Charter represent the shared aspirations of the Canadian people certainly has an appealing ring to it. Public opinion polls show that the vast majority of Canadians favour the Charter and have greater confidence in judges than politicians in protecting their fundamental interests. In addition, the rights contained in the document, such as equality, liberty, and freedom, are ones to which most Canadians appear to subscribe. Nevertheless, this initial appeal is deceiving. As attractive and plausible as these theories and surveys may seem, they do not and cannot withstand close scrutiny. The combined strength of naturalist and positivist theories do not offset the dead weight of their combined flaws. There is a marked deficit in legitimacy and a communitarian slant on rights-talk is little more than cooking the same stew in a different pot. The elaborate theoretical schemes are displays of political style more than exercises in substantive politics. The very fact that there is such disagreement within academia over the general source and broad nature of social consensus hints at the paper-thin cogency of this jurisprudential strategy.

At the heart of my critical challenge is the conflictual nature of rights-talk. Far from reflecting a social consensus or manifesting a natural order, the rights in the Charter mask fundamental social and political conflicts. Indeed, rights-talk is more a discursive site for dispute rather than a sedimented resolution of dispute. So long as these conflicts remain hidden, the appearance of social consensus and, therefore, democratic legitimacy is maintained. However, when these conflicts are exposed, that appearance evaporates. Once the Pandora's box of Charter adjudication is thrown open, it will not only be impossible to press its lid back down, but it will become increasingly unclear how it was ever closed in the first place. The legitimacy of the Charter is once again put back in question; the claimed objectivity of Charter adjudication is revealed as being entirely spurious and its practice as lacking democratic warrant.

To demonstrate and drive home this critical challenge, I will examine some leading and praised examples of contemporary Charter scholarship that espouse the formalist cause. The work of David Beatty and William Conklin takes as its focus and ambition the revival and defence of an explicitly formalistic account of constitutional adjudication. For them, the problem is not with the formalist project, but with its execution to date. While they each approach their task from very different angles and with very different results, they share the ambition of retrieving a formalist credo that will still the doubters' voices for all time. Unfortunately, they struggle in vain as their efforts are as fanciful as they are futile.

THE BEATIFICATION OF THE CHARTER

David Beatty is undaunted by the dismal legacy of legal formalism and unreconciled to the pusillanimity of his erstwhile colleagues. Over the past few years, he has been on a Charter pilgrimage. In a series of books and articles,[21] he seeks to identify and describe the full and true meaning of the Charter's protection of rights and freedoms. He insists that Charter adjudication embodies the cardinal virtues of objectivity and determinacy. Or, more strictly, he argues that whatever the dubious merits of Charter adjudication to date, a proper appreciation of what judicial review under the Charter entails would allow its performance to meet the desired standards of constitutional rectitude and political integrity. For him, the present practice is not only flawed and misguided, but is unconstitutional and calls into question its perpetrators' entitlement to sit as judges: 'There [is] *only one* approach to constitutional review that [is] consistent with the "inner logic" of the Charter, and ... this, and *only this*, vision [is] constitutionally correct.'[22] In short, behind the prosaic and flawed actuality of constitutional law stands the immanent perfection of Coraf, as yet only barely glimpsed and imagined, but soon to arrive in all its resounding constitutionality. It is an affirmation of natural law and formalism on a magnificent scale.

Beatty's claims of objectivity are not of a common or garden variety and go much further than contemporary attempts to establish an account of 'bounded objectivity.' More accurately, he sets himself the task of showing that 'there is a single, unique theory of judicial review that is embedded in the Charter.'[23] Whereas almost all academic commentators agree that any viable account of constitutional law must explain the cases and doctrines that have developed around the principal text, Beatty insists that the truth of the Constitution and the derivative validity of judicial review are entirely to be found in the Charter itself: 'All of the principles and doctrines used by the [Supreme] Court in the interpretation and application of the Charter must themselves be derived from, and be consistent with, the principles and values which underlie the Charter.'[24] The greater part of *Talking Heads* is devoted to explaining how most of the decisions and judgments of the court since 1986 do not do this. Indeed, a more recent essay, 'A Conservative's Court,' has the sole purpose of revealing how almost all the Court's decisions and judgments in 1989 and 1990 were wrong-headed. More than that, he contends that not only are the majority of the judges' approaches and methods incorrect, but they are 'unconstitutional,' in the sense of being outside the Constitution, and the judges' 'entitlement to continue to sit on the court' is called into question.[25]

Accordingly, Beatty does not accept that there is any obligation to recognize as valid those decisions that have or will become so entrenched in the Court's continuing daily practice or customary self-image as to be considered by everyone else as part of the Constitution. Further, he presumably would find it entirely rational and defensible to argue that *all* decisions made by the Court were mistaken and unconstitutional insofar as they failed to respect the intrinsic principles and inner logic of the Charter.[26] The Constitution is never what the judges say it is, because it always stands completely apart from judicial attempts at interpretation and is unaffected by those interpretive interjections or glosses. This, of course, places an immense burden on Beatty in defending his claim to provide an objective account of the Charter. Contrary to even received formalist wisdom, he must demonstrate that the Charter speaks entirely for itself, unaided and unmoderated by its judicial or scholarly disciples. On his own insistence, he must prove that there is one and only one correct mode of judging that can square with the Charter. It is, therefore, fatal to his project to suggest how another reading of the Charter *might* be possible. On the other hand, it is unnecessary for me to prove that Beatty's method is invalid in some final sense or that its outcomes are uniformly wrong; it is enough to show that an alternative reading or set of decisions could also be valid and consistent with the Charter.

His first book, in 1987, *Putting the Charter to Work*, was a confessedly modest attempt to grasp a unique moment in Canadian constitutional history and 'to think out loud' about the 'beginnings of a description of and justification for the practice of judicial review.' It was not intended 'to preclude alternate principles or theories.'[27] Indeed, he thought it best to proceed from the most conservative and least controversial 'traditions of judicial caution and restrain.'[28] However, like Paul on the road to Damascus, by the time he reached his next scholarly port of call, an important conversion of belief and purpose had occurred. While the substantive content of the theory remains the same, it is not put forward as a tentative proposal for adoption, but has attained the objective status of fundamental truth. No longer a suggestive contention about Charter prudence, it has become an inspired account of revelatory wisdom. In short, it is a declaration of the Charter's Beatification.

At the core of Beatty's beliefs is the understanding that constitutional review comprises an institutional conversation of justification about the extent and means by which the goal of equality of self-determination is to be achieved in a liberal democracy.[29] While the primary responsibility for setting the details of this social agenda is for Parliament, the courts have a crucial role to play in ensuring that this legislative duty of social engineering is undertaken in a way that is least restrictive of individuals' freedom. Using *Oakes* as his theoretical landmark,[30] Beatty plots a constitutional map in which section 1 is the 'make or break' of Charter adjudication. Whereas there ought to be general deference to Parliament's choice of policy objectives, the courts must be vigilant and aggressive in policing the means employed to accomplish these ends. As such, section 1 of the Charter is at the interpretive heart of this constitutional compact, and the decision in *Oakes* is its justificatory lifeblood.

Beatty attempts to support the dubious objectivity of this theory by two different routes. One looks to the traditions and wording of the Charter itself and the other focuses on a particular decision of the

Court. Unfortunately, not only do both strategies fail, but each undercuts the possible success and compounds the actual failure of the other. Whereas his interpretation of the Charter looks to the contested decision of the Court in *Oakes* for validation, that decision is itself justified as more of an exegetical rendering of the Charter text than a creative supplement to it. Although Beatty wants to have his cake and to eat it too, his creative appetite lets down his constricting taste. Although he claims that the Charter is not what the judges say it is, he can only make good his claim to objectivity by relying on one particular pronouncement of what the judges said it was. Ultimately, he has to look to the very source of what he most wants to avoid – '[judges'] values and ideological orientations'[31] – to make his objectivist assertions stick. As such, Beatty's own defence of his theory is the best offensive resource for the non-formalist critic.

Rather than begin or ground his objectivist defence in the Charter's immediate text, he starts by surveying the different judicial approaches that took shape in the Charter's first five years. Reducing these to liberal and conservative streams, he measures these competing adjudicative techniques against the basic precepts and values that inhere in the Charter's inner logic. Not surprisingly, for one who had already written a book extolling the virtues of egalitarian liberalism, Beatty dismisses the conservative approach and embraces the liberal method. More than that, he isolates the decision in *Oakes* as best capturing the essence of the Charter: it is the instance of liberal adjudication that most closely reflects the two-step measure of ends and means in *Putting the Charter to Work*. Beatty is adamant in opting for this, not because he agrees with it or thinks it amounts to the best vision of the judicial role in a liberal democracy (which he clearly does), but because it most nearly captures the objective truth of the Charter. The acid test, therefore, becomes whether Beatty can show that *Oakes* is the only and exclusively valid view of the Charter rather than the reflected projection of his own juristic leanings.

In an unanticipated move, Beatty declares that the wording of the Charter is of no particular assistance. Indeed, he takes a positively cavalier approach to the text and any conventional appreciation of judicial responsibilities for interpretation:

> In contrast with conventional wisdom, the liberal method has relatively little to do with defining which interests and activities are protected by the rights and freedoms which the Charter guarantees ... rather than the role of interpreter of

> a constitutional test, the Court's primary function is to evaluate the justifications offered by Governments and their supporters for why a particular social policy had been chosen to be enacted into law. Justification, not interpretation, it transpires, is what the Charter and judicial review is mostly about. Section 1, not the substantive sections in which the rights and freedoms are entrenched, is where all of the action takes place.[32]

This being the case, what is the authority for this deviation from convention and tradition? Through what particular understanding does it 'transpire' that 'justification' is the only valid and unique approach to Charter adjudication? Why is every other formalist's conception of valid adjudication mistaken?

The most obvious candidate for such an authority is 'original intent' – the view of those who actually drafted the document and had the democratic mandate to do so. However, Beatty highlights the conceptual and pragmatic flaws in this move and gives short shrift to it as a valid interpretive device.[33] Instead, he declares that on the basis of the Court's judgments in its first of couple of years, a purposive approach to Charter adjudication is the proper methodology. Recognizing the scope for manipulation and that 'text, context and historical origins all could provide assistance,' he argues that the ultimate purpose of the Charter is 'to be derived from the most basic values and principles that organize and distinguish societies that are free and democratic and those that are not' and that are given form and substance in *Oakes*.[34] Without more argument, he concludes that such a 'rigorous' approach would enable the Court 'to resist any temptation to read the Charter in a manipulative way.'[35]

The audacity of these sweeping claims is only matched by their transparency: the account and defence of purposive judging is riddled with contradictions and non sequiturs. It defies reasonable explanation of how an open-ended methodology can 'ensure the objectivity and integrity of the whole enterprise.'[36] First, all of this seems to rest not on the objective truth of the Charter, but on the reading by one particular set of judges and a single academic of a vague and general constitutional document. Indeed, in brutal contradiction of his operating objectivist assumptions, Beatty justifies this judicial approach as a matter of necessity because 'the Charter is written in large and malleable terms ... [whose] sweeping language ... would allow it to grow and expand.'[37] Second, the alleged authority for this particular judicial method is nothing more than a transient majority of judges who, and this is most important, share Beatty's predeliction for means/ends analysis. He wants to freeze a particular moment in judicial time and treat it as a privileged occasion for objectivist insight; this is a familiar, but illegitimate move. Third, he simply equates purposive judging with liberal judging without any explanation of why a judge cannot identify the purposes of a free and democratic society as genuinely conservative in spirit and scope. All in all, Beatty does a good job at showing how the Charter becomes what the judges want it to be: it does as much their bidding as they do its. None of this is a problem, except for the crucial fact that he is trying to offer a cogent demonstration of how and why this is not the case.

With imagination and industry, legal materials can be organized to support and justify incompatible outcomes. The fact that the general drift of these outcomes corresponds to the orientation of status quo thinking and values is not necessary; it is not a matter of doctrinal rationality, but a question of political orientation. The socioeconomic context is itself largely indeterminate and requires no particular rule for its continued survival. While a shift in the whole regime of legal rules (e.g., contract, property, and family) will be significant, the existence or shading of particular rules (e.g., the postal rules, the finders' rules, and the change-of-name rules) will not be crucial. Moreover, in the same way that the socioeconomic context underdetermines law, that very same law overdetermines the possible outcomes to any legal dispute. There is a general and pervasive indeterminacy that plagues all attempts, not simply jurisprudential ones, to explain social events and to fix social knowledge in any strongly objective way.

More a constructive activity than a given thing, law involves an inescapable dimension of human choice; policy drives legal interpretation as an exercise in operational logic. This is particularly true of Supreme Court judges as they acknowledge openly that their task is not only to apply precedents, but to change and create new ones when circumstances so require. In a crucial sense, therefore, it is never possible simply to 'follow the rules' because the question of what is the relevant and precise rule and what following it entails remains irresolvably contestable. In the traditional notion of judging, each part of its functional equation (law + fact = decision) is insufficiently determinate; the law must be spoken for – it cannot speak for itself.

Even where there appears to be a consensus on the existence of any particular rule, nothing necessarily flows from that concession. Whether a rule exists and what it means are different inquiries. While they are not entirely unrelated, the issues give rise to a different set of conceptual and normative concerns; a person's ability to identify the French language is of little help in determining what any particular example of it means. Rules do not operate as impersonal and dispositive forces in social conflicts. Their existence and meaning are more often the consequences rather than the causes of a particular resolution. Furthermore, even if there is a consensus on the meaning and existence of a particular rule, there is always another rule that competes for application or the dispute can be reclassified into another doctrinal field, for instance, from tort to property or contract.[38] Indeterminacy infiltrates all levels and dimensions of the law; it both energizes and debilitates the interpretive process and search for meaning.

The effort to identify one definitive and normative explanation of that regime is defeated by the fact that a theory will not be able to achieve the appropriate mix of analytical generality and historical particularity. It must run the risk of overinclusion or underinclusion. A theory that merely describes the extant details of legal practice will not be able to predict the direction and nature of doctrinal change; it will cease to be useful at the very time its assistance is most required – the identification and resolution of hard cases. On the other hand, a theory that attempts to move beyond such detailed description will run into two major obstacles. It will be unable to account for a sufficient range of present legal data and lose its descriptive power. Alternatively, it will be compatible with different combinations of legal materials that constitute existing legal doctrine and will fail to deliver on its predictive promise. As all formalistic efforts to justify a theoretical account of responsible adjudication reveal, a solution to this normative dilemma is agonizingly elusive.

Contrary to the traditional view, the law is a locus of conflict. There are a host of different interpretations competing for descriptive and predictive superiority, but none is able to claim final victory. Insofar as uncontested interpretation is only possible where there is a pre-existing and shared set of values, the competing and contradictory forces at work in forging legal doctrine foreclose the establishment of the necessary consensus. Accordingly, legal doctrine is not a reflected embodiment of one indwelling and sufficient theory, but is the formal site for the attempted, but unattainable, blending and reconciliation of competing theories. The temporary accommodations made are more a result of political expediency than moral purity. Although one theory may tend to dominate and infuse the law with its guiding principles, a competing theory will constantly challenge it and provide a debilitating set of counterprinciples. At times, the tension will precipitate doctrinal crisis; at other times, the friction will be subdued and relatively untroubling. Yet, muted or manifest, it fuels and informs doctrinal development. The particular trajectory charted and followed will, at least in part, be a function of the larger historical forces that impinge on the legal and judicial enterprise. Consequently, in this general sense, law is another arena for the stylized struggle over the terms and conditions of social life. In sum, law is politics.[39]

However, it is important to emphasize that a dismissal of objectivist jurisprudence does not commit the sceptic, as Beatty imagines, to a subjectivist account that reduces judging to 'purely personal choice,' a whimsical exercise of capricious opinion or idiosyncratic invention.[40] This depiction of judging is merely the flip side of objectivism. If it is to have any theoretical bite, it will depend upon the possible validity of an objectivist epistemology in which there is only objective truth or subjective opinion. For those like Beatty who do work within such a paradigm, the decision to criticize a judge for his or her failure to follow and respect the presumed objective truth of the Charter carries some very harsh implications. The charge of indulging personal predeliction suggests that knowing the real truth of the Charter's meaning in any particular instance, the judge made a calculated decision to deviate from it. This is tantamount to mala fides. Accordingly, whenever Beatty admonishes judges for using the wrong interpretive method or applying it wrongly, he is accusing them of not only being a bad judge, but also being dishonest and irresponsible judges. As he makes such subjectivist criticism of all the judges at one time or another (when they disagree with the Beatific Charter), including the largely fêted Wilson J., he is really condemning the whole judicial enterprise.

On the other hand, my version of scepticism rejects entirely this epistemological paradigm. As such, it accepts neither the objectivist account of judging nor its subjectivist bête noire. Under the rubric 'law is politics,' I take a very different view of the philosophical status and methodological validity of law's claim to determinacy. Legal doctrine does not conform to any simple internal rationality, nor is it reducible to a cluster of external organizing principles. While there is clearly an inseparable and organic relation between law and politics, there is no one account of that relation that is valid for all time and all societies. Any explanation is itself indeterminate; its character and implications vary with the context. While it is still possible to offer opinion and evaluation, there is no mandate for claims about whether doctrinal materials *necessarily* and *universally* determine results or whether those results are *necessarily* and *universally* good or bad. A sceptical account of law is decidedly against any kind of functionalist or instrumentalist account of the relation between law and politics, whether it comes from the right, left, or centre of the political spectrum. Law is 'neither a ruling-class game plan nor a repository of noble if perverted principles ... [but] a plastic medium of discourse that subtly conditions how we experience social life.'[41]

Legal doctrine is not simply 'out there,' but is always in need of collective retrieval and re-creation. There can be no law without interpretation, no interpretation without interpreters, and no interpreters without politics. Yet doctrine is not nothing, but a special kind of something that has to be interpreted to mean anything. While there will be occasions of Machiavellian manipulation, it is as mistaken to suggest that the judge has complete interpretive freedom as it is to claim that the law effects complete interpretive control. The distinction between 'that to be interpreted' and 'that who interprets' cannot be sustained: doctrine and judges interact to shape each other in a contingent context of political power. Contrary to Beatty's views, judgment is neither the intelligible articulation of objective truths nor the chaotic fantasizing of subjective experience. Consequently, the sceptic is able to deny the idea of objective meaning and, at the same time, to accept that judges largely act in good faith. While it incorporates the judges' sense of felt boundedness, it exposes and challenges that deep set of contestable values on which judges claim to rest their decisions.

Finally, an explanation of the law's indeterminacy does not hasten the demise of democracy, as many traditional writers seem to predict or imply. McLachlin's claim that 'there can be no true freedom without the rule of law' is merely a scare tactic designed to underwrite and warrant the judges' own tenuous power.[42] The critical contagion is fatal to the legitimacy of the adjudicative enterprise, but it is not damaging to democracy. For some, however, subterfuge and dissemblance might be preferable to candour and honesty in facing up to the fact that there is no exclusively principled or objective way to decide intransigent economic and social issues. Yet the response to this abiding difficulty is neither despair nor cynicism. Democratic practice will have to be given priority over legalistic values and judicial practices. The devaluation of the Rule of Law, in a society in which it has come to signify rule by lawyers, is not an occasion to be lamented. Democracy is about popular power, not privileged authority. By encouraging people to understand themselves as the makers of decisions and not as the amanuenses of a received wisdom, they will begin to assume greater responsibility for those decisions and their social consequences; the ensuing society will become truly theirs. In this way, people will grasp that democracy is not about servitude to lordly politicians or imperial judges, but is about personal participation and social solidarity. Power can never be abolished; it can only be entrusted to those whose lives it most directly affects and affirms.

FORMALISM RE-VISIONED

Having long ago abandoned the discredited and transparent values of rule formalism, constitutional scholars turned to purposive reasoning and policy analysis as a means of explaining the licence, limits, and legitimacy of constitutional interpretation and judicial review. Recognizing that any serious account of constitutional development had to take account of larger questions of social justice, mainstream jurists began to look upon legal doctrine as reflecting an underlying political rationality or scheme of social justice that rendered constitutional interpretation and judicial review coherent and legitimate. By adhering to this ideal, judges and jurists could avoid engaging in open-ended exchanges of ideological debate and retain their vaunted democratic independence. Recently, however, there has been a growing consensus that policy formalism has been unable to withstand the sustained attentions of the anti-formalist critics. Traditional scholars extricated themselves from the false security of black-letter rules only to fall victim to the deceptive allure of black-letter theory. The change was one of location rather than of mind. Although they looked beyond the limiting horizons of law and explored the ample attractions of other disciplines, such as moral philosophy and economics, they never disabused themselves of the worth of formalism as an intellectual project and political aspiration. Their ambition was to colonize and exploit these extralegal outposts for the greater imperial benefit of formalism. As such, jurists resorted to 'policy' as a means of securing the crumbling foundations of the traditional legal edifice, not as an opportunity for escaping its undesirable confines.

Undaunted by the demise of policy formalism as a site of intellectual refuge, traditional scholars have again shifted ground, this time to the loftier plane of constitutional 'visions.' While their passion for purposive reasoning and policy analysis has been quelled, their fixation with formalism is unflagging. Of course, it cannot be denied that social visions play an essential role in the development and understanding of constitutional norms. Behind every constitution lies a set of social visions that give it life and meaning. Whether involved in its design or interpretation, all constitutional actors must possess a framework of ideas that helps them to grasp the past tradition of political ordering, the nature of present reality, the possibilities for future action, and the justifications for these understandings. Constitutional visions structure perception and prescription. They inhabit the twilight zone between pure normative abstractions and historically verifiable assertions.[43] Without generative visions, legal reasoning would be reduced to a desultory game of catch-as-catch-can; law's normative dimension would be lost. Yet as a means of prescribing constitutional interpretation or justifying judicial review, visionary formalism is as ill-fated as its rule-bound and policy-oriented predecessors. Formalist fidelity has been purchased at the cost of political transparency. Visionary formalism is even less successful than rule formalism and policy formalism at concealing its political persuasions. The resort to constitutional visions is not so much an attempt to escape from politics as it is an effort to romanticize and exalt a particular form of political insight. This serves to legitimize the activities of academics and judges whose work can be identified with that form. Moreover, the form, while conceded to be political in nature, is represented as operating independently of ordinary ideological conflict. Visionary formalists gain their rhetorical force and constitutional authority by disclaiming their partisanship on contested matters of national politics, even as they claim their authority to make decisive interventions into those matters. Neutrality and impartiality are a function, and not a renunciation, of ideological context.

A leading exponent of visionary formalism is William E. Conklin. The strongest part of his erudite and rigorous scholarship is his exposure of the shortcomings of rule and policy formalism. However, his proposed alternative of visionary formalism is open to the same debilitating criticisms that he uses against these earlier formalist incarnations: he manages to highlight the inevitable failings of formalism in the process of crafting its most sophisticated expression. *Images of a Constitution* seeks to describe the constitutional images held by Canada's judicial and academic elites. According to Conklin, these images are important not because of what they tell us about the Constitution or those judicial officials granted the privilege of enforcing the Constitution, but rather because they are the constitution. Conklin insists that the legal text and the compendium of doctrinal interpretations that have been grafted upon it are the residual deposits of the more dynamic engagement over competing images of constitutional reality: 'A constitution is an image; it is a product of the legal community's imagination. A constitution does not live except through the consciousness of the legal community.'[44]

From this starting point, Conklin identifies three constitutional images that have found expression and favour in the Canadian legal community of scholars and judges: the *historicist* image looks to the history of institutional arrangements as the source of constitutional norms and rests its claims to validity on tradition, reaching its most potent manifestation in the Martland/Ritchie dissent in *Patriation Reference*;[45] the *rationalist* image, which views the Constitution as a self-contained collection of posited rules or values and the rational architecture of the law's internal logic, is celebrated in the writings of William Lederman and P.M. Kennedy;[46] the *teleological* image derives constitutional meaning from the ends toward which society is or ought to be moving and receives its strongest approval in the judicial and scholarly legacy of Ivan Rand.[47]

While each of these images has its practitioners and apologists, Conklin maintains that the rationalist image has dominated Canadian constitutional discourse, although it is not monolithic in its manifestation. On the contrary, he goes to great lengths to show that there has been a continuing tension and variation among three distinct strains of rationalist imagery. *Rule rationalism* sees the Constitution as a comprehensive set of rules or doctrines that can be derived rationally from the constitutional text and from the real or presumed intent of its framers. Conceived in the 1920s, rule rationalism captured the allegiance of Albert Abel, Louis-Phillippe Pigeon, and Jean Beetz.[48] *Policy rationalism* looks beyond the rules to policies or values that are said to underlie the constitutional text. The inquiry remains rationalist in that the policies being sought are assumed to possess an objective identity that can be ascertained through rational inquiry: 'The policy image merely adds a broader resource material (social/economic facts and shared goals) and more diversified techniques of rationality (psychology, theory, and history).'[49] This image was embraced by Bora Laskin, Noel Lyon, and Peter Russell. Finally, *orthodox rationalism* seeks constitutional truth in the interplay between textual rules and extrinsic policies. As expressed in the work of Brian Dickson, Bertha Wilson, and William Lederman, its aspiration is to escape the rationalist confines of both rule rationalism and policy rationalism. Ultimately, however, orthodox rationalists are forced to seek refuge in some form of rationalist discourse. For Conklin, they 'uncontrollably, imperceptibly relapse into rationalist horizons not unlike generations of Canadian scholars before them.'[50]

Having rejected rationalism, Conklin throws his jurisprudential weight behind the teleological image. He maintains that constitutional law should consist of judicial efforts to engage in reflection about the telos to which Canadian society is evolving. However, while constitutional adjudication must involve itself in the potentially open-ended issues of ideal-directed theory, it is constrained by the need to situate such reflection within the historical tradition of social/cultural practice in Canadian law and politics. In this way, according to Conklin, constitutional law not only becomes a dynamic mediation between political theory and legal practice, but also ensures that it contains an appropriate dimension of self-criticism and scrutiny: 'The challenge for the contemporary lawyer is to picture a constitution which allows him or her to question the "givens," to connect the "givens" to universalist human rights claims of theory, and to critique their reified character when divorced from social/cultural practice.'[51]

While this makes for interesting reading, it does little to advance understanding about the operation and legitimacy of constitutional adjudication. Emboldened by the initial power of his categorical insight, Conklin relies upon his taxonomy of constitutional images to develop a full-blown theory of constitutional decision-making. Unfortunately, his normative ambitions outstrip his analytical reach. Indeed, the juxtaposition of quotes from Plato and Derrida on the opening pages of *Images of a Constitution* create a suitable, but unintended, contradictory icon for the ensuing text. For Conklin's espousal of visionary formalism to carry the day, he must demonstrate not only that judicial utterances can be usefully and consistently categorized according to particular constitutional images, but that the images judges hold drive the outcome of the cases they decide. Moreover, if his advocacy of teleological imagery is to pass jurisprudential muster, he must be able to demonstrate that resort to such imagery has justificatory validity in a democratic polity. Unfortunately, Conklin is unable to meet these crucial challenges. By losing contact with sociopolitical reality, his constitutional vision becomes little more than constitutional daydream believing. Conklin is one more dewy-eyed Corafian.

NOCTURNAL FANTASIES

While they may sometimes appear self-contained and exhaustive, constitutional visions are never complete or mutually exclusive. They are inevitably selective in emphasis and embrace. It is their raison d'être to form an accessible distillation of the historical and aspirational elements of our collective and personal lives. Because of their generality and aphoristic nature, they often lead to contradictions between visionary intimations and existential practices and result in incoherences among commonplace patterns of behaviour:[52] the constitutional practice is not always the child of the visionary parent. Constitutional actors are divided among and within themselves about the appeal and efficacy of different visions of constitutional order.[53] The courts and legal doctrine are venues for the ceaseless negotiation of visionary conflict. As there are many different visions at work in its formulation and interpretation, even one judge's contribution to legal doctrine is not a reflected embodiment of one indwelling and sufficient vision, but is the formal site for the attempted, but elusive, blending and reconciliation of competing visions. The temporary accommodations made are more a result of political expediency than moral purity. Although one vision may tend to dominate and infuse the law with its guiding principles, competing visions will constantly challenge it and provide a debilitating set of counterprinciples. At times, the tension will precipitate doctrinal crisis; at other times, the friction will be subdued and less disruptive. Yet, muted or manifest, this antagonism fuels and informs constitutional development.

The example of Bora Laskin, to which Conklin frequently refers, is revealing. Conklin sometimes tries to pigeon-hole Laskin as a policy rationalist and, at other times, he characterizes him as a rule rationalist. Whereas Conklin observes that 'Bora Laskin, as a young scholar, gives policy rationalism a rigour and sophistication unmatched in Canadian constitutional history,'[54] he later contends that 'for Laskin, the teacher, the British North America Act, 1867 posits rules and those rules constitute the exclusive resource material for constitutional law.'[55] In trying to draw a distinction between Laskin as a 'young scholar' and Laskin as a 'teacher,' Conklin is suspiciously silent on the reasons for this change and the identity of the real Laskin. Of course, the fact is that Laskin, like other judges, was quite capable of cutting his constitutional image to suit his political cloth. Thus, while Conklin goes to great pains to contrast the rule rationalism of Justice Laskin with the policy rationalism of Justice Dickson, it is not difficult to find examples that run counter to this assessment. Conklin claims that

> Dickson understands constitutional judgments to be 'value decisions' whereas for Laskin, the judge, values constitute an illegitimate source of law. Dickson incorporates values and public policy as constituent elements of his image whereas Laskin, as a judge, relies entirely upon posited rules for his image of a constitution.[56]

This assessment sits very uneasily with the well-known and pre-Charter picketing case of *Harrison* v. *Carswell*. In that case, Dickson steadfastly maintained that it was not the role of the Court to 'weigh and determine the respective values to society of the right to property and the right to picket' because doing so would raise 'important and difficult political and socio-economic issues, the resolution of which must, by their very nature, be arbitrary and embody personal and economic social beliefs.'[57] On the other hand, Laskin advocated that the Court engage in a 'balancing of interests' in order to further its 'search for an appropriate legal framework for new social facts which show up the inaptness of an old doctrine developed upon a completely different social foundation.' How could Laskin, the great rule rationalist, have so openly embraced an inquiry into policy? And how could Dickson, one of Conklin's prime examples of a policy rationalist, suddenly have become so rule-bound? The answer, surely, is that the images that Conklin projects onto these two judges did not suit their political purposes in the particular circumstances of this case. For Laskin, perhaps because of his experience with labour relations, the rule established by the picketing law seemed oppressive and it was necessary to invoke policy arguments to challenge its continued authority. For Dickson, possibly because of his corporate law background, the same rule seemed natural and desirable; he therefore had no wish to subject it to searching scrutiny.

I do not mean to suggest that Conklin is wrong to argue that Laskin, Dickson, and other jurists have an affinity for one constitutional image over another. On the contrary, he makes a strong case that they do. Where he goes wrong is in assuming that these images actually drive legal outcomes. As the judgments in *Harrison* v. *Carswell* show, judges are quite capable of shifting images when it suits their political purposes: constitutional images are a fungible part of a broader vision of political justice. However, such shifts are rarely necessary; there is usually sufficient scope within a judge's preferred image to fashion whatever results he or she desires. No better evidence of constitutional imagery's indeterminacy exists than that provided by Conklin himself. In discussing the judicature sections of the Constitution Act, 1867, Conklin notes that Laskin's views shifted over time concerning the proper interpretation to be placed upon section 96, the section that provides for federal appointment of superior, county, and district court judges. As an academic, Laskin viewed this section as nothing more than an appointing power and dismissed the 'needless artificiality' of reading section 96 as preserving the judicial functions of section 96 courts. As a judge, however, Laskin embraced such 'artificiality,' holding in *Crevier* v. *A.G. Canada*, that it 'would make a mockery of the Constitution Act, 1867' to allow provincial governments to transfer section 96 powers to provincially appointed appeal tribunals.[58]

Conklin's explanation for this shift is supremely unconvincing. It did not occur because Laskin became disaffected with one constitutional vision and turned his judicial affections to another; it was more than a whimsical change of judicial outfit. As Conklin concedes, both doctrinal arguments are consistent with the judges's rule rationalist image of the Constitution. The shift came about because Laskin moved from a 'textualist' approach to rule rationalism to a 'functionalist' approach to rule rationalism. Notwithstanding its particular leanings and defining characteristics, the apparent indirection of rule rationalism belies its predictive significance and interpretive malleability. Yet the question remains of why Laskin moved from one approach to another. Conklin cannot really expect critics of formalism to believe that Laskin went to sleep as a 'textualist' one night and woke up as a 'functionalist' the next morning: nocturnal visits from some jurisprudential fairy who sprinkles constitutional moondust in judges' eyes are truly fantastical. It is more likely that the move had less to do with the taxonomic niceties of constitutional imagery than with the dynamic forces of social and political power. Rather than Conklin's juristic flights of fancy, a more plausible explanation might be that Professor Laskin identified with the interests of labour tribunals and other administrative bodies, while Judge Laskin came to care more about the parochial concerns of the judiciary and to be influenced by its special interests. If constitutional image had anything to contribute to the process, it was more likely a matter of Laskin's need to maintain his judicial self-image than anything else.

The upshot of all this is that constitutional imagery is much less important in explaining constitutional discourse and decisions than Conklin recommends or predicts. Certainly, 'the expression of a judge's image of the constitution' is not the major source from which 'to understand a judgment as it really is.'[59] On their own, constitutional visions reveal little about legal outcomes. However, this does not mean that they are of no importance to the constitutional critic. Their significance lies in their contribution to the essential task of legitimacy – the effort to convince citizens that the power wielded by the judiciary has an authority and wisdom that transcends the collective views of its existing membership and is thereby deserving of civil obedience. Contrary to the insistence of Conklin and other formalists, constitutional imagery is not a source of determinative reasons for judicial decisions, but rather a mode of rationalization that judges and juristic apologists use to account for decisions driven by forces largely extrinsic to constitutional discourse.

In the same way that the paparazzi who chronicle royal apparel maintain that it is the clothes that make the monarch, visionary formalists perpetuate the myth that it is the image that makes the judge. This shallow pretence is no more persuasive in the judicial arena than it is in the royal realm. Presumably, it is only convincing to those dedicated followers of fashion that have a material stake in the public's continued hoodwinking. It is obviously true that some judges prefer one kind of sartorial rationalization to others and that this inclination may bear some connection to their deeper political predilections. Moreover, it is worth observing that particular styles of discursive dressing may sometimes have to be changed to better produce or match a desired effect. But, when all is said and done, clothes are clothes. And, while the choice of apparel, literally or figuratively, may signal much, rarely will it determine the identity and intentions of the person who is in the clothes. It is the familiar error of, at best, mistaking symbol for substance or, at worst, treating symbol as substance.

Nevertheless, even if Conklin's account of visionary formalism could overcome the fatal weaknesses of incoherence and indeterminacy, the question would still remain of why a democratic polity should be governed by the constitutional and social visions of an elite cadre of political officials. Mindful that in spite of recent and continuing efforts at diversification, the judiciary remains an unrepresentative and relatively homogeneous group, Conklin offers no real defence of the legitimacy of subjecting citizens to judges' partial visions of justice. It is not a challenge to the bona fides of judges to suggest that their largely male, white, heterosexual, Christian, wealthy, and middle-aged identities will influence and shape their acceptance of certain values as fundamental verities. Like all people, judges' images of the good life tend to reflect the limited and, in their case, privileged vantage points from which they survey and evaluate events. As such, judicial imagery is a part of, not apart from, the regularly contested and always contestable context of politics.

This points to a more fundamental problem with Conklin's analysis and visionary formalism in general. By simultaneously discussing differences in constitutional imagery and discounting underlying forces of class and power, Conklin pretends that there is far more room for diversity and radicalism in constitutional adjudication than actually exists. Judges may be free to choose historicism, rationalism, or teleology as an imaginative mode of justificatory argument, but they cannot detach themselves from certain foundational understandings. While the respective rights of picketers and property owners may be modified at the margins, the underlying institutions and distributions of property are not subject to challenge. While the courts may occasionally voice sympathy for the plight of ordinary and disadvantaged Canadians, they remain firmly wedded to a vision of rights that privileges those who wield market power and restricts those who would like to see that power restrained. Thus, despite a considerable change of personnel over the last little while, Supreme Court of Canada decisions remain all too predictable. Changes in constitutional imagery belie a depressingly consistent devotion to a conservative vision of society and its transformative possibilities – plus ça change, plus c'est la même chose.[60]

Evidence supporting this sad conclusion is constantly revealed in the Supreme Court's reactionary assumptions and regressive implications – an emphasis on individual over collective interests, the state as the greatest threat to social justice, negative liberty over positive freedom, and so on.[61] The distinct preference of the courts for the interests of the haves over the have-nots persists in the face of much activity in the rhetorical salons of constitutional imagery. Doctrinal indeterminacy masks and gives way to ideological proclivity. Rather than expose this objectionable state of affairs, academics seem content to record and quibble over the latest trends in the judicial fashions of argumentative attire. This is particularly galling in the work of sophisticated scholars like Conklin. Recognizing that constitutional adjudication takes place in an ongoing context of power relations, he pays only lip-service to this context and makes no real attempt to comprehend the relation between constitutional imagery and the protocols of social and economic power.[62] Moreover, he fails to address the radical implication of the critical idea that 'all knowledge is socialized' – the implication that any attempt to salvage judicial review as a formally viable and substantively democratic enterprise is doomed to failure.[63] In the process, Conklin has reduced the promising insights of constitutional imagery into an escapist exercise in constitutional dreaming.

A CRITICAL AWAKENING

The dubious achievement of Conklin, Beatty, and those tempted by the rhetorical appeal of a legal formalism is to flirt with the kind of demagoguery that Aristotle warned about so long ago – the person 'who asks law to rule is asking God ... and no others to rule.'[64] Their formalist flight to philosophical abstraction is an escape from democratic responsibility. Despite theoretical dreams to the contrary, there is no way to escape the politics of our finetude and land in an infinite realm of pure reason that secures us against the need to make difficult and always contestable choices. Legal theory is the opiate of the lawyering masses: Coraf will not be coming. No theory can be formally necessary as well as materially adequate to relieve us of the painful responsibility of knowing what to do: ideology is inescapable. Accordingly, with a critical awakening, it might be possible to acknowledge that 'justice therefore demands that no one should do more ruling than being ruled, but that all should have their turn.'[65]

Like the law itself, modes of thinking about law have their limits and orientations. As special kinds of social knowledge, explanations are contingent upon and open to constant interpretation and reinterpretation. There is no world of reality that stands apart from the way in which the world is described or judged. Nor is there a way of describing or judging that exists outside the world. Reality and the medium in which it is understood and evaluated are inextricable. Rightness is not about correspondence with an external world nor about solipsistic harmony with our own prejudices. It is to be found in the historical and reflective negotiation between the two. No matter how modernist and sophisticated its accoutrements, no theory (or its scholarly production) exists apart from prevailing social and political practice. The pertinence and value of any legal theory is a function of its interplay with the irrepressibly contingent context of social life whose unfolding it can neither fully predict nor entirely control; the contingent pressures of politics subvert the objectivist pretensions of formalism. As a consequence, the achievement of a just social order cannot be accomplished through a rigorous deployment of perennial legal techniques and immutable structures. Rather, it depends upon an appreciation of and sensitivity to the changing circumstances of political power in particular societies. Of course, it does not mean that because law and politics are fully implicated in each other they replicate each other in a simple or undistorted fashion; the life of the law is more than its internal logic and less than the total experience of social life.

In this chapter I have sought to demonstrate that Charter adjudication is not about the objective interpretation of constitutional rules and their dispassionate application to given sets of social facts. Rather, judicial decision-making necessarily requires the courts to engage in ideological disputation. The courts' unavoidable task is to confront and resolve fundamental social and political conflicts whether they be within rights, between rights, or between rights and claims based on the general welfare. Once this is understood, the justification for the Charter and, in particular, for the legitimacy of the courts' role in interpreting and enforcing Charter rights on the basis of a community consensus or an evolving tradition becomes profoundly unconvincing. Issues like affirmative action, union rights, abortion, and Sunday closing lie at the heart of political controversy in Canada. Their temporary resolution does not reflect a community consensus, but puts into place a conventional morality. Whatever explanation may be offered for handing over decision-making power on these crucial issues to the courts under the Charter, it cannot be justified by the resort to a pre-existing Canadian consensus over 'our home and native land.' The only consensus that may and does shape the work of the courts is that among the community of legal elites.

The irony of all this, of course, is that if there were a true consensus of community values, there would be no need for a Charter of Rights. Judicial review of legal action in terms of its constitutional validity would be unnecessary. The fact is that community consensus runs out at the very time that it is most needed – in the resolution of disputes that arise because of a breakdown, gap, or shortcoming in the extant body of conventional norms. It is not that there is no sense of shared values in Canada, but that there is always one too many set of such values. Canada is a mosaic of different communities, including Natives, Québécois, women, Westerners, WASPs, Northerners, workers, Catholics, Acadians, gays, and so many more. Indeed, the dominant identity of the Canadian cultural and political tradition might well be its toleration and nurturing of local and special affiliations. For instance, in the abortion debate, it is not so much that there is no sense of social solidarity, but that there are two very strong and largely irreconcilable communities that each draw upon and are energized by a different vision of individual responsibility and social justice.

One of the unanswerable questions for those who seek to justify the Charter on the basis of communal values is why the community cannot be trusted to identify and give voice to that consensus through the democratic and legislative arms of government. In recognizing that any consensus is organic and protean, it is difficult to understand why a consensus should be entrenched in a document that is practically impossible to change and is enforced by a group of citizens that are unrepresentative of and unaccountable to the community at large. If there is a detailed and uncontroversial body of extant norms, there will be no need for judicial review. But if there is no such consensus – and there is surely not – the defence of judicial review in terms of such a consensus is futile and misleading. Instead of being disabused by the tribulations of their American counterparts, Canadian judges and jurists seem intent on following that dubious tradition and banging their heads against the brick wall of constitutional legitimacy. How is it, or could it ever be, possible to appeal to an idea (of community, consensus, or tradition) to resolve a division of opinion, when that division arises because of the inadequacy, indeterminacy, or contentiousness of the very idea being called upon to resolve the division? The only hope must be that this exercise will belatedly knock some political sense into them. Unfortunately, if Beatty's and Conklin's work is anything to go by, the effect has been to encourage even more outrageous hallucinatory reveries of formalist fulfilment.

The point that this chapter has tried to make – that Charter adjudication is and can never be objective – is certainly not new, nor is it particularly radical. Indeed, it is the same point that was made over a dozen years ago by another individual who objected to the courts being given responsibility for resolving conflicts of the fundamental nature that the Charter involves. Writing in a case that involved much the same conflict between picketing and property rights as that which arose in *Dolphin Delivery*,[66] he stated that 'the submission that [courts] should weigh and determine the respective values to society of the right to property and the right to picket raises important and difficult political and social economic issues, the resolution of which must, by their very nature be *arbitrary* and embody *personal* economic and social beliefs.'[67] These views were expressed by none other than Chief Justice Brian Dickson. It is surely fantastical to suggest that the enactment of a document like the Charter would be enough to transform those 'arbitrary' and 'personal economic and social beliefs' into an objective and attainable consensus on the meaning and weight of rights-talk in the Canadian forum of political debate. Lord Acton would not be satisfied by that explanation. Nor should we be.

4

An Abstraction of Vision: A Miserable Existence

Doctor Arbuthnot was not far short of the mark: 'Law is a bottomless pit.'[1] It is capable of accommodating all manner of philosphical insight, ideological choice, and hermeneutical possibility. In the three centuries following Arbuthnot's observation, liberal theorists have riled against this existential reality. With a hubris worthy of the Pharaohs, they have sought to dig and shape the legal pit in their own philosophical image. Their goal has been to construct, or to discover, a solid jurisprudential foundation on which to erect their legal edifices. Their imagination and resourcefulness are admirable, but they are to no avail. Although theorists often claim to have succeeded, the foundation inevitably collapses, like a false bottom, disclosing the political chasms beneath. Undaunted, they blame the failure of the particular performance rather than call into question the validity of the general project.

The Charter's enactment has given to the liberal quest a new impetus and a greater sense of urgency. Because the courts are trusted with the overt responsibility to adjudicate upon controversial issues of political confrontation, the stakes are much higher. While success will be so much sweeter and more useful, failure will be so much more bitter and damaging. In league with courts, liberal academics have been busily engaged in the construction of yet another foundation – 'a theoretical framework of constitutional principles' – to give meaning and stability to the Charter enterprise.[2] While judges have followed the time-honoured traditions of the common law and worked in a piecemeal and pragmatic way, it has been left to the academics to draw up the construction plans and to insist that whatever the judges felt they were doing, they were really following some immanent blueprint all the time. Of course, there is disagreement about the precise contours of the judicial artefacts and the details of the architectural design. Nevertheless, all agree that the foundation can be built. Many insist that it has always been there in the hallowed form of rights-talk. It is simply a matter of refining its practice and finding its nature and scope.

However, the practice of rights-talk is the result of political struggle, not an occasion for its resolution. As such, rights-talk is an indeterminate medium that only takes on any definite and determinate meaning within a particular form of social practice and ideological commitment – a vision of politics. Moreover, it is this set of shared values and customary expectations that energize and inform rights-talk; it is not the other way round. While the indeterminacy of rights-talk means that it can be utilized for transformative and progressive purposes, the ideological orientation of rights-talk's underlying vision makes it more amenable to some appropriations and manipulations than others. The predictability of rights-talk and its general political presuppositions rest upon an impoverished and partial vision of social life. As a categoric mode of political argumentation, rights-talk suffers from the debilitating weakness of being based on an alienating, individualistic vision of social life.[3] To be blunt, it provides the institutional and rhetorical means to express a tolerant liberal morality.

The appeal and limits of rights-talk flow from the same sources, for 'at the heart of this ethic lies a vision of the person that both inspires and undoes it.'[4] At the same time that it offers the prospect of empowering individuals and rescuing them from collective tyranny, rights-talk also stifles the possibility of truly progressive social change. As an historical artefact, rights-talk has played a positive role in social struggle and retains obvious strengths, such as the value of human dignity, physical protection, distrust of bureaucracy, and worth of rational justification.[5] However, rights-talk overthrew the divine right of kings, clergy, and aristocracy only to replace it with the sovereignty of the abstract individual – God in more philosophical and less theological uniform. It treats people as abstract individuals rather than as situated citizens whose lives are presently constrained as well as potentially satisfiable within their relational contexts. Like all ways of seeing and comprehending the world, rights-talk distorts as much as it illuminates; it tends to shape the world in its own political image.

The individualistic vision of rights-talk depicts individuals as separate and egoistic, striving for a liberty that is self-regarding and a sociability that is hollow, and with equal capacity to use those rights. As such, rights-talk provides an inherently false account of human community both in its present practice and future possibilities. A rights-centred society becomes little more than an aggregate of self-interested individuals who band together to facilitate the pursuit of their own uncoordinated and independent life projects – a relation of strategic convenience and opportunism rather than mutual commitment and support. While the strict individualism of American liberalism has been tempered and moderated by a communitarian commitment, the Canadian political vision of rights-talk remains too abstract and private: it is insufficiently situated and civic. In order to illustrate and substantiate this critique of individualism, I will concentrate on the use of rights-talk in current North American debates over abortion and poverty. While rights-talk is not always inimical to social transformation, I contend that it is always limiting and limited.

A FLIGHT TO ABSTRACTION

In seeking to establish the terms and conditions for collective life, societies must inevitably engage in the normative struggle between competing social visions. Behind every particular intervention in a political dispute, there stands a framework of ideas that help people to grasp the past tradition of political ordering, the nature of present reality, the possibilities for future action, and the justifications for these understandings. People's competing visionary allegiances are the stuff of political life: 'We are divided, among ourselves and also within ourselves, between irreconcilable visions of humanity and society, and between radically different aspirations for our common future.'[6] Accordingly, the law is an important venue for an extended conversation about the kind of society and individuals that people want to be and become. By engaging in this discursive encounter, people not only help to define it, but are themselves defined by it. More often implicit than explicit, these poetic visions sustain, energize, and animate the prosaic routines of economic and social life.[7] Structuring perception and prescription, they inhabit the twilight zone between pure normative abstractions and historically verifiable assertions. Although largely mythic in source and simplicity, they order reality and become part of our lived experience and self-understanding. By mediating the actual and the ideal, these visions of private ordering simultaneously empower and limit the political imagination. As such, they not only carry strong explanatory force, but they also wield significant moral authority. While they resonate with utopian echoes, they are meant to convey a sense of the attainable and the realistic in historical experience.

That vision commits its adherents to a whole host of foundational premises, insights, and intuitions about the human condition and its potentialities. To affirm a particular vision is to accept a basic epistemology, a social theory, and a human psychology. While they often seem self-contained and exhaustive, these social visions are necessarily incomplete and not mutually exclusive. They are selective in emphasis and embrace. It is their raison d'être to form an accessible distillation of the historical and aspirational elements of our collective and personal lives. Because of their generality and aphoristic nature, they often lead to contradictions between visionary intimations and existential practices and result in incoherences among commonplace patterns of behaviour.[8] Consequently, the doctrinal practice is not always the child of the visionary parent. Nevertheless, although they are indeterminate in the guidance they offer, these visions do push in definite ideological directions and dictate a particular setting of the doctrinal agenda.

In the legal arena, an appreciation of these visions' role and operation is essential to any effort to comprehend the direction and substance of rights-talk. Without such generative visions, law and legal reasoning would be reduced to a desultory game of catch-as-catch-can; the normative dimension of law would be lost. There are many different visions at work in the formulation and interpretation of legal doctrine; legal actors are divided among and within themselves about the appeal and efficacy of different visions of constitutional order. Accordingly, legal doctrine is not a reflected embodiment of one indwelling and sufficient vision, but is the formal site for the attempted, but elusive, blending and reconciliation of competing visions. The temporary accommodations made are more a result of political expediency than moral purity. Although one vision does tend to dominate law and infuse rights-talk with its guiding principles, competing visions are constantly challenging the hegemony of the dominating vision. Rights-talk is characterized by confusion and contradiction; any thought of visionary integrity is historically inaccurate and idealistically flawed. For most of the time, the friction will be subdued and relatively untroubling, but, on ocassion, the tension will precipitate doctrinal crisis. Yet, muted or manifest, this antagonism fuels and informs the doctrinal development of rights-talk.

Rights-talk is dominated by one central vision: *individualism.* While it stops short of libertarian anarchism, it does represent an abstract liberalism. Traditionally inspired by Thomas Hobbes, John Locke, and Immanuel Kant and recently invigorated by John Rawls, Robert Nozick, and Ronald Dworkin, the liberal vision of society portrays people as rational maximizers and self-interested consumers of utilities. There is no available yard stick to make interpersonal comparisons of utility and thereby to generate a plausible account of the public good. While individuals seek to obtain the maximum freedom, to pursue their own freely authored self-interest, their efforts to do so require some security from the subjective and selfish interference of others engaged in the same project. The central contradiction and paradox is that the more freedom that is allowed to pursue such ends, the less security is available against the intrusion of others. In short, individual freedom seems possible only through its collective limitation and negation: my freedom can only be obtained by curbing your freedom and your freedom can only be obtained by curbing mine. As an attempt at mediation, the creation of a political state is posited to replace the anarchic war of all against all with an ordered world. In order to resolve the dilemma of order-and-security, the theory of rights is enlisted to prescribe the extent and manner in which certain freedoms can be limited in order to maintain sufficient social stability and peace to allow greater freedom in general.[9]

The central images of this individualist vision are state distrust and individual liberty. It imagines a world consisting of independent, self-sufficient, and equal persons who confidently draw up and robustly pursue their own life plans. Each individual has a true moral and pre-social self, not contingently sculpted by the social milieu. Normative experience is private and does not lend itself to public reckoning; human fulfilment is a personal odyssey. Within such a society, freedom is achieved when people are treated as an end and not as a means to other people's ends. Society is never more than the sum of its individual parts, nor public morality more than a temporary coincidence of private values and preferences. The state facilitates freedom by imposing a minimum of formal and equal constraints upon people's activities. Society must approximate as closely as possible a voluntary scheme of individual co-operation. Although the possibility or opportunity for fraternal association is not denied, it can only be a personal choice and can never become an integral feature of an individual's identity. Paternalism is to be studiously avoided in economic and political affairs.

The main enemy of freedom is the state and the collective will. Their tendency to abuse power and hamper the heroic individual must be kept in constant check lest the irresistible slide down the totalitarian slope be allowed to begin. This balancing demands a limited, but strong, state that focuses and exhausts its energies and authority in efforts to facilitate the individual pursuit of personal life plans. The upshot is that the state must uphold the crucial institutions of private property and contractual exchange. To do more is oppressive and to do less is anarchic. The state must protect a pre-political sphere of pure autonomy that does not depend for its existence or legitimacy upon the state. Standing above politics, it sets the parameters and standards for the competitive struggle between self-directing individuals. Of course, none of this account is intended to sanction crass egotism. While people ought to be sensitive and generous to those less well off than themselves, altruism is a matter of personal morality or choice, not a collectively imposed obligation. This basic distrust of the state is matched by an equally strong trust and confidence in the capacity and willingness of individuals to make the 'right' choices. As such, there are no general standards by which to judge the substantive worth of individual or collective action for, as the liberal vision most strongly insists, individuals are the best and only measure of such matters.

Informed by such a vision, rights-talk conceives of the very essence of individual identity as being an abstraction from its constitutive connections. An identity is something that everyone has by virtue of their existence as unique individuals. It is almost as if each person is born normatively full-grown, like Zeus' children, with a raw set of values, preferences, and characteristics that can be given (more or less) expression in the historical act of living and socializing. Under this view, freedom is the successful resolution of both the search for that true intrinsic identity and the struggle to live one's life in accordance with its dictates. In this way, relations with other individuals are understood in terms of limitations rather than as vital contexts within which people can (or cannot) become fully human. Liberal rights-talk obliges individuals to view their connection with others and their responsibility for others as a matter of detachment and voluntary choice. There is almost a wilful refusal to recognize the extent to which people are socially situated – a failure to grasp how people shape and are shaped by their structured relations with others.

My critique of abstract liberalism finds its source in the notion that while it is possible to come to know and relate to men, women, and children of different races and cultures, there is no chance at all of meeting 'the abstract individual.' There are Chinese men, African women, and Caucasian children of richer and poorer communities, but there is no universal rights-holder. Indeed, Aristotle hit the critical nail on the head when he concluded that an individual who finds moral fulfilment outside the community is 'either a beast or a god.'[10] In a regime of rights-talk, the abstract individual is a beastly god. A vision of personhood that is so lofty and vague has no relevance to the historical context of real struggles and their resolution. The liberal revolution of rights emancipated the citizens from state tyranny and turned them into free and equal legal persons, but left them at the mercy of private and profit-driven interests. Within this world of anxious privatism, people come to be suspicious of others, and the only bond that holds them together is 'natural necessity, need and private interest, the conservation of their property and their egoistic persons.'[11] Rights become another commodity to be traded in the marketplace of humanity and act as a barrier separating people from genuine communion with their fellow citizens. While the economically powerful imagine that their whole destiny is in their own hands, all people are 'forever thrown back on [themselves] alone, and there is a danger that they may be shut up in the solitude of [their] own hearts.'[12] Moreover, in its rampant universality, rigorous abstraction, and splendid isolation, the liberal individual takes on a very male, heterosexual, European, educated, middle-class character in its orientation, interests, and relation to the world; its productive capacities eclipse entirely any consideration of its reproductive responsibilities.

The liberal account of self, adrift in society and often a stranger to itself, fails to grasp the idea and practice of oppression as being situational and social in nature. It places too much emphasis on individuals and too little on structural arrangements. Collective practices can oppress or ennoble as much as can the isolated acts of well-intentioned individuals who live according to them and whose acts take on meaning within them. Although liberal individualism has eliminated much overt racism, sexism, and homophobia from public life, the institutions and practices that frame the ideas and activities of individual actors remain deeply and systemically flawed: the social whole is often greater than the sum of its individual parts. Discrimination is, at least, as much about the general effects of social practices as the intentions of individual actors. Individuals must go beyond good intentions to transform the political contexts that translate dominant interests into neutral standards, that turn momentary ideas into naturalistic assumptions, and that transform good intentions into bad effects.

By posing the problem in terms of individual action, liberals obscure as much as they explain and resolve particular instances of discrimination only at the expense of perpetuating its deeper effects and causes. Concentrating on individuals' intentions rather than on the victims' conditions of life allows the 'morally blameless' to wash their hands of the problem and makes it all too easy to 'blame the victims.' Racism, sexism, and homophobia are more than the conscious conspiracy of a power elite or the crazed delusions of bigots; it is part of the historical culture, social heritage, and political tradition.[13] As race, gender, and sexuality are constituted in and through social history, racism, sexism, and homophobia are social practices. Being systemic, they permeate both power structures and personal relations. Liberal self-expiation obscures the uncomfortable fact that affirmative sacrifice by the dominant may be the only way to achieve substantial equality for the dominated.[14] By persisting in thinking discrimination is more about personal identity and private attitudes than public actions and social conditions, the chances that liberalism will confound discrimination and establishing a truly egalitarian society are reduced.

Furthermore, liberal theory's insistence on positing individuals as rational, self-interested, and pre-social ethical beings who share little more than an abstract humanity manages to treat everyone the same, while claiming to celebrate the difference and dignity of each. This deficiency is particularly acute in regard to the inclusion of corporations as potential rights-holders. In an early Charter decision articulating the right to be secure against unreasonable search and seizure, the Supreme Court of Canada waxed boldly about the importance and sanctity of human dignity and the need to preserve a zone of privacy from state interference.[15] As crucial and as worthy as these aspirations are, the fact that the rights-holder claiming this protection was a corporate media conglomerate does tend to give the Court's humanistic rhetoric a very hollow ring. The fact is that rights-talk manages to trivialize and devalue profound human interests by equating real people with artificial economic entities.

BEGGING THE QUESTION

Although written 150 years ago, *Les Misérables* still retains an appalling relevance today. Like Victor Hugo's Paris of the last century, the contemporary streets of Canadian cities are fast becoming home to increasing numbers of the wretched and dispossessed. Without support or shelter, beggars abound, but 'become lost in the cold murk that envelops solitary destinies, the distressful shadows wherein disappear so many unfortunates in the sombre progress of mankind.'[16] Insult is added to injury by the fact that although Canada is one of the richest countries in the world, it has almost the greatest disparity between the income and wealth of the rich and poor. The situation is proportionately worse for the young, women, and people of colour. In a country of plenty, homelessness, a condition that affects over 100,000 people, amounts to a national disgrace.[17] The enormity of the problem reduces the pain-searing cry of personal tragedy to the sedated murmur of a collective statistic.

Whereas ignominy thirsts for respect, those who offer charity to the poor do so as much in the spirit of self-righteousness as from a sense of solidarity: philanthropists are too often motivated by a need to assuage their own guilt than by a wish to eradicate poverty. The modern tendency to abstract the poor, to portray them as essentially different and, thereby, to distance the poor from privileged purview and responsibility are part and parcel of the judicial mind-set. However, if judges feel too constrained by the law to tackle head-on the problem of homelessness, academic commentators suffer from no such limitations, nor can they be allowed any such excuses. As especially privileged members of society, they must, like the best kind of fools, go where others fear to tread. Yet, like many well-intentioned philanthropists, legal scholars respond to social problems not with social solutions, but with the bestowal of compassion and legal rights. For instance, in the case of the homeless, considerable scholarly energy is devoted to establishing a right to shelter and defining its nature and scope.[18] In a provocative contribution to the legal debate over rights and begging, American writers Helen Hershkoff and Adam Cohen run this risk of philanthropic patronization. They seek to speak for beggars and to alleviate their condition by arguing that begging is fully protected speech under the U.S. First Amendment. Their larger concern is to engage political attention and, by making 'it impossible for [mainstream listeners] to be oblivious to the poverty in their midst,'[19] place its eradication firmly on the agenda of social reform.

Although Hershkoff and Cohen's general ambition is eminently laudable and worth struggling for, their reliance on rights-talk as a means to that end is ultimately self-defeating. The dubious achievement of constitutional recognition for beggars' rights will likely increase, not reduce, the possibility that 'the poor are spoken of with the kind of dehumanizing imagery that makes it possible for some to deny their existence and to expiate society from any sense of responsibility.'[20]

Indeed, Hershkoff and Cohen beg the very question that they seek to answer – why are there beggars and how might we abolish them, not institutionalize them? – and expiate society from any real commitment to change. Rights-talk portrays and shapes a world that is inimical to the long-term aspirations of all its citizens, especially 'les misérables.' Giving individual rights only responds to the stark symptoms of poverty and may falsely obviate the need to confront the real structural causes of this endemic social disease. Rights-talk's abstract, universal and decontextualized depiction of individuals as moral beings undercuts the have-nots' claims to being treated as fully human and hinders efforts to establish a more egalitarian and empowering vision of citizenship and civic justice.

In their crafted commentary, Hershkoff and Cohen give an effective and cogent demonstration of rights-talk's disabling indeterminacy. Through a dextrous and sophisticated use of normative argument and legal doctrine, they show that 'begging is speech that existing first amendment values and case law protect'[21] and that it cannot be banned or unduly restricted. Of course, Hershkoff and Cohen resist the temptation to insist that this is the one and only true reading of the constitution beyond the cavil of political expediency. Instead, they recognize the critical imperative to accept that there are other plausible and opposing interpretations that could also meet the general criteria of doctrinal fit and normative justification. Rights are part of politics, not a precondition or boundary to the legitimate realm of contested politics. As such, Hershkoff and Cohen offer a compelling exercise in the progressive project of deviationist doctrinalism – the attempt to utilize routinized argumentation to transformative effect without falling into the trap of mistaking the contingently revisable for the revealed truth.[22] However, the fact that the courts have not yet been persuaded by a Hershkoff and Cohen–like brief ought to tip them off to the precarious nature of their undertaking. It should not only remind them of the conservative judicial instinct to side with the established order of things, but also alert them to the ideological orientation of rights-talk that makes it more amenable to some appropriations and manipulations than others.

Rights-talk obliges individuals to view their connection with others and their responsibility for others as a matter of detachment and voluntary choice. There is almost a wilful refusal to recognize the extent to which people are socially situated; a failure to grasp how people shape and are shaped by their structured relations with others. In particular, liberal theory's reliance on a depiction of individuals as rational, self-interested, and pre-social ethical beings who share little more than an abstract humanity flatters to deceive: it treats everyone the same while claiming to celebrate the difference and dignity of each. It is as though everyone is a potential beggar. Even for progressive critics like Hershkoff and Cohen, moral autonomy and democratic citizenship amount to little more than being abandoned to one's own devices and being put at the mercy of one's enabling or disabling social setting. In this way, rights-talk fails to comprehend that coercion can come in many different and subtle forms; oppression is neither exhausted by the power of the purse nor limited to the authority of the state. For instance, within capitalist society, the category of the 'abstract individual' becomes very classist in substance and orientation: rights-talk provides itself with little scope within which to recognize material deprivation and the resulting social oppression as the sociocultural norm. Rights-talk posits an almost libertarian vision of the morally autonomous being as one committed to robust self-reliance and fierce competitiveness; the spectre of the 'hard-working citizen' is always in mind.

An important corollary of this informing vision of social well-being is the understanding and assumption that it will be possible for beggars to alleviate their own suffering. Once beggars are empowered by a suitable set of rights and fired with an earnest sense of disciplined industry, this deliverance will be achievable without the rest of society having to change or sacrifice anything. Although peddled as a practically viable and eminently desirable ambition, it is really a highly objectionable and socially disingenuous vision of dystopian dimensions. Again, it places the burden on the already disadvantaged and relieves the presently advantaged from doing much at all. Furthermore, it continues the pretence that the extant economic order is only a neutral backdrop against which bargaining, exchange, and the accumulation of private property occur, but which itself has little impact on the nature and effects of such transactions. This, of course, is a canard. Detaching form from substance, liberal theory compresses life into constricting forms and turns questions of power into a discourse of power.[23]

A central claim made by Hershkoff and Cohen in support of a right to beg is that it can foster a sense of social solidarity and mutual responsibility that is essential to the establishment of a truly communal society: 'The beggar implicitly proposes the communitarian vision in which citizens have a responsibility for each other's survival' and, as speech that engages, begging 'has the ability to create social bonds between speaker and listener.'[24] While the recognition of the need for solidarity is crucial, Hershkoff and Cohen's proposal is the very negation of a truly egalitarian community. The relational engagement between beggar and listener is based on the most egregious imbalance of power. It does not cultivate a 'bond of empathy,'[25] but perpetuates a one-sided and hierarchical relation of dependence in which poverty offers and society accepts. It arises in a plea of supplication, is consummated as a squalid bargain, and is performed through an act of pity.

Rather than break down the gulf in power between rich and poor, legitimating beggars' rights pretends that it can be bridged by the most impersonal and patronizing of charitable gestures. By granting formal status to the unfortunate beggar, Hershkoff and Cohen mistake the aristocratic affectation of noblesse oblige for the truly democratic spirit of communal welfare. It allows the haves to salve their troubled conscience by a conspicuous display of private charity to the have-nots. It is surely a cruel conceit to suggest that in this way beggars serve an important social function 'in permitting others to discharge their religious obligation to give charity.'[26] To rhapsodize the beggar in such terms is almost tantamount to asking victims of a vicious assault to feel comforted by the fact they have acted splendidly by allowing psychopaths to gratify their antisocial behaviour. Surely this is the worst form of rationalization and one that does little credit to either victim or perpetrator; it is dehumanizing and demeaning. Moreover, in the mutually supportive relationship that is supposed to characterize begging, Hershkoff and Cohen's fixing of moral and cultural stigma on the listener is perversely misascribed: 'The soul in darkness sins, but the real sinner is he who caused the darkness.'[27]

Intellectual charity and political naïvety are not what the dispossessed want, but what they despise. As Nietzsche stingingly observes:

> Among helpful and charitable people one almost regularly encounters that clumsy ruse which first doctors the person to be helped – as if, for example, he 'deserved' help, and would prove to be profoundly grateful for all help, faithful and submissive. With these fancies they dispose of the needy, as of possessions, being charitable and helpful ... from a desire for possession. One finds them jealous if one crosses or anticipates them when they want to help.[28]

By institutionalizing and legitimating the position of 'beggar,' Hershkoff and Cohen do 'les misérables' the considerable disservice of entrenching the fact of poverty rather than working to eradicate it. The most that begging does is to provoke charity, often generous, and alleviate immediate need, always important. But it in no way changes the general and continuing situation that permits and often condones the poverty that begets the beggar. These destitute souls beg not for alms, but for an end to their plight as hapless hostages to capitalist fortune: it is public transformation as much as private charity that they seek.

Like most rights in the liberal vocabulary, the right to beg is formal and not substantive. Admittedly, begging helps to counteract the view that 'poverty in America is either non-existent or insignificant' and 'makes it impossible for [mainstream listeners] to be oblivious to the poverty in their midst,' but it fails to generate any substantive response by way of a corollary right or otherwise.[29] As a kind of speech, begging is fully satisfied by permitting individuals to give voice to their complaints, but without any obligation on listeners to make any substantive response to those pleas. This liberal vision of begging depicts a just society as one in which the achievement of moral autonomy can be effected without concern for serious economic equality. Indeed, taking seriously the idea of a right to beg confirms that in contemporary society, property still remains the measure of all things. Without property, beggars are barely people: they are almost nothing, because they own almost nothing. Echoing the sentiments of the nineteenth-century industrial elite, the vast majority of people continue to believe that all human beings have a real existence only if they make money or help to make it.[30]

It is crass to talk of a person's self-realization in circumstances in which 'she is destitute and needs help.'[31] To speak in such terms is to fall victim to the idealist temptation to treat freedom as a purely metaphysical state of mind; people can be free even in the most dire of material conditions, provided that they have the liberty to think and speak for themselves. It is a pretence of the privileged to talk of agency in such circumstances. This amounts to the violence of abstraction and is the philosophical kissing-cousin of rights-talk in the dysfunctional family of liberalism.[32] Such political theorizing commits a grievous form of intellectual harm that gives fraudulent legitimacy to the content and consequences of contemporary living. The right to beg beggars us all.

Like everything else, the problem with poverty is that its abasements become bearable to its wretched victims and that it is accepted as inevitable by those who perpetuate its condition. Although rights activists like Hershkoff and Cohen might castigate the judges and mainstream society for perpetuating a phantom normalcy in which the problems of 'les misérables' are diminished and dismissed, they themselves manage to perpetuate that condition. By allowing beggars the constitutional privilege to 'speak to the broad society about the pain of being poor,'[33] they give formal recognition to the poor as natural residents of contemporary American society. This moves people to anguish, but not to action. It is not formal status or rights that they crave, nor what we should wish to bestow. Rights only work for those who are already privileged. To others, they are a travesty of justice. It is change, not its promise, that is needed. Neither patronizing nor romanticizing 'les misérables,' the progressives' ambition must be to embrace everyone within the arms of a society that truly cares for the plight of all. To do otherwise is to run the risk of turning on its head Anatole France's ironic lament for 'the majestic equality of the laws, which forbid rich and poor alike to sleep under the bridges, to beg in the streets, and steal bread.'[34]

It is not enough to invite beggars to the bourgeois banquet so that they can, at least once, experience the good life. This not only demeans the guests and makes the hosts feel undeservedly beneficent, but it works as an almost celebratory occasion for 'the way things are.' To paraphrase Marx, the beggar is not freed from the tyranny of private property, but receives the dubious right to beg for it.[35] Not only does a right to beg not change the underlying structure of private property and its unequal distribution, but it places that very structure of capital accumulation outside the activist agenda of transformative possibilities. Moreover, those who are presently privileged and commited to eradicating poverty must not be content to speak for and on behalf of 'les misérables.' They must have a place of their own from which to speak and nurture a voice of their own in which to speak. Beggars are only saved when they no longer exist. Their salvation demands nothing less than that their suffering become ours too.

Any non-liberal vision of social justice must understand and be prepared to alter fundamentally the structural conditions that entrench the misery and humiliation that is the enduring lot of the panhandler. A progressive campaign for moral self-realization and political enlightenment must address these deep sources of institutional injustice that frame and valorize the lives of rich and poor alike. In contrast to the individualist cast of abstract liberalism, a competing vision would not understand society as a crude aggregate of separate things, but as connected cells in a thriving organism. Individuals are not universal and abstract moral entities, but are situated within a local and concrete context; they are political beings with particular historical and social affiliations. As between people, a sense of belonging and reciprocal responsibility for others would be fostered. Instead of a freedom that is contractual in origin and static in nature, there would be a more organic and dynamic understanding of freedom. Accepting that the social whole is much greater than the haphazard aggregation of its individual parts, personal worth and self-esteem would be embedded in and nourished by affective affiliations: 'Solidarity is the social side of love.'[36] Personal liberty without public responsibility is, at best, hollow and unsatisfying; at worst, it is uncivil and corrupting. Instead of relying upon transcendent values and abstract rationality, the search for social justice is based upon a practical reason that is contextual and contingent in character; flights of metaphysical musing become hopelessly fanciful and indulgent. The political agora and the economic marketplace would cease to be simply arenas for the confrontation of competing wills and the satisfaction of individual wants, but would become crucibles in which to forge a common good.

THE INVISIBLE WOMAN

As a matter of public discussion, abortion is constantly thought about, but is never entirely thought out. Debate is as old as society itself and promises to continue for as long again. The political contestation around abortion is quite recent. It is only in the past couple of decades that the engagement has moved into the legal sphere and begun to dominate legal theorizing about law and rights. Rather than bring clarity, order, and restraint to this perennially contested topic, law has tended to exacerbate the tensions and differences among the protagonists. Indeed, the debate over the legality and permissible limits of abortion is a classic example of legal argument: everybody talks, but few listen; everybody has an opinion, but few agree; much is said, but little is accomplished.[37] The issue is profoundly divisive and is likely unable to be resolved to everyone's satisfaction. It has become a lightning rod for competing ideological views on the family, the state, sexuality, poverty, and morality. However, the more limited focus of my attention is on the inappropriateness of rights-talk and its impoverishing effect upon public debate. In particular, I want to concentrate on how the abstraction of rights-talk contributes to law's patriarchy by rendering women invisible and preventing their empowerment as full and equal citizens in a democratic society.

While the discourse around abortion is about women's lives, it has been dominated by men. Treated as a matter for religious, medical, and legal enquiry, the debate has been confiscated by these largely male professions. For these men, abortion is not a women's issue, but 'it was their issue about their "issue".'[38] Furthermore, the general terms and conditions of that debate have been largely male in substance and expression. Discussion always manages to be about something or somebody else other than women and their (lack of) freedom to control their own bodies – fetuses, fathers, children, doctors, lawyers, economists, philosophers, and so on. Indeed, for the very reason that it is about women's lives, abortion has not been given the prominence in social reform and action that it deserves. However, because of its importance to women's lives, it is crucial that the debate over abortion and its social practice must be resolved by and for women.[39]

Apart from its debilitating indeterminacy,[40] the abstract, decontextualized, and universalized language of rights portrays and shapes a world that is inimical to the long-term ambitions of women to be treated as fully human. In short, it fails to take them seriously *as women*. While the achievements of rights-talk have been considerable for the emancipation of women in many areas of social life, it has proved sorely inadequate to the task of ensuring that women are able to take control of their own bodies. Women's moral and physical autonomy often amounts to little more than being abandoned to their own devices and being put at the mercy of their disabling (or enabling) social setting. This sense of non-attachment from others 'is not the way women generally think about themselves and is utterly inappropriate as a description of a woman who is pregnant.'[41] Within liberal society, the category of the 'abstract individual' becomes very patriarchal in substance and orientation: rights-talk provides itself with little scope within which to recognize women as members of oppressed groups or male hegemony as the sociocultural norm. Not only does liberalism posit a male vision of the morally autonomous being as one committed to robust self-reliance and fierce competitiveness, it manages to assume that reproduction and child-rearing will take care of themselves.

In its failure to take women seriously, liberal theory offers women a Hobson's choice: they must deny that an important part of their moral and social distinctiveness derives from their reproductive capacities if they are to obtain full moral standing, or they must reduce themselves entirely to their reproductive identities and become dependent, second-class citizens, trapped within the confines of their own biological distinctiveness. For the liberal individual, pregnancy is an aberrational condition and is to be tolerated rather than integrated into the life experience of the polity. As a deviation from the male model of physical integrity and psychological development, childbirth is seen, at worst, as a kind of illness and, at best, as a mechanical exercise that leaves women unchanged and unaffected in their sense of themselves and their relations to others. Rather than be a profoundly revealing challenge to the abstruse character of individual autonomy in the liberal world view, women's reproductive experience is trivialized and marginalized. As Ursula Le Guin describes it, rights-talk gives no discursive space or value to women's lives:

> We are told, in words and not in words, we are told by their deafness, by their stone ears, that our experience, the life experience of women, is not valuable to men – therefore not valuable to society, to humanity. We are valued by men only as an element of their experience, as things experienced; anything we may say, anything we may do, is recognized only if said and done in their service.
>
> One thing we incontestably do is have babies. So we have babies as the male priests, lawmakers, and doctors tell us to have them, when and where to have them, how often, and how to have them; so that is all under control. But we are *not to talk about* having babies, because that is not part of the experience of men and so nothing to do with reality, with civilization, and no concern of art.[42]

The most revealing illustration of the absurdity of liberal theory's abstract individualism is its depiction and understanding of the fetus. From its moment of conception, the fetus is the archetypical abstract individual: it is the perfect inhabitant of the liberal society. Unencumbered by historical circumstances and disconnected from social relations, it is the very epitome of the Hobbesian citizen – the solitary being who, uncorrupted by and not responsible for others, is in a natural state of autonomy. In a more modern allusion, Barbara Katz Rothman has declared that 'the fetus in utero has become a metaphor for "man" in space, floating free, attached by only the umbilical cord to the spaceship.'[43] In its innocent and splendid isolation, the fetus represents the elusive and vacuous nature of freedom in a liberal theory of rights-talk. Such an abstraction illuminates the perversity of depicting social life in such ahistorical and asocial terms.

Far from being unconnected and independent, the fetus is totally dependent on the pregnant woman for sustenance and survival; it is at its most completely helpless when it is at its most completely autonomous. It achieves its abstract freedom at the cost of lived existence. By refusing to acknowledge the basic connectedness of people and their inter-dependence, abstract individualism can only give the fetus a visible presence in rights-talk by rendering the pregnant woman invisible. Robbed of her separate identity, she is reduced to a convenient machine for the fetus's incubation and denied her own entitlements to social respect and political recognition as a full and equal citizen.[44] Taken on its own terms, therefore, rights-talk reduces humanity to an empty abstraction. In so doing, it manages to treat some entities as more deserving of human solicitude and other entities as less deserving. A fetus is neither a person nor not a person; it is itself, a fetus, and must be so treated as a unique entity. In the extreme world of rights-talk, it is either the full liberal individual or nothing. And that is no solution at all.[45]

Another troubling feature of abortion rights is their negative aspect. Under a liberal theory of rights-talk, the basis of individual freedom is the absence of collective constraint and interference: individuals are most free when they are left entirely to their own devices and desires.[46] However, when it comes to abortion (and many other issues), the very arguments that are used to ground and police the woman's right to choose an abortion handcuff its proponents' capability to develop and substantiate that right. There are very definite and conservative limits to rights that are based on a 'keep the state out' philosophy of political action and moral choice. The notion of freedom as privacy is disastrous for any full development of a progressive policy on abortion. Not only does rights-talk artificially and harmfully treat the fetus and the pregnant woman as separate and competing persons, but it also abandons that woman (and any child that is subsequently born) to the socioeconomic vicissitudes of real life. After all, access to abortion is not an abstract problem for abstract women. The real difficulty is for young, unmarried, poor, and, often, black women.[47] In short, the privacy of such women can leave them free to be and do nothing. Moreover, rights-talk relieves public and private elites from any justified responsibility to take positive steps to ensure that women have actual and realizable choices in determining the course of their reproductive lives.

The initial attraction and ultimate failure of rights-talk as a progressive means for achieving reproductive justice are well evidenced by the judgment of Bertha Wilson in *Morgentaler*.[48] Her opinion stretches the limits of rights-talk in the cause of women's liberation, but still remains within its confining discourse. For her, the constitutional issue was not about procedural fairness, but went squarely to the substantive question of 'whether a pregnant woman can ... be compelled by law to carry the foetus to term.' She had little doubt that such a compulsion struck at the very heart of personal liberty. A woman's decision to terminate her pregnancy was not simply a medical one, but one that has 'profound psychological, economic and social consequences for the pregnant woman.' Indeed, while men cannot relate to such an agonizing decision other than in an objectifying way, the pregnant woman is faced with living with a decision that 'deeply reflects the way the woman thinks about herself and her relationship to others and society at large.' Accordingly, because the criminalization of abortion treated women as 'the passive recipient of a decision made by others' to use her body for the most intimate purposes, Wilson concluded that women did have a constitutional right to an abortion: 'Can there be anything that comports less with human dignity and self-respect?'[49]

Nevertheless, in spite of her decision's progressive cast, Wilson falls victim to rights-talk's conservative ideology. First, she follows the 1973 American decision in *Roe* v. *Wade*[50] and holds that, although the state has no justification to interfere in the very early stages of pregnancy, the state's interest in protecting the fetus increases and becomes more tolerable as the pregnancy develops. However, she is reluctant to suggest any specific guidelines and feel that such matters should be left 'to the informed judgment of the legislature.' This is a strange way to protect women's dignity, self-respect, and freedom from state interference. Second, while Wilson insists that women's choices ought not to be confined to 'any one conception of the good life' and that a woman is neither 'a totally independent entity disconnected from society' nor 'a mere cog in an impersonal machine in which her values, goals and aspirations are subordinated to those of the collectivity,' she interprets women's freedom as being negative and solitary. She perpetuates the notion that the state that governs best is the state that governs least: 'The rights guaranteed in the Charter erect around each individual, metaphorically speaking, an invisible fence over which the state will not be allowed to trespass.'[51] In effect, Wilson's adoption of an individualistic ideology abandons women to their own devices and stymies the struggle to encourage government to fulfil its progressive obligations to provide appropriate reproductive health facilities and services.

The negativity of rights-talk results from the liberal insistence on dividing the world into public and private spheres.[52] The courts are constrained to view the state as almost the exclusive source of oppression and to treat the private realm as an unencumbered sphere of freedom. While the state can be a culprit, victims often suffer oppression at the hands of private actors and through structures of private power. As the American Supreme Court so succinctly expressed it in *Harris*, 'although government may not place obstacles in the path of a woman's exercise of her freedom of choice, it need not remove those not of its own creation.'[53] Such platitudes only add insult to injury. Women can only get an abortion if they can find a doctor to do it and have the financial resources or funding assistance to pay. Without adequate resources or funding, abortion remains accessible only to the privileged. In such circumstances, a putative right to an abortion is cold comfort. Again, those who cannot afford such expense are in that position because of personal failings and not through any systemic fault with the polity. As Rhonda Copelon summarizes it:

> To treat a woman's poverty and her inability to exercise choice as a consequence not of market conditions and public policy, but of private fault is a dangerous fiction built upon another aspect of the separation of the public and private spheres. It rests on the idea, central to capitalist patriarchy, that the family unit has the responsibility of being economically self-sufficient. Not only does this notion of privatization permit the state to escape responsibility for the tragic conditions of people's lives, but the ideology of private responsibility also makes it possible to blame the poor, who are overwhelmingly women, for their inability to be self-sufficient.[54]

A progressive vision has a different understanding of social life and its possibilities for justice. It does not, as some rights enthusiasts contend that it should, cast women as 'Charter rights-holders first, breeders second.'[55] Instead, it insists that women are always to be treated as citizens, not as rights-holders because that obliges them to cease being women, and certainly never as breeders. A progressive approach would accommodate the fact that women are different from men in their reproductive characteristics, understand the sociopolitical relations that frame and valorize those facts, and ensure that any understanding of what it is to be a full and equal citizen incorporates the vital material dimension of women's lives.[56] Moreover, a progressive society would be genuinely concerned with the substantive quality of children's lives and not simply their mere existence. Too often, those who claim to defend fetal rights confine their attention to a successful birth, with little interest in the child's life in its fuller sense. By reluctantly choosing abortion, many women do so, not because they are indifferent to human life, but because they value life enough not to subject their potential child to living in a world that has little hope of being better than their own.

An essential feature of a truly progressive vision of reproductive well-being is the recognition that subordination is reinforced by ignoring the relevance of social conditions that give rise to that subordination in the first place. Consequently, a non-liberal theory of public responsibility begins with the inseparable connection between social conditions and the individual exercise and experience of personal autonomy. So instructed, it looks beyond the negative legalisms of rights-talk to the affirmative politics of a needs-oriented social agenda. As a practice of communal solidarity, it concerns itself as much with social welfare as it does with individual privacy: formal autonomy and substantive equality become pervasively related and mutually supportive.[57] Accordingly, any satisfactory debate about abortion must also be about universal health care, housing, day care, employment, sex education, literacy, and so forth. Unless the problem of abortion is located within this broader and deeper social context, it will never be resolved in a way that fully respects and values women and children.

A more positive and less rights-oriented vision of social justice would not be premised on liberty as negatively and abstractly defined. Freedom is more than a lack of collective interference; it is the establishment of positive opportunities for substantive action. A progressive vision would look to the state to stand by and empower women so that they would have the true autonomy to make decisions for themselves, have those decisions respected, and work toward providing the social conditions and institutional resources to give effect to those decisions. Within a society in which there were real choices available for women, it might be possible for women to engage in genuine debate about the nature and limits of choice. In short, the most pressing challenge for progressive scholars and activists is to establish a social life in which the need to choose abortion would be greatly reduced – a world in which women and children could be equally and fully human.[58]

SLOUCHING TOWARD GILEAD

In her novel *The Handmaid's Tale,* Margaret Atwood charts the moral landscape that makes up the mythical state of Gilead. It is a future world of right-wing fundamentalism in which women cannot work, hold property, learn to read, or make any choices about when and how they will engage in motherhood; their sole function is to bear and rear children. All of this is done in the name of and for the greater glory of the theocratic state. The central figure in this dystopian fable is Offred, a member of the handmaids' ranks, whose designated role in life is to serve as a surrogate womb for the infertile Commander class. In conveying the wretched experience of what it means to be a woman in a world where women's lives are exclusively determined by their reproductive biology, she confides that 'I used to think of my body as an instrument ... Now the flesh arranges itself differently. I'm a cloud congealed around a central object, the shape of a pear, which is hard and more real than I am.'[59] It is a chilling prospect and one that is not so distant from present reality as many might wish or think.

Atwood's fictional Gilead evolved out of an apathetic liberal democracy that turned a blind eye to the slow erosion of women's – at the best of times – tenuous moral autonomy by neoconservative fundamentalism. Although less dramatic and more benign, the current backsliding on the promise of equal respect for Canadian women's entitlement to control their own reproductive lives threatens to do the same. The historical development of fundamental human rights has thus far reflected only the political struggles of men and has ignored the needs of women caused by their particular social and biological role in reproduction. Respect for the essential personhood of women requires that these needs be given the full protection extended through such traditionally sacred rights as freedom of speech and belief. As Bertha Wilson so uncompromisingly expressed it, the decision to reproduce or not to reproduce 'is properly perceived as an integral part of modern woman's struggle to assert her dignity and worth as a human being.'[60]

The frightening events around the plight of Chantal Daigle in the summer of 1989 place the limitations and dangers of rights-talk for women's empowerment into sharp and disturbing relief. While the Supreme Court of Canada in *Daigle* v. *Tremblay*[61] made an enlightened stand on behalf of one beleaguered individual woman (and is rightfully deserving of praise for so doing), it relied on a rights-based mode of analysis that left in place a systemic program of patriarchial control by the state over women's reproductive lives and legitimated rights-talk as a way of comprehending women's oppression. Apart from its debilitating indeterminacy, the chosen language of rights portrays and shapes a world that is inimical to the long-term aspirations of women. Its abstract, decontextualized, and universal depiction of individuals as moral beings undercuts women's claims to be treated as fully human and hinders efforts to establish a more egalitarian and empowering vision of social justice.

The engaged and situated circumstances of this unforgettable episode in Chantal Daigle's life make for harrowing reading. By presenting a personal narrative through Chantal's (and Jean Guy Tremblay's) words, it might be possible to gain a richer understanding of this slice of real life. Drawing on affadavits and press clippings, I will attempt to construct, albeit imperfectly and incompletely, the social and personal context in which this case and women's predicament around abortion generally is situated. While there is no available vantage point from which to gain unmediated access to Chantal Daigle's experience,[62] the following narrative is intended to offer an alternative account of Chantal's summer to that crafted by the courts:

> Like most couples, Chantal Daigle and Guy Tremblay met in an entirely prosaic and unexceptional way. In November 1988, she was a 21-year-old waitress who was at the Radio Shack store in a local mall getting her answering machine fixed. She struck up a conversation with the salesman behind the counter. He was four years older than her, six feet tall, and dashingly handsome. They began to see each other regularly and soon were in love. After a few months, they moved in together the following February. Things seemed wonderful at first: 'I was overwhelmed by him at the start. I was blindly in love, but things deteriorated.'
>
> They set the date for a summer wedding to be held at the end of July. But this was not the first time that Guy had been engaged. Three years before, he had been painfully jilted. His former fiancée had answered 'no' on the altar when the priest asked, 'Do you take this man to be your husband?' 'Chantal was my last hope. I said to myself that if it didn't work out with her, I wouldn't start again with another woman. Sincerely, I couldn't love anyone else.'
>
> After moving in together, Guy asked Chantal to stop using contraception. Although she felt that she was too young to start a family, he was quite insistent. 'I didn't want to, but it was so difficult to say no. I wasn't sure about myself anymore. He made me feel as if I didn't have a right to make decisions. He checked my menstrual dates with me. He told me that if I had a baby, he would feel that I was really and truly his.'
>
> She stopped taking the pill. By March, she was pregnant. However, once she became pregnant, he seemed to change. He became physical-

ly and verbally abusive: 'He said that if I continued to be pig-headed, either he or I would end up on the pages of *Allo Police*.'

As her pregnancy proceeded, his possessiveness and violence increased: 'I was scared of him. I wanted to leave him and didn't know how because he was threatening me constantly to disfigure me and to subdue and control me once and for all. He threw me on to the floor even though he knew I was pregnant.'

When the month of their wedding came, the abuse had reached a crisis point: 'During another quarrel on 1 July, he grabbed me by the neck and squeezed tightly, saying I was too sociable and accused me of lying to him.'

By this point, Chantal felt that she could not go on living like that anymore. Nor could she face bringing a child into such an abusive relationship. In early July, she packed her things and moved back to her father's home. She told Guy that she was ending their engagement and her pregnancy. She made an appointment to have an abortion a couple of days later.

But when she phoned home en route to the clinic, she found that he had sought and been granted a court order the day before. The injunction barred her from having the abortion or doing anything to endanger her pregnancy before a full judicial hearing in ten day's time.

Guy had found his lawyer through one of the customers at the car dealership where he had begun to work as a mechanic. Chantal found a lawyer too and filed an affidavit describing his abusive conduct toward her. She explained that she wanted nothing more to do with him: 'If I had gone ahead and had our baby, he would always have had a hold over me. He would have had to keep seeing me to see the child. That isn't my idea of what a family should be.'

By now, the media had got hold of the story. An anonymous donor offered Daigle $25,000 to carry the pregnancy to term. With a public conduit, Tremblay made further declarations of intent: 'I love her, and what I did right now is not just for me, it's for her too.'

On the day of the hearing, pro-choice and anti-abortion demonstrators massed outside the courthouse. A plane overhead carried a banner, reading 'S.O.S. – life for the baby fetus, its father and mother.' Justice Viens ruled that Chantal had no compelling reasons for interfering with the right to life of the fetus that she carried and prohibited an abortion. Chantal was shocked, but put on a brave face: 'I feel like a victim. I have more rights than a 20-week-old fetus. I still have hope and it is still my choice.'

Guy greeted the news of his victory with hugs for his lawyers and supporters and with a cry of 'mission accomplished.' He smiled across the courtroom at Chantal for the first time that day. She never looked back or acknowledged him as she left the courtroom with her family.

Two days after the ruling, she received leave to appeal the decision to the Quebec Court of Appeal. On the same day, Chantal received a message through the media urging her to think twice. It was sent by Barbara Dodd, a Toronto woman who had successfully fought a similar injunction only weeks before, but had later undergone a change of heart after being counselled by anti-abortion activists. Tremblay echoed Dodd's sentiments: 'I know she is going to regret everything if she has an abortion.'

Chantal replied, also through the media: 'The only thing I would regret is having the baby and he is the one who would make me regret it.'

Tremblay ignored her stated intentions that she would never return to him. He announced that he intended to raise the baby with her as his wife: 'She said she doesn't want to see me no more but she's going to have to if she has an abortion because it's not going to be finished. I think every man is possessive but that's no reason to kill a child. I don't think it's really her heart talking in this decision. It's her family. It's the pro-choice people and the media.'

By the day before the appeal, Guy had formulated a backup plan: 'There's no question of Chantal keeping the baby ... Either she comes back to live with me or my parents are going to keep it.'

By his parents, Guy meant his father and step-mother. He explained that his unwillingness to leave the fetus in the custody of Chantal resulted from the abuse that he had suffered at the hands of his natural mother: 'I had problems with my mother. She's responsible for this bump that I have on the back of my head. She hit me with a hockey stick when I was 11 years old and fractured my skull ... I didn't have a fun childhood and if I want this baby, it's because I don't want it to live the way I lived.'

Although he had been convicted of assault in another situation in 1982, Guy shrugged off Chantal's accounts of his brutality: 'Everything she's said in the newspapers and on television about me is false. I never beat her and I never prevent her from seeing her friends. It's true that I shook her a bit, but every couple has fights ...

I never hit her hard enough to leave marks ... Maybe I pushed her around a little, but that's normal for any couple.'

A week after the hearing, the Quebec Court of Appeal upheld the injunction in a split decision. Again, the majority found that Chantal's reasons for seeking to end the pregnancy were not sufficiently grave. Chantal's lawyers sought leave to appeal to the Supreme Court of Canada and were granted a hearing en banc two weeks later on 8 August. Chantal was already over 20 weeks pregnant and beyond the cut-off date at which Canadian hospitals will perform abortions except in medical emergencies. She would remain eligible for procedures at clinics in the United States until her 24th week and vowed to await the decision of the Court.

In the meantime, as opposing activists demonstrated across the country, Guy again had a change of heart over the future of the fetus. He decided that Chantal would raise it with financial contributions from him: 'I thought about it and you don't take a newborn baby away from its mother. At the beginning, I had it in for Chantal because of what she was putting us through.'

On the morning of 8 August, lawyers for Guy, Chantal, and various intervener groups in support of both sides made their submissions. Chantal was not present. After the lunch break, Chantal's lawyer rose to tell the court that he had been able to confirm information given him by the minister of Justice – Chantal had gone to Boston, in disguise and under an assumed name, and had had her abortion. Guy was incensed: 'She just killed my child ... I'm going after her. I have to talk to my lawyer about what charge, but we're going to pursue her.'

After a brief recess, Chief Justice Dickson announced that the hearing would continue. By the end of the day, the Court delivered a unanimous decision without reasons granting the appeal and quashing the injunction. Pro-life demonstrators were distraught; the women who had brought toys and stuffed animals for 'Baby Daigle' were reduced to tears on the steps of the Supreme Court building. Gilles Girondin, an anti-abortion activist, issued a statement: 'This child has lost his life and this child was practically the child of Canada. We've been spending months out of our lives ... trying to save that child's life.'

Chantal was relieved: 'I had left him and he wanted me back at any price. But I wasn't going to stay with a man who was violent, insanely jealous and wanted to control every aspect of my life. I didn't want to be a single parent bringing up a child alone... If he was capable of pushing me around, he would have been capable of doing violence to a child, so it was partly to protect that child that I aborted it.'

When the Supreme Court released its written reasons in mid-November, Chantal made a terse statement: 'Twice, they didn't listen to me, but this time they took into account what I and my lawyer said.'

When she was named 'Newsmaker of the Year' by *Chatelaine* magazine in December, Chantal was subdued: 'People across the country know my name, and law students will study my case as part of their courses, but what I would really like is to be forgotten.'

THROUGH THE LAW DARKLY

Legal discourse is a particularly potent tool for negotiating and constructing social reality. It is one of the ways society defines itself and presents the world to itself. While the state often relies on crude force or threats to achieve its ends, the law's strength and long-term viability stem from its success as a sophisticated and ideological mode of world-making. The discursive practices that comprise the language of the law structure the world in particular and partial ways: 'Law is a reiterated failure to classify life.'[63] Being normative in nature, it operates as a gatekeeper of the mind that all factual entrants must not only respect and obey, but that designates them as valid and relevant facts in the first place. As an intelligible description of and mutual prescription for action, legal discourse predisposes its speakers and listeners to certain interpretive choices and social stances. Located and sustained by historical conditions and circumstances, the discourse is socially imposed and, what is often overlooked, unconsciously assumed by its individual users. Indeed, its efficacy is attributable to its achievement of an ostensibly robust, plausibly coherent, and functionally dependable image of social life and control.[64]

The staple feature of modern legal language is rights-talk. The law insists on characterizing and categorizing social interaction as occasions for the exercise or breach of legal rights. When individuals' relations are represented through rights-talk, their dealings are forced into a particular linguistic and, therefore, ideological strait-jacket. By speaking in that way, the legal system has adopted a very partial idiom and has set aside other ways of describing their shared experience. For example, the sterile and impersonal style of rights ignores the understanding of the event as an immediate, interpersonal act of subtle and mixed expectations and interpretations. Rights-talk has achieved an objective existence and is treated as something to be grasped and wielded. Rights-talk is not simply a taxonomic device to organize and engage the world, but brings into existence a world and a way of ordering people's roles in it. Moreover, it has brought into play a whole paraphernalia of understandings about citizens' past conduct, present intentions, and future dealings together. In effect, they have had created for them a distinct past and future scenario for their experience. Discourse has worked a practical and significant exercise of power. By filtering it through the sieve of abstract rights-talk, a rich and complex experience has been diluted and sanitized. Any situation's significance for the participants has been transformed and often impoverished.

Chantal Daigle's own account of her harrowing experience stands in stark contrast to the bloodless recounting of the courts and its impoverishing reliance on rights-talk. The courts framed the whole dispute between Chantal Daigle and Jean Guy Tremblay as a matter of clarifying and enforcing the respective rights in play: 'This case raises fundamental problems of evaluation and balancing the rights of the pregnant woman, the potential father, and the unborn child.'[65] Although the Quebec Court of Appeal was more explicit and open, the Supreme Court of Canada's decision was also underpinned by the rhetorical foundations of rights-talk. The decision bears all the hallmarks of rights-talk – rampant indeterminacy, abstract analysis, patriarchial prejudice, and political naïvety. The fact that the two courts arrived at different results is not significant in this regard: the disagreement was over whether they could find a sufficient jurisprudential basis for the relevant rights and not whether rights should be dispositive of the dispute.[66] Indeed, the Supreme Court made it clear that not only was 'the recognition of rights' at the heart of its inquiry, but, by so limiting its inquiry, it could resolve the case in a neutral and non-political way, without having to stray onto contested ideological terrain:

> The court is not required to enter the philosophical and theological debates about whether or not a foetus is a person, but, rather, to answer the legal question of whether the Quebec legislature has accorded the foetus personhood. Metaphysical arguments may be relevant but they are not the primary focus of inquiry. Nor are scientific arguments about the biological status of a foetus determinative in our inquiry. The task of properly classifying a foetus in law and in science are different pursuits. Ascribing personhood to a foetus in law

> is a fundamentally normative task. It results in the recognition of rights and duties – a matter which falls outside the concerns of scientific classification. In short, this court's task is a legal one. Decisions based upon broad social, political, moral and economic choices are more appropriately left to the legislature.[67]

The first difficulty with the judgments is the general indeterminacy and imprecision that surround and penetrate the preliminary act of determining whose rights are in play, what are the parameters of those rights, and how any conflict between those rights is to be resolved. Although it is never expressly stated, the fact that there is no real position of compromise on abortion – that women can or cannot have an abortion when they decide to have one – is a spectre that haunts and invalidates many of the courts' efforts at rights analysis. As in most other situations, rights-talk is a zero-sum game: what is given to one can only be taken at the expense of another. It provides no space or vocabulary in which to express the complicated and competing considerations that might frame and affect a woman's personal decision of whether or not to proceed with her pregnancy. Rights-talk is not only silent about the relative weighting of such factors, but offers no guidance on how an individual might go about making such a decision. It abandons women to themselves and denies them any discursive or moral resources through which to understand, evaluate, and reach their own decisions. Rights-talk is dumb on the use of rights: all exercises of rights are as good or as bad as any other.

None of this is to be taken to suggest that women should not have a full entitlement to determine the course of their pregnacy and overall reproductive life. Any progressive vision of social justice would ensure that women have such a final veto over what happens to their bodies. After all, there is no way to protect fetal life without controlling women's bodies. However, in affording equal and open access to adequate health care, there is a communal responsibility to promote a vigorous dialogue among women about abortion in which there would be a willingness to listen, an openness to change, and a confidence that any final decision would be with the woman herself.[68] In such a supportive and democratic environment, it might be possible for women to be both pro-choice and pro-life – a recognition that abortion should be freely available, but that the value of life should be robustly defended. This would entail an understanding that life was not only about birth, but encompassed living in its fullest sense, and that abortion might be the least worst alternative in particular circumstances. Rights-talk is incapable of fostering or coping with such dialogic engagement. Also, in a progressive milieu, women could both decide to abort and grieve the loss of their potential child without being criticized as acting wrongly or inconsistently. Without guilt, she would accept that her regret and anguish would be over the circumstances as to why she had to have an abortion rather than the fact of the abortion itself.

Although most of the judges in *Daigle*, some begrudgingly,[69] began from the basic assumption that a woman does have some kind of right to an abortion, they all contended that her right had to be understood and exercised in light of others' relevant rights. More significantly, they insisted that it had to be exercised reasonably. In so doing, they highlighted the limits of rights-talk at the same time that they relied upon it. Unequal to the task it sets itself, rights-talk has to be supplemented by a prior, partial, and, in this instance, patriachial view of reproduction. As Bernier puts it:

> It is accepted that if a pregnant woman has a right to an abortion, it is not an absolute right which she can exercise arbitrarily, as she pleases, at her sole wish, at any time before the birth.[70]

> A person who freely does an act must assume its consequences. Pregnancy is not in itself an infringement of the physical integrity of a woman, an interference with her body, but a function which is a fundamental part of her nature. The rule of nature is that a pregnancy must be carried to term. The right to voluntarily terminate it constitutes an exception to this general rule. To arbitrarily have recourse to this without reasonable grounds constitutes at any stage of a pregnancy an abuse of right.[71]

In order for rights-talk to retain a semblance of political neutrality, many of the judges' analytical efforts are devoted to elucidating whether there are any other competing rights that can be said to curtail the pregnant woman's right. The most obvious candidate as a competing rights-holder is the fetus. All the judges maintain that the fetus has a status as a separate entity from the pregnant woman whether as a fully independent person or as a potential person to be protected in the public interest. Whereas the majority gave counterbalancing weight to the fetus as an equal rights holder,[72] the minority saw it more as an outer limit on the woman's ability to exercise her right.[73] The problems with this kind of analysis are manifold, but the two most telling criticisms deserve special attention.

First, the terrain of rights is unidimensional: people must not only be rights-holders to count, but are reduced to nothing but rights-holders. Abstracted from social setting and political conditions, each rights-holder is treated as being exactly the same and as being endowed with exactly the same claims to the state's protection and support. There is no analytical room or formula through which to recognize and respond to the difference in actual circumstances between one rights-holder and another. Moreover, once the fetus is recognized as having an equal status, it becomes easy to present the conflict of right in a very partial and weighted fashion. LeBel's judgment makes this move neatly:

One cannot deny the importance of the inconvenience and the problems that the pregnancy itself often gives rise to. It also involves restrictions on a woman's life. The birth entails certain risks and often suffering. The life of the appellant will not be the same for several months. Finally, it will create a relationship with the child which will see it granted various rights by law after its birth as against its two parents. Moreover, if the injunction is not granted, the life of the foetus is terminated, it will not live. What must be balanced, is the immediate end of the existence of the foetus and the inconvenience and important restrictions on the life of the appellant. At this stage in the development of the child, the balance of inconvenience clearly appears to favour the foetus and would justify the application for an injunction.[74]

When depicted in this manner, it seems a dereliction of moral responsibility not to prefer 'the fetus's life' over 'the mother's inconvenience.' Yet such a conclusion builds on the second infirmity of rights-talk: it fails to place a woman's pregnancy in its proper social, biological, or psychological context. It is ludicrous to think of the fetus as 'a living human entity, distinct from that of the mother that carries it.'[75] Only in the abstract and unreal universe of rights-talk is it possible to detach the fetus from the life and body of the woman. In the most profound sense, it renders women invisible as actual people and reduces them to the status of 'gravida.' When pregnant, women are unavoidably bound up in a whole set of relations with others, which, depending on the circumstances, will be both a burden and/or a blessing. Chantal Daigle's pregnancy reinforces that view. In particular, the separation of the pregnant woman and fetus flaunts the experience that women undergo and report. While the particulars vary from pregnancy to pregnancy and with its social context, childbirth is a transformative process that happens not simply *in* them, but *to* them. As Chantal Daigle knew, her life would never be the same again whether she proceeded with her pregnancy or not; abortion seemed the least damaging and more appropriate option for her and her potential child.[76]

Of course, none of this means that 'this would be the same as considering the child conceived but not yet born as a non-entity.'[77] It is only rights-talk that posits such a ridiculous alternative. The fetus is not a person, but a potential person, and, as a potential person, it is not a non-entity. It does and should have significance in the moral ordering of the world. It is only within the narrow provenance of rights-talk that those who support a pro-choice stance are interpreted to treat the fetus as a non-entity and undeserving of concern or consideration.[78] The real question is who is entitled to give weight to and make any decision as to its fate. This must surely be the prerogative of the pregnant woman. There is no authority – moral, political, constitutional, or otherwise – to remove from her the possibility (and responsibility) of making that decision and putting it into effect. As part of the woman, the fetus can never be separated from the life of the woman, and no decision can be made on behalf of the fetus that does not infringe a woman's security in her own body.

The second candidate as a rights-holder, for placing in the balance against a woman, is the father. While the Supreme Court of Canada rejected the existence or recognition of any such rights, the Quebec Court of Appeal was strongly approving of fathers' rights. Although supported by his colleagues in the majority, Bernier voiced the most extreme statement of the position:

> But when the interests of the mother are contrary to those of her unborn child, when she wishes to terminate her pregnancy in a situation where the public interest is not involved, it is unquestionably the right of the father, on serious and reasonable grounds, not contrary to the interests of the unborn child, to oppose the abortion. This legal interest is based on the very fact of conception which both the father and mother were the cause. It is his child as much as it is the mother's, neither more, neither less.[79]

To equate the position and moral claims of a copulating man with that of a pregnant woman is repugnant and defies even the weak logic of the theory of rights itself; the momentary contribution of semen surely cannot be equated with the period and qualitative dimension of gestation. Moreover, rights-talk inhibits any inquiry into the motives or behaviour of the father and treats all fathers as having equal moral standing. Within its perverse normative universe, the rapist or abuser has as much a moral claim to 'preserving the parent-child relationship which flows from his potential paternity'[80] as has the woman's caring or supportive partner. Also, rights-talk polarizes the issue by making the views of potential fathers either all-important or of no consequence at all; there is no room to suggest that, in certain circumstance, it might be appropriate to consult the potential father, but without giving him any legal control over the woman's decision. Recognizing fathers' rights in any stronger sense gives men a formal control over womens' lives that supplements and strengthens the existing informal controls of social relations that they already enjoy. Within such a scenario, it is the woman who runs the risk of being 'a non-entity' and becoming 'anyone's property'[81] but her own.

All of this rights-talk takes place in an abstract realm that ignores the social realities of a patriarchal society in which reproduction takes place. The courts' understanding of what it is for 'a person ... [to] freely do and act'[82] is naïve. What might be 'freely done' today for a man is not the same as what amounts to voluntary choice for a woman. As Chantal Daigle's own account shows,[83] the experiential facts give the lie to the claim that 'the birth was desired and planned for by the couple.'[84] Her plight also exposes the crass indifference of the court's observation that 'I would be sinking to speculation if I were to venture to predict the effects that the birth of the fetus would have in the present circumstances.'[85] Similarly, an acknowledgment of social realities undercuts many of the anti-abortion proponents' arguments. They claim to root their convictions in respect for the sanctity of human life. But the life they seek to protect would seem to begin at conception and end at birth. This narrow vision inexcusably ignores the fact that denial or access to safe abortion services will put the lives and well-being of countless Canadian women in jeopardy. Prohibiting or restricting reproductive choice, while adequate day care and social support services continue to be denied to women, will not eradicate the need or desire for abortion. Rather, it will compel beleaguered, poor women to once again risk septicaemia and death at the hands of unscrupulous back-street butchers or bring an unwanted child into the world. A return to those dark ages would be a sad legacy. It remains the case that the greatest threat to the fetus is not from the pregnant woman, but from a society that fails to address issues of poverty, violence, illiteracy, and so on.

In Atwood's Gilead, women and men of good faith perceived the dangers of the oppressive denial of reproductive choice only when such measures had already rendered them powerless to resist. Taking seriously applications for a court-ordered injunction by a jilted and abusive lover to deny a woman access to a lawful abortion is precisely the sort of first step down the path to a biologically determined future against which Ms Atwood's heroine counsels vigilance: 'Nothing happens instantaneously; in a gradually heating bathtub, you'd be boiled to death before you know it.'[86] The sane and just response is to pull the plug on this rising tide of moralism and to consider seriously the idea of giving women *full* control over their own bodies and lives. Rights-talk is incapable of achieving such a progressive ambition. It is long on talk about personal dignity and equal respect, but short on giving substantive effect to that rhetoric. It grants women equal standing as responsible and autonomous citizens, only to snatch it away in one of the situations when they most need it. When decisions concern their reproductive lives, women revert back under rights-talk to the demeaning status of children – treasured, but not fully trusted to think and act for themselves.

CONCRETE CLOSING

In contrast to liberal lawyers and jurists, I remain an unrepentant Arbuthnotian. Of course, I do not deny that the Charter reflects a particular vision of social living and justice – to do so would flout reality and be both naïve and dangerous. I maintain that the coherence of the Charter vision is grounded solely upon the ideological assumptions of its framers and interpreters. These liberals mistake their own creations for the hard rock of hermeneutical necessity. The platform on which the Charter is built is attached to nothing; it hurtles through the Arbuthnotian void, giving the appearance of support only to those who are perched precariously upon it and falling at the same rate of speed. As such, it might be tempting to dismiss the Charter enterprise as 'nonsense without stilts.'[87] To do so, however, would be to miss the major point. The construction project undertaken by the courts and the liberal commentators may be without foundation, but it carries political clout. The Charter is a potent political weapon, one that is being used to benefit vested interests in society and to weaken the relative power of the disadvantaged and underprivileged. Moreover, it is not simply that the particular decisions reached are regressive in result. While, to be sure, many are, the problem runs much deeper. Decisions are made in the context of, and are the product of, a very partial vision of social life and political justice.

Rights-talk's abstract individualism demands that the rich complexity of social life be crammed into a simplistic and one-dimensional frame of reference. To reduce the high-tech television advertising of large corporations and the pathetic pleas of street-corner beggars to the simple and equivalent exercise of their speech rights or to equate a woman's agonized decision to end her pregnancy with the vengeful wishes of an abusive lover is as offensive as it is wrong-headed. It is to miss so much that is relevant to a proper understanding and resolution of the problems of power and responsibility in a society that claims to be democratic in practice and ambition. Indeed, rights-talk will never allow the marginalized and disenfranchized to be 'admitted as full and equal members and citizens in any country known as "democracy".'[88] The development of a communal responsibility or civic duty is stymied by the obsessively individualistic and self-regarding quality of rights-talk. Provided individuals are acting within their rights, there is neither occasion nor cause for complaint. As such, it is an impoverished and impoverishing medium of political discourse that makes people hostages to their worst selves and strangers to their better selves.

When people's lived experience is filtered through the distorting lens of rights-talk, the world is presented in the absolutist and static terms of a black-and-white photograph and results in a monochromatic diminution of democratic politics and its vivid possibilities. This abstract and still-life snapshot of social living contributes to the failure to see and participate in the historical world as an iridescent and dynamic experience in which power has so much to answer for and achieve. When the limiting discourse of rights-talk and the dull refraction of its abstract vision are abandoned, it might be possible to comprehend the buzzing world of real-life social interactions in more than drab shades of existential grey. Instead, with a change of visionary focus, the world might represent itself in the full spectrum of bright blues, yellows, and reds for people's delight and edification.[89]

5

The State of Rights-Talk: Private Rights and Public Wrongs

Beware then the heathen gods; have no confidence in principles that come to us in the trappings of the eternal. Meet them with gentle irony, friendly skepticism and an open soul.

– Learned Hand

Contrary to popular impression, the twentieth century has not been the century of the individual. Nor has it been the century of the government; both have always been prominently around in one form or another. It is the century of the corporation. Although there seems to be an institutional tendency to collective amnesia, it is indisputable that the modern corporation exercises a degree of economic and social power that is of the gravest significance for the condition of the Canadian polity. The chief executives of multinational firms wield awesome power over social affairs and personal choices: they are the new feudal barons. From McDonald's to General Motors and from CTV to Bell Canada, corporations are the primary loci for making decisions about the distribution of the important human and economic resources that so deeply affect people's lives. There is no choice in dealing with corporations for their activities pervade the whole social fabric – how we put food on the table, what food we put on the table, what we pay to put food on the table, and what food we think we should put on the table are all questions that are deeply shaped by the actions of corporations and the life images that they project. Under the illusion of commercial service, corporate managers are leading public policy-makers.

These developments raise major problems. The most pressing and troubling is that of democratic legitimacy and accountability: 'Why should the rights of ownership prevail over the rights of democratic citizenry in determining who is to manage the affairs of a business enterprise whose policies might directly affect as many as half a million employees, and whose choice of product, location, and technology touches entire communities and beyond?'[1] The answer is, in large and profound part, related to the polity's persistent attachment to a liberal theory of the state, especially the distinction between public undertakings and private interests. Even at the end of the twentieth century, it remains true that 'the moment we utter the words "the state" a score of intellectual ghosts rise to obscure our vision';[2] those of Mill and Dicey are still among the contending phantasms. The major source of bewitchment is the conceptual tendency to insist that the state is synonymous and coterminous with government. A failure to appreciate that government and its agencies are only one part of the state stalls any progress in checking the abuse of power in modern society. Indeed, concentration on the governmental sectors of the state as having a unique status in liberal law and theory has served to perpetuate and justify the abuse of power in other regions of the state. Outside the conceptual provenance of the liberal state, corporations are left to their own devices.

The response to this state of affairs is not to tinker with the operational rules, but to change the game entirely. Accordingly, the target of this chapter is the state or, more accurately, current ways of thinking about the state. Most lawyers' allegiance to particular theories of the state is unconscious and, therefore, all the more potent in operation. Legal efforts at social change and transformation are hamstrung by an analytically impoverished and politically inadequate understanding of the identity and character of the Canadian state. The identity and character of the state is not so much a technical question of descriptive accuracy as it is a political question of normative worth. No definition of the state results from a passive observation of social life or, least of all, legal doctrine, but from constitutive and prescriptive judgments about the world. As such, participation in law generally, and in constitutional law in particular, involves a taking of sides in the struggle for and over power. Discussion about the state and corporations is a practice that obliges people to discuss the character and quality of social experience generally. By interrogating the idea of the state, society might begin to take responsibility for the existing conditions of social life and force itself to address the abiding question of any political theory: what is the proper and best way to live?

In addressing that question, my hope is to provide a more informed and progressive theory of the state that can act as a better basis for the practical advancement of democratic politics. After a brief sketch of the impoverished notion of the liberal state in the corporate age, I will focus on recent legal decisions under the Charter that combine to reveal the present state of judicial thinking on the issue of the public/private distinction.[3] The difficulty for the courts is that the very reasons that oblige them to address this troubling matter also prevent them from bringing it to a satisfactory conclusion. Indeed, in this important sense, the conceptual dilemma at the heart of legal doctrine is liberalism's pervasive dilemma writ small. Insofar as the courts' rhetoric must bear some connection to social reality in order to preserve their political legitimacy, the courts must ensure that they act effectively and consistently to remedy alleged abuses of power. But, in so acting, they make the greatest challenge to the rhetorical foundations of their political legitimacy. The judges are like political Charles Blondins. While it is difficult enough to negotiate the Niagara Falls of politics on any rhetorical tightrope of legitimacy, it is fatal to attempt the feat with a frayed or non-existent tightrope. That judges seem to effect such a crossing and are only occasionally seen to crash into the political waters beneath is more testimony to the public's induced credulity than the judges' superhuman agility. As such, legal doctrine is an optical illusion of the first order and its practitioners are magicians of deserving repute. Yet the excellence of their craft ought not to blind people to the emptiness of their achievement.

THE CORPORATE AGE

The fact that corporate power and influence are so thoroughly pervasive in the larger and smaller matters of contemporary life in Canadian society is itself cause for considerable concern; the structural connection between private economic power and public political authority is democratically unsettling. However, this is made doubly troubling by the additional fact that there is also an increasing concentration of corporate assets and ownership in relatively few hands. For instance, since 1980, the top 25 corporations' share of Canadian corporate assets has risen by 14 per cent, and nine families control almost half the value of the 238 corporations that make up the TSE 300 index.[4] Also, a few corporations dominate large sectors of the economy. For instance, in mining, 5 per cent of the corporations have over 90 per cent of the assets, equity, and profits; in manufacturing, 2 per cent of the corporations have around 80 per cent of assets, equity, sales, and profits.[5] All in all, Canada possesses an economic structure that stands in stark contradiction to its proud proclamations about its democratic process in which power is distributed equally among the citizenry and its exercise is accountable to the polity at large.

While the state has played an enormously expanded role in structuring the economy and has acquired significant corporate holdings in competitive sectors of that economy,[6] corporations have managed to exercise increasing control over the economy at large and over the discrete functioning of government departments. This influence is exercised in various ways. There exists a high degree of overlapping membership in so-called public and private organizations at the top level of management; high-ranking politicians and bureaucrats come from or go to organizational positions in the corporate elite, and lasting ties are nurtured between the two sectors.[7] Also, the idea of 'agency capture' – in which the bodies to be regulated begin to set the agenda for, influence the problem-solving mentality of, and dominate information available to the agencies intended to do the regulating – is more the rule than the exception. The strategy is transparent: the weaker and more manageable private power consents to the fictional authority of the nominally stronger, but more diffuse, power in return for the right to do almost whatever it wishes.[8] Apart from constant and sophisticated lobbying, the media are dominated by the Canadian corporate elite and reflect its views; almost 50 per cent of the controllers of the leading media firms are also directors or executives of elite Canadian corporations.[9]

Unfortunately, at the same time as corporate power has increased, the effectiveness of the traditional devices to control it have decreased. The legitimacy of corporations is suspect. The institutional check of economic competition, if it ever truly existed, is no longer a viable instrument of corporate regulation. The concentration and growth of corporate power has enabled corporations to control more than be controlled by the disciplinary impulses of a market economy. Furthermore, partly as a consequence of this development, the claim that the separation of corporate management and ownership would guard against untrammelled power has managed to facilitate the opposite result. As corporations come to resemble large-scale bureaucracies more than commercial entrepreneurs, corporate managers begin to maximize their own utility and not the company's profits; they become as much the scriptwriters of the economic drama as actors in its unscripted performance. Efforts to remedy the situation have tended to be directed toward legitimation of the status quo, and little commitment has been made to the genuine dissipation of concentrated corporate power.[10]

At the heart of the problem is the need to exert effective and legitimate control over corporate activities and introduce accountability to these private centres of accumulated power. However, the continuing attachment to a liberal theory of the state, with its insistence on preserving a separation of the public from the private and of the economic from the political, has proved to be a major stumbling block. While private actors are permitted and encouraged to engage in the worldly pursuit of economic gain, public officials are expected to act as civic angels in the communal service of more heavenly ambitions.[11] Already struggling to keep pace with modern changes in social organization, liberal theory exhausts itself in vain efforts to tackle and control abuses of power; practical reality intrudes upon theory's fantasy. In modern society, economic wealth gives rise to a potent source of political power; the celestial chorus sings in a remarkably rich register. Liberal theory recognizes this difficulty, but insists upon treating the confluence of economic and political power as a remediable malfunction than as a structural flaw in the theory itself. As such, the liberal theory of the state makes democracy safe for corporate power: it becomes a credo for the winning elite in the constitutional game of economic power.

Any attempt to ground a sharp and consistent distinction between government action and private activity is misguided. There are, of course, differences between the government and so-called private centres of power. Such dissimilarities must be respected in the design and implementation of regimes of liability, control, and accountability. In short, allowance must be made for a greater differentiation of immunities, privileges, and liabilities between government and civil actors; different questions must be asked as well as different answers given. However, notwithstanding this, there must be a much greater appreciation of the similarities between the exercise of government and private power and their shared potential for abuse. A crude bifurcation of the social world into the government and its citizens is simply untenable in a modern political economy that nurtures all kinds of institutional hybrids and aspires to principles of democratic governance. The state consists of much more than the government, and the governed are much less than everyone or everything that is not the government. By refusing to acknowledge the crucial importance of corporations and similar institutions in contemporary social life, such theorizing ensures that large sections of the state will remain beyond the reach of civic control and the grasp of popular accountability. In short, 'the large corporation [does not fit] ... into democratic theory and vision.'[12]

There are many consequences and corollaries to the traditional way of thinking about the state and corporate power, but the major effects are twofold. By treating corporations separately from the state, liberal theory overlooks the important influence of corporations over the government both directly and indirectly through the economic clout that they wield in modern society. Second, by treating corporations as being the same as citizens, it ignores the exercise of power by corporations over citizens and fails to provide any effective means by which citizens can challenge that power in the name of democratic justice: most people must be employed by a corporation to live, and the fear of poverty is the greatest form of political control. Each effect combines to insulate corporations from democratic regulation and to facilitate the insulation of their economic and, therefore, political power; they are the favoured and bastard offspring of traditionalists' marriage to the public/private distinction. Depending on whether the entity in question is deemed to be public or private, an abusive exercise of power will either be held to a full set of operating standards and invalidated or it will be left to the abusing institutions' own corporate conscience and the dubious discipline of the marketplace.

RIDING THE DOLPHIN

When it comes to the courts' constitutional forays into these matters, the public/private distinction has proved very useful. It has been found to be a convenient front for a whole host of conflicting and challenging issues that seem to defy any simple or lasting resolution. Doctrinal manipulation of the public/private distinction is employed by the courts to decide cases in an ostensibly technical manner and to avoid the impression of deciding on the political merits of the case. The ideological underpinnings of the public/private distinction are by no means determinative in each and every case; they do not demand or sanction a particular set of detailed outcomes. However, they do energize and inform the interpretation of the Charter and push its enforcement toward certain types of conclusions. As imagined normative bottom lines, these deep-seated premises allow the legal community to maintain institutional legitimacy by pretending to be exercising its considerable power in accordance with ostensibly neutral and formal directives. By so doing, lawyers and judges are able to duck the real and difficult issues of substantive justice that underlie and are hidden by their professional commitments. The result is power without responsibility or accountability; this is not the apotheosis of democratic politics, but its nemesis.

By way of enhancing a more progressive project of social and economic relations, I will identify and criticize the discredited vision of the state and the public/private distinction that judges and lawyers rely upon in their routine practices. More often implicit than explicit, this liberal vision is part of the institutional architecture of Charter jurisprudence. However, in the seminal case of *Dolphin Delivery*,[13] these ideological commitments and their frailties were revealed in stark detail for all to see. The Supreme Court of Canada delivered a judgment that let the political cat out of the constitutional bag and into the critical light. Although welcomed in some quarters, the decision has received almost universal criticism, in whole or in part, from the academic community. Yet, for all the apparent force and heat of their words, these critics manage to operate within and actually reinforce the ideological paradigm in which the courts work; they are both the critics and conservers of the liberal credo.

Dolphin Delivery was always destined to be an important and troubling case. It was the first major decision by the Supreme Court of Canada that directly concerned the rights of labour under the Charter. Moreover, it raised a fundamental dilemma of political magnitude in the context of an ostensibly 'technical' question of legal interpretation. The case concerned an industrial dispute between the Retail, Wholesale and Department Store Union (RWDSU) and Purolator Courier Inc. Representing the locked-out employees of the company, the union believed that Dolphin Delivery Ltd., another courier company, was acting as a business ally of Purolator. The union decided to picket Dolphin's premises. However, before it could do so, Dolphin sought and obtained an injunction from the British Columbia Supreme Court against RWDSU to prevent the picketing. The injunction was granted on the basis of the Court's finding that the alleged relationship between Dolphin and Purolator was unproven and that RWDSU's proposed 'secondary picketing' constituted the common law tort of inducing breach of contract between Dolphin and its employees. The matter fell to be resolved under common law because Purolator, an interprovincial undertaking, was subject to federal labour law, and the federal legislation was silent on the legal status of secondary picketing.

The particular constitutional issue raised by the case was whether secondary picketing was a protected activity under the Charter's guarantee of 'freedom of expression.' Because of the factual context, this in turn raised major questions about the reach of the Charter, particularly whether it applied to private litigation and/or the common law. In appealing the decision to grant the injunction, RWDSU was unsuccessful before the Court of Appeal and the Supreme Court of Canada. In the Supreme Court, the seven-member bench unanimously held that the granting of the injunction and the common law on which it was based were beyond the scope of Charter scrutiny.[14] The leading judgment of the Court was given by McIntyre J. The judgments are collectively inscribed with many of the (mis)informing assumptions and argumentative motifs that characterize traditional ways of liberal thinking about the state and, also, the limitations of the ingrained habits of the legal mind. In short, it is a paradigmatic example of the falsity and function of the public/private distinction; it illustrates the centrality of the distinction to the continuing legitimacy of the judicial enterprise at the same time that it reveals its analytical transparency and ideological sway. The reasoning offered in support of the holding can be summarized in the form of seven sequential propositions:

1. The Charter applies to the common law (592).
2. The Charter does not apply to 'private litigation divorced completely from any connection with government' (593).
3. The Charter applies to the executive and legislative branches of government, but not to the judicial branch (598–9).[15]
4. The Charter applies to the common law 'only in so far as the common law is the basis of some governmental action'; thus the Charter does not apply to the common law in its regulation of relationships among private actors (599 and 603).
5. The Charter does not apply to court orders issued pursuant to the common law (600).
6. The Charter applies to legislation in its regulation of relationships among private actors (600–3).
7. Where the Charter does not apply to the common law, 'the judiciary ought to apply and develop the principles of the common law in a manner consistent with the fundamental values enshrined in the constitution' (603).

It takes little critical intelligence to realize that there is an obvious inconsistency among these propositions. The giveaway is the Court's holding that while the Charter applies to legislation regulating private relationships, it does not apply to common law rules that do the same.

Consequently, while the Court starts off by maintaining that the Charter applies to the common law, its conclusion is completely at odds with this assertion. By the end of the judgment, it is clear that the Charter does not apply to the common law – there must be some additional governmental presence or involvement to attract Charter scrutiny. McIntyre J. seems to have reached these contradictory conclusions by basing his first assertion, that the Charter applies to the common law, on an interpretation of section 52 of the Constitution Act 1982 and his second assertion, that there must be some additional governmental presence, on an interpretation of section 32(1) of the Charter. Yet, while this helps to explain his reasoning, it does not alter the fact that the two assertions ultimately cannot be reconciled with each other. While it would be tempting to write off this internal contradiction as evidence of a confused and incompetent judiciary, such an assessment is both too harsh and too kind. It is too harsh because the dilemma that the Court found itself in was not of its own making; it is a reflection of the inherent contradiction of liberal ideology in a positivist age. It is too kind because the political implications of the contradiction are more pervasive and pernicious than if it had been a product of mere confusion or incompetence. Like its marine counterpart, *Dolphin* shows that beneath the doctrinal surface, there is a whole world of political action and social agony.

THE LIBERAL STATE

The Charter is, at root, a liberal document. Its enactment was a constitutional affirmation of liberal faith. The whole framework and tenor of the Charter reflect traditional liberal values; it arms individuals with a negative set of formal rights to repel attempts at government interference. This is not to deny that the Charter contains traces of a more positive and communitarian strand of politics. Guarantees of language rights, the reasonable limits clause, protection for affirmative-action programs, and references to the preservation of aboriginal and denominational school rights are evidence of such thinking.[16] However, the important thing to note is that with the exception of language rights, these communitarian concerns find voice only as qualifications and limitations to Charter guarantees. Thus, while they may occasionally serve as brakes on the full expression of Charter rights, they do not alter the fact that liberal individualism is the engine that drives the Charter carriage. Thus, in *Hunter* v. *Southam Inc.*, Dickson C.J. was able to say that the purpose of the Charter is 'to constrain governmental action inconsistent with those rights and freedoms [enshrined within it]; it is not in itself an authorization for governmental action.'[17]

The liberal theory of the state is essentially a philosophy of distrust. The perceived threat to social justice comes from despotic official rule whether in the form of a tyrannical dictator or from collective and undisciplined popular power. The role of the state is restricted to setting the stage for intelligible action by self-possessed and welfare-maximizing individuals. Indeed, some modern liberals still go so far as to depict the minimal state as the corollary of a natural economic competitiveness between contending entrepreneurs: 'The state itself (an all-encompassing protective association) may be regarded as a market phenomenon which emerges from a competitive process in the market for protection.'[18] Under the Charter's individualistic vision, the main enemy of freedom is not disparities in wealth or concentrations of private power, but the state. Although such a fear is not entirely groundless, its exaggerated and blinkered focus makes liberals blind to the threat of unchecked private power and to the valid role of government as a promoter of liberty, particularly for the disadvantaged and oppressed.

As such, the Charter's incorporation of liberalism as the dominant Canadian ethos is mistaken. It is neither descriptively accurate of existing social and political conditions nor prescriptively desirable as a future model for social and political life. Although this liberal theory of the state has played a major historical role in resisting aristocratic rule and improving the lot of the common citizen, its political pertinence and merit no longer obtain in contemporary Canadian society. The harsh fist of the political despot has been replaced by the smiling face of the corporate executive. Power remains exercised over rather than by citizens. Liberalism's trivialization of corporations' power continues the powerlessness of ordinary people. In this sense, liberalism's promise far outruns its performance. In short, it lacks any viable explanation of exploitation: it is a Micawberesque view of social life. By failing to recognize that political equality demands prior economic equality, liberalism turns a blind eye to the disproportionate political influence of the economically strong. In doing so, it renders its own efforts at egalitarian reform marginal and cosmetic. The welfare state operates to mitigate the harshness of a market economy, not to replace it with a more democratic mode of economic distribution.

Derived from the writings of John Locke and Thomas Hobbes, and developed in modified form by Robert Nozick and John Rawls, the liberal theory of rights and political justice is premised on the belief that individuals possess a pre-political sphere of pure autonomy and freedom that does not depend for its existence upon the state. In this scenario, individuals are independent and complete entities who interact with others out of a begrudging necessity to better satisfy their self-regarding wants and preferences. At the heart of this liberal compact is the foundational criterion that the state must remain entirely neutral toward people's differing conceptions of the good life. Accordingly, the major function of a liberal charter is to police the boundary that separates the political and the collective from the pre-political and the personal – to contain the state so as to prevent it from intruding, in its utilitarian zeal, upon the 'natural' realm of individual liberty. The major difficulty confronting adherents of liberalism is identifying the line that separates the domain of individual liberty from the domain of state action. This problem is less daunting for proponents of natural law who can at least claim that the boundary is a product of the natural order of social life and justice.[19] While naturalists seek to 'find' that elusive line, positivists struggle over where to 'draw' the line. The line drawers may be a more advanced and sophisticated bunch than the line finders, but they are part of the same intellectual heritage and political tradition.

For positivists, however, the task of determining where the public sphere ends and the private sphere begins is an intractable one. With no natural authority on which to rely,[20] the distinction between the public and the private seems beyond objective or neutral assessment; they are driven to depend on the unreliable signposts to prevailing social mores and political consensus. Indeed, the line drawers tend to hide rather than dispense with their naturalist affiliations; they draw their lines in accordance with an undisclosed, but very real, map of ideological commitments. Modern liberals draw upon an historically specific and idealized version of bourgeois Western democracy in the 1960s. For instance, Ronald Dworkin trumpets a liberal theory of constitutional justice that defends state neutrality as the best way to promote equal concern and respect for each individual and their diverse conceptions of the good life. However, in fleshing out this skeletal premise to support equality of opportunity rather than equality of achievement, Dworkin and his followers, like David Beatty, are forced to take a stand on a particular substantive theory of the good life and to undermine liberalism's foundational criterion of neutrality.[21] Consequently, liberalism becomes not a meta-language of moral neutrality, but an ideological vision of substantive politics that embraces values like social peace, privacy, diversity, affluence, and the Rule of Law and favours entrepreneurial individuals who are driven to exploit their advantages for their own advantage. While many will (and will not) be attracted by this vision, it needs to be defended on its own substantive terms and not justified by resort to the liberal metric of moral neutrality.[22]

In the nineteenth century, jurists of a positivist persuasion thought that they could finesse this difficulty by relying upon the distinction between the market and the state. The political orthodoxy of the day enabled them to assume that the bounds of private action were drawn by the invisible hand of the market whose operation was, in turn, directed by the strong arm of the common law. An abuse of power occurred when the state, or someone acting through or on behalf of the state, interfered with or failed to protect such common law entitlements. There was no empirical analysis into the actual quality of those rights and their exercise. Instead, the courts engaged in an analytical enquiry as to whether the state was involved or not. If it was, remedial intervention through the courts was warranted; if not, those affected had to lobby for political reparations through the legislature. The emphasis throughout was upon whether the impugned act could be identified with the formal attributes of governmental authority and not upon whether it had actually inhibited or damaged the interests of particular citizens. Pedigree and form, rather than effect and substance, were the standards for evaluating impermissible behaviour.

The difficulty with this view was that it contained the seeds of its own destruction. Absent some theory of natural rights, the labelling of market activity as 'private' and regulatory activity as 'public' can be exposed as wholly arbitrary and contingent. Without an acknowledged 'natural order,' the market is simply one choice among many regulatory regimes for economic activity. This, in turn, means that the state is implicated in the market in the same way that it is implicated in any other political choice made within its territorial jurisdiction: the market is one form of state-sanctioned arena for social interaction and economic exchange. The state's claim to sovereignty implies that a decision not to intervene and regulate, or mere inaction, is as much a governmental responsibility as a decision to do so. Thus, the attempt to limit state activity to efforts directed at changing the status quo is misconceived; the state is equally implicated in the retention of the status quo. Acquiescence and action are merely flipsides of the same governmental coin.

An interesting doctrinal example of the flipability of the public/private distinction involves two notorious English cases on racial discrimination. In *Charter*, a Mr. Shah was refused membership to the East Ham South Conservative Club. He alleged that this was because of his race. The legislation provided that it was 'unlawful to any person concerned with the provision to the public or a section of the public ... of any goods, facilities or services to discriminate on grounds of race.' Engaging in a highly formalistic analysis, the House of Lords decided that whatever was not public must be private and that as a social club was private, it could not be public.[23] It concluded that the government had no business interfering in people's private lives. However, in *Applin*, the law lords held that efforts to dissuade couples from fostering black children were unlawful as they were fostering children in the care of the local authority and, therefore, were 'a sector of the public.' Although the 1968 Act outlawed public acts of discrimination, it left intact a private person's common law rights to discriminate 'to their hearts content.'[24] Throughout the judgments, emphasis is placed on the extent to which the foster parents are *in loco republicae*. Insofar as family, often and traditionally thought of as archetypically private, can be classified as a public institution, it seems both functionally and analytically unsound to find that clubs cannot also possess the necessary attributes of public identity; the status of clubs and families is a substantive matter of context and perspective. Furthermore, in light of these anomalies, Parliament amended the legislation in a somewhat ironic manner: it declared that clubs with over 25 members were to be within the scope of the Act (i.e., public) and that foster parents were to be outside of it (i.e., private).[25]

Moreover, from a positivist perspective, common law protection of private property and freedom to contract must themselves be characterized as a form of state activity.[26] The plea by free-marketeers and their ilk that government stay out of our lives – that the state that governs least is the state that governs best – is as contradictory as it is disingenuous. Judicial enforcement of private property and of contractual rights is as coercive to those who do not share in their benefits as confiscation is coercive to those who do share in them. In other words, the relevant issue is not whether the state ought to intervene. The state is already there; the only question is on whose behalf state power should be exercised. As Duncan Kennedy puts it:

> The private owner's 'freedom' to exclude others from his possessions has as its corollary his 'power' to control the lives of those who cannot live without access to the means of production. Admission to use of the property is the carrot, exclu-

sion the stick that orders our lives. It is a familiar notion that, through the definition and enforcement of legal rights in things, the state is deeply implicated in the particular order that emerges from the inter-action of private individuals.[27]

At bottom, the crude separation of society into either the state or the citizenry cannot be sustained. The state is implicated in all activity that takes place within its boundaries. It is the state that determines and constitutes within itself the particular mapping of society into different regions of public authority and private liberty: the private is a function of the public. The realm of so-called individual freedom is brought into existence by and thrives through the choice of public power. Of course, it may be the decision of a public and democratically mandated body to authorize certain organizations to act as a self-possessed and welfare-maximizing agent. However, with the recognition that such 'private' entities are legitimated through public power and not defined in contradistinction to public power, the pursuit of private interest will be viewed and understood in a different light than liberalism recommends. The public/private distinction offers a misleading framework for normative analysis and regulatory justification. A recognition that the state is implicated in the establishment and exercise of public duties and private power entails a different agenda and political context for their evaluation and legitimation. In particular, it ceases to be a question of whether to regulate, but becomes a matter of how and when to do so; the shift in focus has considerable substantive effect.

Accordingly, the public/private distinction is not an indifferent structure that provides a convenient framework for debating and deciding the distribution of political power. It skews that debate and prods its resulting decisions in particular directions. The entitlements of private property owners exist only insofar as the state is prepared to recognize and lend support to those entitlements in the face of competing claims. What is referred to as 'private power' is, in reality, public power that has been delegated to certain individuals and that can be wielded in a largely unchecked and democratically unaccountable way.[28] This exposure of the illusory nature of the public/private distinction also lays bare the underlying fallacy of liberalism. If the distinction between the public and the private is without substance, the liberal enterprise of seeking to police the boundary between the two spheres is, at best, futile and, at worst, ideological. Whether it is a question of line finding or line drawing, it is a formal fraud that perpetuates a substantive injustice.

THE ROCK AND THE HARD PLACE

The liberal vision of social life and justice is not only intellectually discredited, but it fails to present an even rudimentary picture of the contemporary workings of Canadian society and government. The welfare state has long since come of age in Canada. However, the tragedy of Canadian jurisprudence is that the liberal vision still holds the legal intellect and political imagination in its inequitable grip. The Supreme Court's judgment in *Dolphin Delivery* is the clear product of such impoverished thinking. Moreover, although the academic response to the decision was one of widespread criticism, it shares the same ideological assumptions and standards. The pre- and post-*Dolphin* commentary on the reach of the Charter – the line between public and private action – is all of a piece. It speaks in the elitist and anachronistic language of nineteenth-century liberalism, although it often feigns a more modern and sophisticated accent. Whereas one group quibbles over the si(gh)ting of any line between public and private terrain, another group proposes that the Charter has a potential application to all social life.

A claque of academics welcome the attempt to draw a line between the public and private sectors of social life and to confine the Charter's application to the former.[29] For them, it is simply a matter of drawing the line in the right place according to the Charter map's textual coordinates. For instance, in his comment on *Dolphin*, Peter Hogg contends that McIntyre J.'s cartographical interpretation is mistaken and that his line drawing therefore is inaccurate. Hogg agrees with McIntyre that 'the best reading' of the Charter is to restrict it to government action so that 'there is a private realm in which people are not obliged to subscribe to "state" values and into which constitutional norms do not intrude.'[30] However, he is troubled by the Court's decision about whether the Charter applies to the courts themselves. Preferring the result and reasoning in *Rahey* and *B.C.G.E.U.*,[31] Hogg criticizes *Dolphin* for its failure to acknowledge that the making of a court order would supply the requisite degree of governmental action. While Hogg shares the courts' concern not to extend the Charter inadvertently to all kinds of non-governmental activity, he believes that such an undesirable outcome can be avoided by holding, as *Dolphin* did, that the Charter does not apply to these rules of the common law that regulate relationships between private parties. While these two statements are logically entailed by his major axiom about the Charter only applying to government action, they are little more than an attempt to preserve the discredited public/private dichotomy by obscuring the line beneath a new, but equally arbitrary, distinction.

Given that the state is implicated in virtually all forms of so-called private activity, the question of whether that involvement manifests itself as a crystallized rule of the common law, a court injunction, or some less obvious form is completely beside the point. This can be illustrated by considering the facts in *Re Blainey and Ontario Hockey Association*.[32] In that case, the Ontario Hockey Association (OHA), a 'private' body, denied Justine Blainey the opportunity to play hockey in a male league. The courts had to decide whether the practices and rules of the OHA were authorized by government. According to the test enunciated by Hogg, a negative answer would be required: there was no common law rule and no court injunction specifically authorizing the OHA to deny women access to its leagues. Yet this conclusion is misleading. Whether OHA's legal authority to deny Blainey the right to use its facilities flowed from the complex tapestry of common law property rights or from a single jurisdictional thread, the fact remains that it was a power conferred upon it or sanctioned by the state.

The arbitrary nature of Hogg's distinction is further evidenced by its indeterminacy. What may appear as private activity in one factual context can be transformed into state action in another. All that is required is for the actors to position themselves so that the underlying presence of the state is driven to the surface and forced to reveal itself. Suppose, for example, that Justine Blainey decided to flout the OHA's decision by chaining herself to the boards of the rink whenever an OHA game was scheduled. Further, suppose that in order to enforce its decision, the OHA sought an injunction to have her removed for trespassing. According to Hogg, Blainey could now invoke the Charter to resist the OHA's action. Yet the only difference here is that by challenging the OHA's assertion of its property entitlement, Blainey forces the state's support of that entitlement out of the legal shadows and into the political light of day, where it is much less persuasive.

Recognizing and conceding some of these difficulties, a less traditional group of liberal scholars eschew such dubious distinctions and reject the public/private dichotomy.[33] They acknowledge that any attempt to draw a coherent and principled line between the public and private realms of life is ill-fated. The nexus between the state and the challenged action is never sufficiently close to rule out any private behaviour and is always too loose to catch only public activity. Moreover, they argue that even if a line could be drawn there is no convincing political justification for doing so. Accordingly, it is best to be rid of the distinction altogether and make all social activity open to potential Charter scrutiny; the decision whether to intervene in a particular case will be driven by an examination of the substantive values and interests at stake. For instance, in a particularly trenchant criticism of *Dolphin*, David Beatty concludes that McIntyre's efforts to interpret the courts and common law as not part of the government is not only conceptually confused, but results in the courts being above the Charter: it is 'elitist and anti-democratic' and 'will act as a cancer on the moral authority on which the very life of the judiciary depends.'[34]

The constructive consequence of this critique is the recommendation that constitutional norms ought to apply to and inform all facets of Canadian life; Charter justice must be available in the private and public realms. Yet, for all their apparent perspicacity and just instincts, these scholars are blind to or refuse to see the full implications of their critique. Without some notional sphere of private autonomy to be preserved from the intrusions of others, whether it be the state or other individuals, the knit of constitutional rights and freedoms starts to unravel. If the state is implicated in all forms of societal activity, Charter claims cease to be about the protection from state interference of some preordained realm of individual autonomy. Instead, they become ideological claims about the appropriate allocation of state powers and social resources among individuals. The negative notion of liberty – a freedom to be let alone to enjoy one's assets without governmental interference – becomes incoherent. The question of whose entitlements are to be protected from whose interference becomes a matter of contested political choice rather than the correct application of abstract principle. Accordingly, if there is to be any genuine constitutional sense or meaning, the role of the state must be completely revised and people's understanding and relation to it transformed.

Without any workable distinction between private autonomy and public power, the courts' legitimacy and efficacy are dealt a fatal blow. Without such an allegedly natural sphere of private liberty to be protected, the defence of citizens against official tyranny becomes a hopeless exercise: the judicial lions will be chasing their own tails. Indeed, liberal critics who advocate no potential limits to the Charter's reach have thrown themselves onto the horns of a painful dilemma. Unless they are prepared to develop a substantive vision of distributive justice, they have no metewand against which to measure the social value of any particular act or state of affairs. Without such an operative baseline, there is only a desultory ad hockery. If they do develop such a vision, they will have reneged on liberalism's vaunted claim that 'the liberal state must be neutral on ... the question of the good life.'[35] As such, any proposed vision of substantive justice will enjoy no prior claim over competing visions of a liberal or any other persuasion. Moreover, any move in this direction would oblige liberal critics to accept the impossibility of a neutral or apolitical mode of Charter adjudication – a conclusion that no stripe of liberal, naturalist nor positivist, can countenance.

The practical implications of this theoretical shambles are devastating for courts and for liberal theory generally. The reliance on early-nineteenth-century ideas to tackle and resolve late-twentieth-century problems is like trying to repair a computer with a hammer and chisel: it will do much more harm than good. Working from a positivist tradition in a postrealist age, Canadian judges struggle to make any sense of a liberal charter of rights. Without clearly defined realms of public and private activity, 'constitutional rights become affirmative duties on governments to intervene to redress deprivations in civil society.'[36] Neutrality ceases to be a plausible characteristic or attainable goal of judicial review. For instance, imagine the archetypal dispute between the person who wants to take property to satisfy life-sustaining needs and the property owner who claims a right to dispose of it as he or she wishes. Liberals seek to resolve such disputes by resort to the spurious rhetoric of rights. Yet, lacking the mythical support of a public/private distinction, any efforts to reach coherent solutions become impossible without addressing the deep normative assumptions that rights-talk masks and seeks to finesse. By confronting the complicity of the government in all forms of social (mal)administration, the courts would have to take responsibility for the social conditions that resulted when its ostensibly neutral decisions meshed with the existing patterns of power and the play of private activity. The distribution of wealth and power would be firmly within the judicial bailiwick, and ideology would be inextricably on the jurisprudential docket. Without the reassuring disguise and rhetorical trappings of liberal legalism, the judicial lions would be out of their lair and revealed as the rampant beasts they always were.

In light of these difficulties, it is not hard to see why the Supreme Court in *Dolphin Delivery* was faced with an unenviable task. On the one hand, the Court had to accept the fact that it would stretch things too far to pretend that the common law was 'non-law' or 'found law.' Even the most formalistic of contemporary lawyers must acknowledge that the common law is a creation of courts, not a product of providence. Of course, judges still want to cling to the myth that an act of common law creation is and continues to be neutral and distinct from politics. The judges' self-image is that of passive referees who develop the law in an even-handed and impartial manner. Yet even this view must have posed difficulties for a court dealing with a case involving industrial torts in the *Dolphin* context. The invention of the tort of inducing contractual breach in the nineteenth century is a notoriously crude example of judicial power being mobilized to further the interests of employers at the expense of the labour movement.[37] Perhaps for this reason, McIntyre J., while insisting that judges act as 'neutral arbiters' when they *apply* the law, is strangely silent on the question of how that law was created in the first place.[38]

On the other hand, the Supreme Court could not have interpreted the Charter in a way that would have required it to abandon liberal conceptions of the state and of the judicial role. To have done so would have compelled the Court to have confronted the complicity of the state, *including the courts,* in all forms of social activity. This in turn would have required the Court to have embraced an overtly political role for itself. It would have had to acknowledge constitutional responsibility for the social state of affairs that resulted when its ostensibly neutral decisions combined and reacted with 'private' activity. Existing distributions of property, wealth, and power would have been up for grabs in an ideological battle over the content of such guarantees as liberty, security, and equality. Moreover, without the reassuring disguise and rhetorical trappings of liberal legalism, the courts' participation in the ideological debate would be naked and, as such, an affront to liberal sensibilities.

The Court in *Dolphin* found itself between a rock and a hard place. The rock was represented by the incoherence of the public/private dichotomy in a postrealist age and the hard place by the overtly political character of Charter adjudication in the absence of a public/private cushion. Given this uncomfortable state of affairs, the Court's only choice was to produce a judgment as contradictory and incoherent as liberalism itself. The product was a decision that appeared to recognize the positivist nature of the common law, but, at the same time, sought to preserve the semblance of a public/private distinction by excluding that law from Charter scrutiny. What has so bitterly offended and annoyed liberal critics is the transparency of the exercise. Rather than obscuring the liberal dilemma beneath layers of pseudo-profound abstraction (about the distinction between common law rules that regulate relationships between private parties and those that do not,[39] or between agencies that perform public roles and those that do not,[40] or between laws that authorize unconstitutional conduct and those that merely permit it[41]), the Court ensured that the incoherence of the public/private distinction was laid bare for all to behold.

As if this were not enough, the Court highlighted this incoherence through its invocation of the Ontario Court of Appeal's decision in *Blainey*.[42] One aspect of that case concerned the constitutionality of section 19(2) of the Ontario Human Rights Code, a section providing that 'the right ... to equal treatment [with respect to services, goods and facilities] ... is not infringed where membership in an athletic organization or participation in an athletic activity is restricted to persons of the same sex.' The Court of Appeal held that this section contravened the Charter's guarantee of sexual equality. In *Dolphin*, McIntyre J. refers to this aspect of the *Blainey* case as an example of a sufficiently 'direct and close connection' between the claim advanced and some 'element of government action' to warrant Charter scrutiny. The difficulty with this view is that the effect of the Ontario Human Rights Code, when studied closely, was merely to preserve the common law. The provision did not itself discriminate on the basis of sex; all it did was to exempt from statutory prohibition sexually based distinctions made by athletic organizations. In other words, the legislature could have achieved the same result by drafting a provision that read: 'Notwithstanding the right to equal treatment, the common law shall continue to apply where membership in an athletic organization or participation in an athletic activity is restricted to persons of the same sex.' Alternatively, the legislature could have specified those organizations that were bound by the statutory prohibition on sexual discrimination and omitted athletic organizations from the list. Thus, the government's 'direct and close' involvement with the conduct complained of in *Blainey* in fact went no further than permitting the common law regime and its political morality to continue. Yet, if this is sufficient government involvement to attract Charter scrutiny, it is difficult to see why the federal government's failure to alter the common rules at work in *Dolphin* did not also provide the necessary 'element of government action.' Indeed, it is difficult to see why the failure of government to proscribe any conduct that violates constitutional norms would be beyond the scope of the Charter.

ANOTHER FINE MESS

The legacy of *Dolphin* has been predictable, painful, and political. The courts' attempts to follow *Dolphin*'s elusive logic have not only failed to extricate them from the doctrinal horns of the liberal dilemma, but have managed to impale them further. Ad hockery has been combined with ideological intimation to provide a dog's breakfast of Charter jurisprudence. This unappetizing concoction is particularly evident in the Supreme Court's two post-*Morgentaler* decisions. Although neither case was primarily about the Charter's reach, both relied explicitly upon the distinction between public power and private action. Whereas *Borowski* exposed the vacuity of the courts' insistence that there is a qualitative difference between governmental action and inaction, *Daigle* reinforced the entirely negative thrust of rights-talk and its blatant injustice.

Borowski involved a challenge to the alleged failure of the Criminal Code to prevent the abuse of fetal rights. Since the Supreme Court had struck down sections of the Criminal Code regulating the availability of abortion over twelve months before, the Court held that there was no legislation that could be tested against the Charter's constitutional standards. The Court refused to act in a vacuum and rule on only hypothetical possibilities: legislators act and judges react. However, Sopinka left open the possibility that if new legislation found its way back to the courts, it might be found that fetal rights do exist. However, if that occurs and the courts recognize the existence of fetal rights, it will mean that constitutional rights will have been actively injured or ignored in the considerable time that it will take to get the case back into the courts. Regardless of what constitutional right is at stake, this is surely an intolerable situation even by the courts' own lights of constitutional propriety. It is ludicrous for the courts to treat a further *Borowski* challenge as moot. A decision not to do anything is as much government action as a decision to do something by way of legislation. The courts' persistent failure to recognize this fact invalidates much of its jurisprudence to date. Indeed, Sopinka's assertion that 'in the absence of legislation, there is no government action to bring the Charter into play' is plainly false.[43] Apart from Parliament's positive decision to do nothing, the government is actively involved in the present provision of abortion services through its funding and regulation of hospital facilities. To suggest otherwise is an act of wilful oversight.

In *Daigle*, the Supreme Court refused to acknowledge that the Charter was implicated or anyone's rights were infringed in a potential award of an injunction to Tremblay to prevent Daigle proceeding with her abortion. Noting that there must be some sort of state action before Charter rights can be invoked, the Court refused to intervene in a civil action between two private parties: 'The argument which alleges that the Charter can, on its own, support the injunction at issue fails to impugn any state action.'[44] If an injunction were available in such circumstances, Chantal Daigle's *Mortgentaler* rights would be worthless. It is truly absurd to think that the courts can announce that a woman has constitutional rights in regard to abortion, but proceed to issue an injunction preventing her exercising those rights. Adding insult to injury, the courts' justification would be that her rights are not being infringed as the applicant is a private party and not the state.

The full extent of the doctrinal and political quagmire that the courts have landed themselves in is best revealed in the *McKinney* quartet.[45] Having sown the wind in *Daigle*, they reaped the whirlwind in *McKinney*. In these decisions, an attempt was made to explain exactly what amounted to 'government' under the Charter's section 32. The pivotal question was whether people's constitutional rights had been infringed by the operations and decisions of hospitals, universities, community colleges, and similar public institutions. In a technically complex and inordinately prolix judgment, seven judges managed to exacerbate an already bad situation. Accepting an important distinction between government policy and private activity, they sought to give definition and justification to such a constitutional contrivance. Already buffeted by the critical blasts from *Dolphin*, the Supreme Court located Charter jurisprudence on the proverbial ground between a rock and a hard place. Accordingly, there now exist two equally and distinctly unenticing alternatives of political process and social justice. Whereas one has the courts decide everything in line with judges' visions of social justice, the other installs an almost libertarian theory of private rights and public wrongs. In such environmental conditions, a protracted period of constitutional calm is unlikely and living is likely to be bleak and desperate.

Although there was a baffling permutation of agreements and disagreements, the judges divided between those who wanted to limit the Charter's reach and those who wished to extend it as far as possible; the former concentrated on the meaning of government action and the latter focused on the meaning of private actions. Led by Justice La Forest and joined by former Chief Justice Dickson, a majority held that while a community college was part of the government, hospitals and universities were not. For these judges, the Charter is essentially an instrument for checking the powers of government over the individual: 'Only government need be constitutionally shackled to preserve the rights of the individuals.'[46] The appropriate test was one of the institutional or structural connection of public institutions to government proper. While private activity might offend individual rights, it can be regulated by government or made subject to human rights codes. Consequently, although universities and hospitals perform public services and are largely government-funded, they are autonomous in their decision-making. On the other hand, community colleges are established by the government to implement government policy and are 'simply in form and in fact part of the apparatus of government.'[47]

In leading the three judicial dissenters, Justice Wilson rejected and regretted the narrow formalism of the majority's approach. Agreeing that the Charter did not apply to strictly private matters of litigation, she insisted that constitutional rights do have legal salience when citizens deal with public constitutions. While the level of government funding was not determinative in identifying such Charter-vulnerable bodies, she set out a three-part test for deciding whether public bodies were subject to Charter review: Does government exercise general control over the body in question? Does that body perform a traditional government function or one that has become the responsibility of the state in contemporary society? Is the body authorized by statute to promote an objective that is in the broader public interest? On the basis of these questions, Wilson concluded that universities, hospitals, and community colleges all fall within the reach of the Charter and could infringe citizens' constitutional rights. However, in a wonderful affirmation of law's indeterminacy, the other two dissenters disagreed over the precise application of the test; they did not include universities within the ambit of Charter litigation.

As the opinions of Wilson's dissenting colleagues illustrate, the problem with both the majority's and minority's tests is that they are incapable of fulfilling their intended purpose. They amount less to bright lines than to a penumbral fuzziness. In their attempts to be comprehensive and consistent in their dualistic cataloguing of public institutions, they succeed at being both over-inclusive and under-inclusive. Although the majority's emphasis on institutional pedigree renders inquiry into the functions of public bodies irrelevant, such an analysis results in public bodies that perform private functions being always open to Charter review and private bodies that perform public functions being always closed to Charter review. Such a scheme has no sense or justice for the citizen on the receiving end of institutional abuse. Moreover, it is mistaken to contend that any loss in substantive consistency is compensated for by a gain in operative certainty: 'The existence of control is the only sure guide to whether the function is one of government to which the Charter should apply.'[48] Decision-making autonomy is never an all-or-nothing affair, but is always about more or less control over particular activities. For instance, the extent of the universities' autonomy is not so indirectly tied to government funding; questions of staffing, enrolment, and long-term planning are dictated by government's commitment to continuing levels of funding and the universities' adherence to government policy. Accordingly, 'control' is no more (and no less) 'sure' than a functional analysis. Each proposed test cannot attain any level of operational efficacy without constant resort to contestable and contested political values.

The minority's approach is equally fraught with imprecision and indirection. In trying to stretch the notion of state action to cover a variety of public institutions, it fashions a constitutional test that is capable of encompassing all kinds of private activity. This is particularly so in the case of corporate practices. Under Wilson's tripartite test, there is nothing to distinguish between most public agencies and private institutions. For instance, a publicly funded school and a private educational company are similar in functional terms: each is created and controlled through statute and performs an educational function that is promoted and mandated by government. The same is true for private health companies and private security companies. As such, the decision to exclude corporations from Charter challenge cannot be sustained under any functional test. In a world in which the state involves itself in all dimensions of people's lives, efforts to distinguish public bodies from private organizations on a functional basis are doomed. Moreover, the courts' arbitrary and ideological solicitude for corporate independence is particularly striking when set against decisions that place Charter responsibilities on statute-authorized law societies and even on private persons when making citizens' arrests.[49]

Although those with more progressive instincts will likely side with Wilson's approach, it is an ideologically dangerous course of action. As with all the other judges' opinions, her judgment's working assumptions go to the heart of the democratic compact between those who are entitled to rule and those who are ruled over. The enactment of the Charter and its judicial elaboration have presented the Canadian polity with a stark and limiting choice. On the one hand, there is the option of a two-tier culture of politics in which private abuses of power are treated much less seriously than public ones: government is always cast as the villain and private bodies as the victims – in effect, an official ideology of public wrongs and private rights. This is the view of *McKinney's* majority. On the other hand, there is the choice of a more integrated system of justice in which almost all questions of individual entitlement and public policy fall to be decided by the courts. There would be no issue of allocated efficiency, distributive equity, or private fairness that would be outside the judges' potential jurisdiction or notional competence. Democracy would be reduced to a matter of lawyerly virtue, and justice would become a judicial affair of noblesse oblige. This is effectively the implication of Justice Wilson and her minority colleagues' views.

In facing such a choice, democracy is placed in an impossible bind. Citizens can opt for an anachronistic theory of (in)justice, a judicial republic, or even a frightening combination of both. However, those who recoil from the prospect of a libertarian ideology will also have cause for concern with the minority approach. Contrary to Wilson's belief, the application of a functional test cannot pretend to be engaged only in disputed applications of abstract principle: it is fully implicated in hotly contested matters of ideological substance. While some might be content to trust their political fate to liberal judges like Wilson or Dickson in such ideological confrontations, they might be less sanguine about deferring to an increasingly conservative bench. Perhaps most troubling of all is the fact that this choice will not be made by the people at all or their democratically elected representatives. The constitutional die was cast with the Charter's entrenchment in 1982; the power of choosing has already been ceded to the judges, the new proconsuls of popular politics. Whichever way the taxed judges choose, it is a sad situation for a nation that prides itself on its commitment to democracy. As citizen Ollie might have said to politician Stan, 'This is another fine mess you've got us into.'

CUTTING EDGE

The public/private distinction may be theoretically incoherent, but that does not mean that it lacks political purpose. On the contrary, the distinction produces a discernible ideological thrust and direction to the courts' work. The effect of limiting Charter application to actions of the legislative and executive branches of government is to exclude from Charter scrutiny the major source of inequality in our society: the maldistribution of economic wealth and political power. When confronted with questions of Charter justice, the judges, like Lord Nelson, turn a blind eye to underlying disparities in wealth and power. If both eyes were permanently denied constitutional sight, this might not be so bad – a judiciary deprived completely of Charter vision is a not uninviting prospect. However, the courts' selective blindness in relation to 'private' inequities is offset by an acuity with respect to 'public' denials of individual rights. The result is a judiciary that disregards primary causes of social injustice in its determination to restrain the arm of the state best equipped to redress those causes — the democratic limb represented by the legislature and the executive. Put simply, the Charter can be invoked to challenge the Combines Investigation Act[51] but not the combine.

The presumption underlying the public/private dichotomy is that existing distributions of wealth and power are a product of individual initiative as opposed to state action. Conveniently overlooked is the fact that such distributions and their accumulations generally depend for their very existence and legitimacy upon a panoply of state-supported laws and institutions. The Charter incorporates and builds upon these assumptions. Moreover, it is not just that existing distributions of wealth and power are removed from Charter scrutiny; such distributions form the base line or 'natural foundation' upon which Charter rights are grounded and against which the constitutionality of state action is to be judged. For example, the right to equality does not promise substantive social equality in the liberal scheme of things. Rather, the right is restricted to requiring equal treatment by the legislative and executive arms of the state. For this reason, section 15 of the Charter does not place affirmative duties upon the state; it is satisfied by 'equal' legislative inaction as much as it is by 'equal' legislative action. Provided everyone is disentitled to benefits 'equally,' the requirements of section 15 are met. Thus, a decision of the Nova Scotia Court of Appeal remedied the failure of provincial legislation to provide welfare benefits to single fathers by striking down the provision that bestowed such benefits upon single mothers.[51] Even after *Schachter*,[52] it is still open to government to lower or eliminate benefits to all welfare recipients as a way of satisfying its egalitarian responsibilities. In such a social vision, equality is reduced to a matter of hollow form rather than a commitment to substantive justice.

Similarly, the right to freedom of expression, in the words of the Federal Court of Appeal, 'is a freedom to express and communicate ideas without restraint ... [and] not a freedom to use someone else's property to do so.'[53] The implication is obvious: property is the foundation upon which Charter rights are conferred, protected, and enhanced. The less property people have, the less they can exercise and enjoy their rights. As such, there is a strong correlation between finance and franchise. In our technological society, wealth is a pre-condition of being able to speak broadly and effectively. Although anyone can stand on the street corner, only the rich can have direct access to our homes through the costly channels of the media. When the rights of property owners and speakers collide, speakers stand dumb before the trumping claims of property. While the courts invalidate legislation that seeks to restrict the exaggerated impact of the wealthy on electoral campaigning,[54] they uphold manufacturers' claims that their freedom of speech is infringed by legislation that restricts advertising in English.[55]

Anyone who doubts the foundational nature of common law property rights after the decision in *Dolphin Delivery* need only consider the following example. Suppose that the common law prohibition on secondary picketing considered in *Dolphin* had been embodied within legislation. Further suppose that the Court had decided that this legislative prohibition violated the Charter and should therefore be struck down.[56] Where would the Court then have looked to determine the legal rights and obligations of the parties? Presumably, the common law would fill the constitutional void. It will come as no surprise to those with any knowledge of the history of labour relations that the common law treats secondary picketing as a tortious and unlawful act. On the basis of the Court's decision in *Dolphin*, the perverse outcome would be that the same prohibition would now be deemed acceptable because it was mandated by the providential common law. Whatever its fate elsewhere, the common law has been reinstalled by the Charter as 'the brooding omnipresence in the [Canadian] sky.'[57]

The public/private distinction also permits the judiciary to influence subtly the results of the Charter game in accordance with judicial values. In particular, it enables courts to decide whether certain entities ought to be subjected to or exempted from Charter scrutiny based on an ostensibly neutral determination as to whether they are 'public' or 'private' in nature. Indeed, the consequences go further. The decision that an entity is 'private' not only permits it to act without fear of breaching the moral imperatives contained in the Charter; it makes it more likely that that entity will be permitted to mobilize the Charter as a weapon to resist government regulation and to insulate itself from popular scrutiny and control.

The courts' treatment of corporations under the Charter provides an excellent example. It takes little legal imagination to construct an argument showing how the activities of modern corporations can be attributed to the state. Corporations, after all, are creatures of statute; their existence and the extraordinary powers they wield are a product of legislation and can be legitimately eliminated by government fiat.[58] Corporate survival and welfare depend on the continuing availability of legal sanctions and support. Corporations are the creation of the government, and, relying on the coercive authority of the courts, any redistributive consequences attributable to corporate activity involve the government. Moreover, even under the analytical script of the public/private distinction, what may appear as private activity in one social context can easily and always be transformed into public action by a re-description of the circumstances. All that is required in the social drama is for the relevant actors to reposition themselves so that the state moves from the wings into centre-stage.

Yet, despite the transparency of the public/private distinction, the Supreme Court has simply assumed that corporations are 'private' entities. Accordingly, not only are commercial corporations and associations generally considered to be outside the scope of judicial review, but they are accorded the same rights as citizens to challenge the administrative and legislative acts of the government. For instance, in *Hunter* v. *Southam Inc.*, section 8 of the Charter was interpreted as conferring a privacy right upon corporations and, in *Big M Drug Mart*, a corporation was permitted to invoke the right to freedom of religion to challenge a law that was deleterious to its economic interests.[59] Indeed, Southam Newspapers and Big M Drug Mart are treated like citizens and become citizens. But, surely, to treat Southam Newspapers, a multimillion-dollar financial outfit backed by huge financial institutions, and an ordinary citizen in the same way by granting them the same constitutional protection is to ignore wilfully the social reality of power. The effect is that corporations are doubly insulated from public scrutiny and control; they can resist attempts at democratic regulation by calling the courts in aid, and they can largely rely on the courts not to interfere in their own activities. As such, the public/private distinction frustrates rather than facilitates any democratic aspiration or practice in controlling corporate affairs.

The approach of the Supreme Court to corporate power and other established professional interests, such as lawyers and doctors,[60] can be contrasted with its approach to trade union power in the round of freedom of association cases decided after *Dolphin*. Continuing a long tradition of judicial antipathy to the labour movement, the Court refused to grant constitutional protection to the very core of union activities: collective bargaining and striking.[61] Not surprisingly, one of the reasons offered by the Court to support this decision was the 'public' nature of union power. Speaking for the majority in the *Alberta Reference*, LeDain J. stated that such union rights 'are not fundamental rights or freedoms' because 'they are *the creation of legislation*, involving a balance of competing interests in a field which has been recognized by the courts as requiring specialized expertise.'[62] Exactly how these labour creations of legislation are different from the corporate ones is never explained or justified. Similiarly, Sopinka's announcement that 'bargaining for working conditions is not, in itself, a constitutional freedom of individuals' is especially hard-hearted in light of the courts' solicitude for corporate rights to free speech and religion.[63] Thus, while 'private' corporate teams get a chance to score on every Charter shot, 'public' union teams have trouble even getting onto the ice. Of course, if the Court follows through on its suggestion that union power is 'public,' labour may yet get its chance to enjoy some Charter action – playing defence.[64]

The platform of liberal legalism on which the Charter is built impoverishes politics and ensures that any attempt to challenge its individualistic structure is effectively defused. The courts' response to the claims of constitutional protection for unions and their political activities is illustrative of this mind-set. In *Dolphin*, for instance, the Supreme Court insisted on treating picketing as a speech activity by individual workers. While this is a necessary classification under Charter thinking, it fails to recognize that picketing is intended as a group act of industrial resistance. To characterize picketing as an exercise of individual speech rights robs it of its broader and more radical political significance as a challenge to prevailing social conditions and thinking. Similarly, in the freedom of association cases, the Court based its refusal to grant constitutional status to the right to strike on the view that people cannot obtain more rights by joining a group than they could possess as individuals.[65] Yet the whole idea and existence of a union is to establish a collective solidarity and presence that can overcome workers' vulnerability to the greater power of employers. Limiting union rights to those that can be exercised by members individually is to subvert the whole raison d'être of unions. The refusal to recognize such rights is a punishing betrayal of the hopes and opportunities of working people for an improved life. Unions are reduced to one more interest group in the ethical bazaar of pluralistic politics, where all are welcome provided they are liberal.

BRIGHT LIGHTS

A new relation between citizen and state demands a new democratic theory of power. In particular, it requires a recognition of the need to face head-on the question of what kind of society people want and ought to be able to have; there is no excuse for hiding behind the false front of the public/private distinction. As a just program of politics, democracy cannot remain indifferent to the substantive outcome of political choice. Corporate power must be placed firmly within the ambit of democratic accountability. A distinction must not only be drawn between wants and needs, but social needs must be ranked in terms of how urgent, basic, and legitimate they are. However, by arguing for an expansive notion of politics that is intended to encompass all facets of social life, there is the obvious danger that even the most intimate occasions of people's lives will be exposed to the threat of collective interference and regulation. While I do not want to trivialize the seriousness of such a fear, there is a possibility of exaggerating its risk. For some, privacy can be a sanctuary in a sordid world, and the anonymity of public life can be a blessing. Yet, for others, privacy can become a prison and public anonymity can exacerbate social isolation and disaffection.

An abandonment of the public/private distinction does not mean that everything is hauled into the public space in which individual citizens lose all sense of privacy or personal autonomy. Nor does it mean that the non-conformist or loner will be dragooned into public life. What it does mean is that there will have to be a collective and democratic accounting of those moments and activities when society at large should devolve full power and authority to individuals and establish a space in which they can be immune from collective interference.[66] Autonomy will not be construed as a collective abandonment of individuals to the good or bad fortune of their personal circumstances, and solidarity will not be utilized as a socializing process for recalcitrant or eccentric individuals. As with establishing an appropriately progressive response to abortion, it will be seen that autonomy, participation, and substantive equality are inseparably connected.[67] Rather than a once-and-for-all reckoning, there will be a continuing and evolving responsibility to negotiate a balanced polity. Democracy is not about judicial revelation by way of quasi-divine respect for an allegedly neutral meta-language of political responsibility, but about popular engagement among citizens in an effort to devise and establish the terms and conditions for their own personal and collective existence. In short, liberalism has run its course.

Within such a democratic theory and practice of politics, the future role of the courts will be extremely limited. In a fully democratic polity, *judex leonis* would very likely become an extinct species. Because the doctrinal light they give forth obscures the path forward to administrative democracy as much as it illuminates it, judges will have to be content to glow dimly and not yearn to shine brightly. In case there is any doubt, I must emphasize that mine is not a call to extend judicial review to corporations. It is a plea to abandon the liberal idea of the state that informs the judicial enterprise and that gives a spurious legitimacy to constitutional law. Democracy is not enhanced by strengthening the judicial arm of the state. Far from loosening the grip of the economic elite on the public policy-making agenda, judges tighten the establishment's hold on its substance and style. Judges and the corporate elite would not be allies in a democratic alliance but partners in a constitutional crime. Moreover, such one-eyed allies could rule only in the kingdom of the blind and the deaf where democracy is unseen and unheard. Judges, bureaucrats, and businesspeople must be prepared to devolve their considerable power to the citizens in whose name they claim to act, but whose powerlessness they continue to ensure. While there will still be a need to resolve disputes in even the most democratic of societies, the resort to an unaccountable tribunal of so-called professional experts inhibits the development of a truly democratic character that cherishes and exploits the possibilities for active participation.[68] The law's empire is built upon the frustrated dreams of a democratic imagination.

6

Down the Yellow Brick Road: Rights Talk Back

At the end of the Yellow Brick Road, the Guardian of the Gates required Dorothy and her motley friends to don green spectacles. Ostensibly to protect them from the searing brightness and glory of the Emerald City, these cinematic glasses enabled them to be dazzled by the verdant brilliancy of the wonderful City and to be impressed by the majesty of the Wizard – 'I am everywhere, but to the eyes of common mortals I am invisible.'[1] In L. Frank Baum's classic tale, the quirky quartet were at first in awe of the ubiquitous Great and Terrible Oz. Initially believing that his assistance was imperative if their deepest wishes were to be fulfilled, they came to realize through dint of their own efforts that he was only a wizened old man who had to rely on props and pretences to maintain a semblance of authority and respect. He was in fact nothing more than the Great and Terrible Humbug. As such, *The Wizard of Oz* is a more light-hearted and less pessimistic rendering of Beckett's *Godot*.

In the context of law and legal theorizing, Baum's tale works to fine allegorical effect. It is a beguiling fable of commonplace credulity, professional complicity, and innocent exposure. Like the Charter, the Wizard is sustained in his power as much by the willingness of the City's burghers to suspend their common sense and to see what they were expected to see as he is by his deceptive deployment of hegemony's privileged accoutrements. Although hyped as sophisticated and state-of-the-art, contemporary jurisprudential writing is also the stuff of fairy tales; it is in theoretical and practical disarray. The glasses are beginning to slip and, in a manner of speaking, something not green is peeking through. Yet, unlike in *The Wizard of Oz*, the stakes are much higher and the consequences are more real.

In this chapter, I intend to survey and respond to the varied and spirited responses that have been made in the Canadian literature to the critical assault on rights-talk. As with Dorothy's journey, there are three sets of eclectic companions on the jurisprudential trek down the Charter's Yellow Brick Road: the pragmatists, the relationists, and the socialists. Each revisits rights-talk for different reasons and attempts to revitalize it in different ways. There is Brian Langille, who wants to lay a jurisprudential foundation for the pragmatic restoration of democratic faith in judicial activism and the legal process. At a less rarefied level, Jennifer Nedelsky and Leon Trakman seek to restructure society in line with a more relational ethic that incorporates a dialogic understanding of rights-talk. Finally, there is a group of socialists who, although once staunch critics of rights-talk, want to tap its transformative potential and harness it to an egalitarian vision of justice. Despite their protestations to the contrary, each of them attempts to salvage the judicial enterprise from conceptual disaster and normative bankruptcy: the humble appearance of the non-formalist presentation belies the hubristic reality of the formalist ambition. By way of conclusion, I sketch a more postmodern approach to Charter lawyering.

THE PRAGMATIC TURNING

Legal theorists have learned well from their practising colleagues. Dogmatism and intransigence help neither the jurisprudential campaign nor the forensic encounter. The ability to shift critical ground as the circumstances dictate marks both the deft legal theorist and the skilled advocate. Although alternative pleadings may work in litigation, they cripple in jurisprudential exchange. The defence of the legitimacy of adjudicative power has led to some subtle but substantive alterations in argumentative stance. Over the past decade, judicial apologetics have abandoned strong claims of objectivity in favour of more humble assertions of determinacy. Pragmatism is distinctly back in vogue and its virtues of intellectual self-discipline, professional craft, and traditional respect are regularly extolled. It is a 'back to basics' movement whose legitimacy is found in Cardozo's pronouncement that 'the philosophy of the common law is at bottom the philosophy of pragmatism.'[2]

Embarrassed by the more extravagant conceits of their predecessors, pragmatists accept that a strong defence of judicial objectivity is doomed and concede that legal reasoning can no longer be treated as deductive at heart. The best that can be hoped for is to view law as a gradual accretion of conventional wisdoms that, in the form of rules and principles, give determinate guidance to the judges. From a pragmatic perspective, lawyers and judges are practical people who pursue practical ends through practical means. As such, legal pragmatism is not so much a philosophy or methodology, but a way of life: it nurtures an existential ethic of inquiry rather than inculcates a catechism of substantive outcomes. Resisting its grounding in anything outside of the lived life of law itself, it is practised and renewed through daily acts of legal reasoning; it tends to the *ad hoc* rather than the *a priori*. In this way, legal pragmatism treats truth and correctness as experiential and experimental rather than apodictic and apocalyptic; judgment is about nurtured prudence, not revealed knowledge.

Such pragmatists find no single algorithm for decision-making, only a pot-pourri of methods that incorporates contextual, historical, human, deliberative, and normative components in all their complexity and ambiguity: instrumentality and situatedness are the watchwords of the pragmatic revival. Under pragmatic tutelage, therefore, law becomes a practical activity that bears more resemblance to carpentry than it does to mathematics. Like most practical skills, it is acquired by the experience of doing it and is handed down from practitioner to practitioner. Valuing technical accomplishment over political insight, it is about knowing the ropes.[3] In this practical calling, lawyers' highest achievement is not in the reduction of law's operative precepts and maxims to an elaborate and exhaustive system; rather, it is to be found in the performance of an acknowledged master craftsperson whose work epitomizes as it celebrates the law's basic precepts and maxim. As Brian Slattery explains:

> Deciding constitutional cases is a practical art, just like playing baseball, raising children, writing short stories, cooking a good meal, diagnosing an illness or governing your country. Good constitutional decisions are made, not by logical deductions from explicit constitutional standards, but by tapping one's tacit knowledge of the practical workings of the constitutional system and its implicit values and principles, which the explicit standards only partially and palely reflect. To attempt to use these standards as the sole basis of decision will be like trying to learn driving from the provisions of the *Highway Traffic Act*. The fact that the standards are in themselves indeterminate does not mean that the decision-making process that they govern is arbitrary or unconstrained. It only means that the practical knowledge that guides and constrains the decision-making process cannot be adequately stated in words. The subtlety of that

practical knowledge and the large number of variables that it embraces mean that verbal formulations of the basic precepts of good constitutional practice will tend to be abstract and indeterminate. Thus, the indeterminacy of general constitutional standards is a reflection of the fact constitutional decision-making is a highly concrete and contextual art that requires experience and skill and more than a little wisdom.[4]

A jurist who has attempted to flesh out and support these claims for a pragmatic theory of law is Brian Langille. In a series of essays,[5] he has sought to salvage the legal enterprise from the storm whipped up by strong sceptics. He wants to show that for all their huff-and-puff, they fail to shake the foundations of law's legitimacy and are themselves 'driven to arational, psychological, modes of explanation ... reification, mystification, and other "subtle" ideas.'[6] While acknowledging that law involves politics, Langille insists that legal argument and adjudication are not fatally indeterminate and ideological, but share in a distinctive and defensible mode of objective discourse. For him, jurisprudence can be said to be directed toward answering two separate, but related, questions. The first is analytical and asks whether legal argument is a coherent enterprise; the second is normative and inquires whether the law is ethically or politically good.

According to Langille, the conceptual apparatus that I utilize – 'a negative non-foundationalism' (474) – to demonstrate the incoherence of the legal enterprise deprives me of any ground from which to mount my political 'tirade against both the Charter and the dark forces of "liberalism"' (482).[7] While critics like myself do 'good work' in criticizing judicial efforts to apply the Charter, such sceptical arguments are of dubious conceptual provenance:

Yet, on their own theoretical terms, it is difficult to know what status these arguments have. For them, at least when they speak theoretically, the Charter and all attempts at Charter discourse are to be regarded as islands of false consciousness in a sea of nothingness. The lesson is that they are better off jettisoning basic theoretical assumptions which are their own unique mixture of very strong versions of the four critical arguments of indeterminacy, subjectivity, contradiction, and mystification. Their strong identification with extraordinarily strong versions of these theses undermines their critique and makes their plea for a more egalitarian conception of law and social justice theoretically empty. (485)

Unfortunately, a Wittgenstein-inspired Langille proves too little and too much for his own analytical and political good.[8] He proves too little in that the normative consequences of my analytical critique are far from fatal; while they are 'ungrounded' in the sense that they possess no absolute or foundational authority, they are not by that very fact illegitimate or illusory. On the other hand, he proves too much for his own normative good. His own attempts to discredit my deconstructive line of critique leave him with no critical perspective from which to analyse the alleged coherence of the legal enterprise or to evaluate its merit; he is reduced to defending what is for no other reason than because it is. Criticism becomes an act of description and, as Wittgenstein might have put it, legal theory 'may in no way interfere with the actual use of [legal] language; it can in the end only describe it. For it cannot give any foundation either. It leaves everything as it is.'[9] Law and legal theory are what lawyers and legal theorists do – nothing more and nothing less.

Langille's rendition of the anecdote of the drunk and the lost keys inadvertently captures the nature of his position and the vacuity of his claims about law's grammar. A drunk loses a set of keys in the dark. When questioned as to the point of looking for the keys under a streetlight, the drunk replies that it is light there. While this is amusing, it is probably less so than Langille's rejoinder: 'The Wittgensteinian response is terribly straight-forward – you must look where the keys are' (501). It is a trifle trite and hugely unhelpful to proffer such advice when the whole incident is premised on the fact that the drunk does not know where the keys are. As with keys and drunks, so with lawyers and law. In the case of the legal theorist, it is not only the location of law's key that is in dispute, but the very existence of such a key. For Langille and others who drink the intoxicating draughts from this particular Wittgensteinian well, the mere uttering of 'open sesame' will be enough to unlock law's treasure trove of elusive conceptual jewels.

Langille's criticisms about the sceptics' claims of linguistic indeterminacy and the radical subjectivity of ethical judgment miss the mark. As I have tried to explain,[10] Langille exaggerates the consequences of a responsible scepticism, ignores the historical point of the critical exercise, and takes the political edge off the critique. It is definitely not the sceptics' case that there can be no general consensus on the shape and substance of past legal doctrine nor that the resolution of particular cases cannot be predicted with a reasonable degree of confidence. But it is very much the case that law fails to meet its own proclaimed standards of rational justification and cognitive clarity. Unsupplemented by external influences and values, legal doctrine can *never* of itself determine the 'correct' and 'unique' answer to a particular dispute. Any fragile consensus about meaning or any confidence in prediction does not arise from inside doctrine, but is given to doctrine from outside.

Legal doctrine is not simply 'out there,' but is always in need of collective retrieval and re-creation. The past is unknowable in and of itself. The past has passed and was what it was, but it is up to those who follow to decide what it is and will become: the future of the past is a present and continuing responsibility. Tangled in a skein of fact and fancy, history can never be excavated in its unadulterated immediacy, but can only be experienced second-hand. Consequently, meaning is always provisional, in that it is always open to (re)interpretation, and conditional, in that it is only knowable from an interpretive perspective. Legal reality is the historical function of the ideological commitments that constitute a legal community at any given time, a community whose identity and expression is itself an interpretive artefact that is never 'self-present as a positive fact.'[11] To put it in Langille's term, even 'agreements in judgments are themselves the object of interpretation,' not its ground. None of this is intended to deny the shared, if elusive, sense of doctrinal intelligibility that everyone experiences at some time. Indeed, in the theoretical interrogation of 'shared meaning,' there is an implicit and unavoidable reliance on the practice of shared meaning.[12]

Similarly, once this understanding of the indeterminacy critique is grasped, Langille's arguments about radical subjectivity are undermined. While indeterminacy leads to choice, it does not mean that that choice is the sovereign prerogative of a radical subjectivity. I reject the caricatured suggestion that judges are consciously manipulative ideologues who combine in machiavellian manner with their colleagues to implement a clear and self-serving scheme of social (in)justice. It is as flawed to propose that the judge is everything as it is to suggest that the law is everything. Although there are frequent instances of overt manipulation, legal doctrine amounts to more than the residual traces of the judicial mind's unbounded freeplay. The posited distinction between 'that to be interpreted' (doctrine) and 'that which interprets' (judge) cannot be sustained.[13] Neither doctrine nor lawyer exclusively controls meaning. Each is implicated by and in the other. Both doctrine and lawyer are shaped by their political milieu; they interact and interpenetrate to generate legal discourse and its 'reality.'

A CRAFTY SUGGESTION

Apart from the invocation of trusted Wittgensteinian wisdom to scotch the sceptics' claims, Langille relies on the *Philosophical Investigations* to suggest an alternative view of legal argument – one that might underscore rather than undermine the viability of legal discourse. He contends that a proper understanding of Wittgenstein reveals that the role of the jurist is 'not to build up theories, but to dispel confusion' (486). In a very concrete sense, Langille wants to rekindle the Hartian notion of law as a social practice and form of life in which jurisprudential explanation is made from a distinctly internal perspective.[14] The crux of his account of law is that it is not about interpretation as a mental mode of passive reflection, but it is about the worldly *activity* of playing the language game: 'Obeying a rule is not a product of thinking, but of acting' (490). To understand legal language means to be an expert on legal techniques; it is a matter of application, not interpretation. As such, law can only be understood and participated in as a form of life that one does not so much know, but rather lives: the lawyer is more a mundane bricklayer than a metaphysical architect. Legal discourse is a grammatical exercise in which 'there is nothing we can do beyond giving examples and insisting upon practice in order to communicate all we ourselves know' (491). Legal theorists must be content with conveying the soothing message that 'this is just the way things are' (493).

Unfortunately, rather than accept law as one more way of coping, pragmatists, like Langille, cannot resist the temptation to turn it into a way of knowing. They mistake consensus for neutrality and press practical reasoning into service in the formalist workhouse. Trying to make a theoretical method out of an experiential muddle, the pragmatists want to practise practical reasoning in a non-practical way: their analysis almost exclusively concerns textual and argumentational matters. They pay little attention to the actual social context in which disputes arise or to the political consequences of decisions: an attachment to and immersion in the relevant doctrinal tradition satisfy the condition of situatedness. For pragmatists, law continues to serve as the principal discursive device for deciding who speaks when, in what voice, and with what authority. Their firm ambition remains 'to strike bottom' and to build the legal enterprise on secure epistemological foundations.[15] Indeed, contrary to their philosophical protestations, they are decidedly not pragmatists.

The major problem with Langille's account is that it is not so much an invalid or controversial explanation of law's viability as it is a denial of the possibility of any explanation at all. By reducing legal theorists to mere grammarians – or, at least pretending to – he seems not only to trade in a profound resignation and obeisance to the status quo, but to glory in the presumed apolitics of this stance. The concession that law and its interpretation is purely a matter of social fact robs Langille of any way of evaluating its content or conclusion. When he approves my pointing out 'the weird and untenable distinctions the courts have managed to draw' (485), it is baffling to understand on what basis he makes these remarks. For him, good law is simply what good lawyers do and good lawyers are those who have become efficacious at whatever it is that lawyers do. It is a tautological gospel of expertise in which the expert is someone who has made a habit of engaging in a particular activity: the standard of good lawyering is quantitative, not qualitative. Langille begins and ends his arguments at one and the same place, namely 'the way things are.' Far from being a celebration of the professional ideal, Langille has effected its ultimate disparagement.

The consequences of this *grammatical jurisprudence* are far from benign. It is not so much that Langille removes most of the interesting and normative questions from the jurisprudential agenda, but that he answers them by default. What interests are served by legal discourse? How does it justify its power and authority? How does law shape the conditions and status of ordinary citizens? Why and how does law change? Insofar as legal discourse is what lawyers say and lawyering amounts to what lawyers do, law will reflect and embody the values, aspirations, and interests of those who constitute the legal profession at any given moment – a predominantly male, white, middle-class group. In short, Langille has made a blatant attempt to convert technique into substance and has effected a 'retreat to the elite.'[16] It is a desperate and transparent effort to preserve the legitimacy of legal values by invoking the naked authority of judicial popes and lawyerly princes.[17] As such, legal theory is the opium of the masses and legal theorists become traffickers and traders in this narcotic practice.

Like linguistic grammarians, Langille wants to claim that while law's grammar is neutral, it does not mean that it is value-free. The familiar norms and standards of law's grammar – 'consistency, even-handedness, and equal treatment' (485) – are uncontroversial and can be acclaimed by all. But this is very wishful thinking. Grammar does not spring full-grown from the head of Zeus; it is customary usage that has ossified and forgotten its organic pedigree. It is not that such values are necessarily bad (although those referred to by Langille are woefully vague), but that they require a defence and not a ritual affirmation. All grammar is an ideology by which the custodians of the status quo impose their own values on the greater community. The idea of 'correct' or 'standard' English is little more than the English used by the educated, upper middle-classes. The language of other groups, like women and blacks,[18] is not inferior or any less logical; it is simply not in a political position to assert itself. Grammar is the calling card of privilege and power.

On his own and in more specific terms, Langille's account is 'deeply shallow' (456). Even if law is an activity, it is a self-conscious activity of justification. Legal doctrine is not simply a collection of litigational outcomes, but a depository of justificatory arguments. There are not libraries of judgments instead of lists of decisions for nothing. Law is an institutional practice of warranting the deployment of threatened coercive power and of fixing certain readings of text with authoritative force. The struggle for meaning and the establishment of determinacy take place in the context of prevailing power relations. While Langille seems to deny their presence in his rendition of law's language game, they provide the very context and conditions for its possibility. For instance, in typical lawsuits, litigants and judges will disagree over the meaning of a particular rule or set of principles. Of course, the judges' interpretation will always prevail as they have the inside track. In the language game of law, the judge always holds the trump cards. The Jacksonian credo is regnant: 'We are not final because we are infallible, but we are infallible only because we are final.'[19] It is a matter of power, and far from resiling from this fact, Langille embraces it and elevates it to an axiomatic insight of jurisprudential merit. When the scam of playing theoretical tailor to the legal emperor is exposed, the only traditional response seems to be to rejoice in and solemnize their nakedness, not to condemn or chastise it. The critical task is to replace this pontifical idea of law with a more secular and democratic version.

Like so many formalists, Langille assumes the very determinacy whose existence he sets out to prove. The stipulation that there must be a preconscious agreement or shared judgments for any stability or possibility of meaning begs the central question to be answered: What is the source, nature, and worth of agreements and judgments? While there must exist some shared judgment to make general communication possible, it does not follow that it will be sufficient to foreclose disagreement in particular circumstances. Indeed, Langille's pronouncement that 'there is as much stability as there is' (493) does not preclude the assessment that there may be very little stability at all. For instance, Langille seems to approve of the observation that 'if, as a matter of fact, there were radical disagreements in application of expressions defined by reference to samples, there would no longer be these language games' (492).[20] The current state of jurisprudential play and legal doctrine gives the lie to the fact that there is a workable extent of stability/determinacy that renders the internal practice of legal discourse coherent or viable. It is not legal technique that resolves cases, but the values that give rise to and sustain the extant techniques. As Langille might put it, indeterminacy and disagreement are the way it is and that are just the way it is.

Many of the points made can be brought together and reinforced by Langille's example of mathematical rule following. The puzzle is to determine which two numbers come next in a series 1, 3, 5, 7 ...[21] The answer is obviously uncertain: 9, 11 ... (odd numbers); 11, 13 ... (odd prime numbers); almost any numbers (serial repetition of six random numbers). Langille accepts the force of the sceptical attack and concedes that the fact that 'neither precedent nor intention can give or dictate the outcome ... is true,' but he considers that to be 'unimportant' (488). For him – and Wittgenstein is again the source – the challenge is not to seek vainly to plug the gap between the rule and following the rule, but to look at and determine existing practices and understandings. The only way to know the correct answer is to learn and be instructed by what others do: 'There is nothing we can do beyond giving examples and insisting upon practice in order to communicate all we ourselves know about the use of [such] concepts' (491).

Where does all this leave the student of mathematics or law? The only Langillean answer must be: Who knows? If 'precedent' and 'intention' are no guide, the hapless student is on her or his own. In such circumstances, it makes no sense to require a following of existing practice when the character of such practice is the very matter at issue. Even to advise a choice for elegance or symmetry seems self-defeating and question-begging. Whatever the case in mathematics, the legal situation is doubly or even trebly problematic. Judges have a tendency to change the operating rules, as it were, in mid-series. Like peripatetic gamblers, they sometimes roll the adjudicative dice for odd numbers, at other times for prime numbers, and occasionally for random numbers. Moreover, what is completely overlooked by Langille and others is that there is no sure method of ascertaining which cases correspond to which numbers. If we accept that chronology is an unreliable guide, a case might be number 3 today, 1 tomorrow, and 5 the day after. Consequently, even if Langille's espousal of an activity-based explanation of legal meaning is taken seriously, it not only cannot get past the finishing line, it cannot even get the hermeneutical project out of the starting gate. Running on the spot passes for Langillean progress.

In attempting to demonstrate the groundlessness of my own critique, Langille has highlighted the profoundly conservative politics of his own grammatical offering. In one sense, he needs no standard against which to measure the coherence or value of legal doctrine because, on his own terms, things are the way they are; there is no point in agonizing about them because they could not be any other way. This, of course, defies any sense or understanding of history; Langille's failure to discuss or mention legal doctrine is not coincidental. Things can be different, and the fact that we have made things what they are means that we can remake them differently. To believe or suggest otherwise is a capitulation to the tyranny of the status quo. And to produce theories, in the name of 'meaningful criticism' (485), that seek to undergird such beliefs or suggestions is a shameful abdication of the jurist's intellectual responsibility.

As regards my own position, I plead guilty to the charge that I work to 'debilitate ... [and] trivialize ... constitutional interpretation' (473). However, I do not accept that I 'misdirect ... reflection upon [those] issues' (473). By depicting constitutional interpretation as an inextricable web of political power and legal principle, I hope to direct attention to the inescapable political quality of Charter adjudication. The search for some solid epistemological or methodological foundation on which to stand bears witness to our unwillingness to take responsibility for ourselves and the fate of others. There is no way to escape the politics of our finitude and land in a timeless domain of pure reason or unadulterated practice where life's always difficult and often painful decisions can be made for us. Although there is no relief from that responsibility, there can be an empowering satisfaction in facing those dilemmas and resolving them for ourselves. Because society determines its own collective values and arrangements, it is resoundingly unjust to allow one group to hold a disproportionate sway over the terms and conditions of social life. On a sceptical account of law, the appropriation of political discourse by the elite voice of lawyers in the name of pragmatism is to be lamented and resisted; it offends and inhibits the aspiration to progressive or egalitarian governance. It will be in spite of and not because of constitutional litigation that justice will most often be achieved. It is only through an unwavering commitment to democracy, as a substantive form of life, that we can really make 'criticism ... and rebellion meaningful' (505). More than that, democracy can help give meaning to our lives as citizens of a common humanity.

GETTING ON THE RELATIONAL TRACK

Langille's work is not the only kind of neopragmatism to enter the constitutional and jurisprudential fray over rights-talk. Whereas Langille reconstitutes a moderate brew, other scholars have cooked up a more progressive and palatable concoction. These commentators have given up the painful attempt to distinguish what goes on in court from what takes place in other arenas of political debate. For them, law provides another site for normative conversation and deliberative dialogue rather than a specialized contribution to that debate. Indeed, they accept that law is woefully indeterminate and cannot meet its own foundational standards of rationality, objectivity, and neutrality. In place of this traditional understanding, they propose an expressive conception of legal reasoning that is more open and less determinative and that views legal questions as matters to be answered through conversation and deliberation rather than by logical proof. In their progressive hands, practical reasoning becomes a thoroughly political way of coping; it does not confuse consensus with neutrality. The criteria for good judging cease to centre on style and form, but direct themselves to a decision's substance and consequences.

One who has gone down this progressive track is Jennifer Nedelsky. She maintains that whatever the original purpose and present reality of Charter adjudication, it is possible and desirable to utilize the courts as part of 'a dialogue of democratic accountability.'[22] Contrary to traditional analyses, the central constitutional challenge is not to balance the tension between democratic process and judicially enforced individual rights. Both of these ideas and institutions are complementary and actually require each other for their own full realization. In order to appreciate fully their mutually reinforcing qualities, Nedelsky insists that rights-talk not be framed in the limiting metaphors of boundary and separation, but be set in a discursive context of relationship and connection. To be effective, rights should imply the need for participation in collective governance as well as evince a concern for individual autonomy. In this way, the courts might become a better institutional setting that nurtures the kind of rights-talk that enhances democracy by enabling 'people [to] deliberate on the patterns of relationship that they want to characterize their society.'[23] It is an optimistic effort to restore and realize jurisprudence's pride in the emancipatory project of liberal democracy.

Another who has pursued the pragmatic path with equal sophistication, but to more practical effect, is Leon Trakman. With a rare combination of theoretical erudition and street savvy, his *Reasoning with the Charter* challenges the traditional conception of rights-talk and judicial decision-making as being narrow, abstract, and disingenuous.[24] He recognizes that any radical analysis of legal reasoning must go beyond methodological skirmishing and situate its epistemological challenge within a broader political critique of law. Taking an optimistic view of the courts' capacity to transform society and their own self-image, he advocates a style and standard of judicial performance that accepts the courts as political through and through. Enjoying a situational advantage over other governmental agencies in listening for marginalized voices, the courts can act as conversational partners in achieving liberty and justice in the flawed actuality of modern democratic politics. As such, judicial activism is encouraged and justified as a way of making the substantive best of a bad constitutional job in the modern project of democratic renewal.

After an exhaustive and exhausting survey of Charter jurisprudence, Trakman concludes that the present pseudo-rationality of constitutional review must be abandoned in favour of a mode of dialogic reason that is normative, contextual, perspective, and interactive. Judges err when they assume that 'the nature of rights is self-evident; that those rights are graduated according to a discoverable hierarchy ... and that justice is achieved by the neutral application of those principles to specific cases.'[25] Moving from a negative and individualistic view of rights to a positive and communal one, he wants to move beyond the public/private schism and reconstitute public life more in the image of a civic republicanism than a stale liberalism. To operationalize this relational approach, Trakman reclaims the voice of rights-talk by reconstituting and revitalizing it in accordance with a relational dynamic. Junking the notion of rights as a set of fixed and abstract claims, he revalorizes it as a conversational discourse through which to establish community in the struggle for meaning. Detached from extant protocols of power, a concrete and expansive version of rights-talk can empower the marginal at the same time as it challenges the status quo: 'Both fundamental rights and substantial justice are contingent upon normative properties that a diverse discourse instils in them.'[26] In the Trakmanian scheme of things, substantive empathy is the order of the day and not an impoverished autonomy. He looks to society more as an organic set of relational interests than an agglomeration of atomistic individuals.

As a spur to implementing this progressive approach, Trakman suggests that judges recognize that law establishes the values that constitute objectivity and lack of perspective. By recognizing their own situatedness and perspectival understanding, judges might abandon the illusion of neutrality and begin to hear and empathize with diverse points of view through vigorous conversational engagement. In this way, Trakman envisages the courts as the crucial interpretive forum for a communal conversation in which the voices of the excluded can join and transform the dominant discourse. Within such a vision, the Charter becomes 'a monitor of social action and a focal point for communal dialogue.'[27] In short, the courts will become a venue for a social dialogue whose substantive content is forged through its contingent and conditional practice; judges will assume the role of dialogic facilitators and communal consciences.

It is important to note that Trakman's book, as compared with Langille's essays, is not simply an arid and abstract endeavour. As befits his pragmatic and situated aspirations, it is jam-packed with practical illustrations and concrete examples. His sweep of Charter jurisprudence is as comprehensive as it is insightful. In particular, he uses the judgments of the courts in the *Morgentaler* abortion decision as a testing ground for his deconstructive criticisms and his reconstructive proposals. For Trakman, the challenge is to move beyond the worn judicial vocabulary of individual rights to 'a social conception of reproductive freedom [that arises] in a communal discourse about the relationship between pregnant women, as a group, and the life of the polity.'[28] In this ambition, he offers a tantalizing glimpse of how a revised judicial version of rights-talk might meet the formalist demands of more traditional theorists and the political criticisms of more radical critics.

In assessing the success of Trakman's project, it is not difficult to appreciate his scholarly sophistication or his democratic motivations. In this sense, his project is worthy of considerable admiration and respect. Yet, for all its wit and wisdom, Trakman's tract is a dangerous document. Although some will defend its persistence with court-based dialogue as the preferred mode of social policy-making as simply accepting the inevitable, *Reasoning with the Charter* runs the real risk of making too good a job of a democratic bad lot. It is naïve as a matter of normative description and dubious as a matter of transformative politics. Like too much modern legal scholarship, Trakman's proposals seek to salvage the adjudicative enterprise rather than junk it: it is little more than a warmed-over dish of old formalism. The fact is that the courts are as much a part of the problem as the solution. Judicial conversation is the antithesis of democratic dialogue, not its apotheosis.

First, as Trakman himself so amply demonstrates, the present practice of Canadian judicial decision-making is clearly found wanting in terms of its approximation to Trakman's conversational criteria of merit. He writes that 'Canadian courts, led by the Supreme Court, have adhered to a distinctly propertied conception of private rights in recent years.'[29] In this, Trakman and I are in complete accord. However, where we part company is over the courts' willingness or capacity to change. To imagine that existing judges are capable of moving beyond their traditional habits and truly engaging in a free-wheeling exercise of this kind of dialogue is highly unlikely. What Trakman's suggestion is more likely to do is to dignify the continuing adherence to a mock-legal ratiocination with the legitimating veneer of civic conversation. Despite its deceptive appearance, the reality will continue to be the privileged few imposing their vision of justice on the disenfranchised many.

In their jurisprudential optimism, Trakman and Nedelsky leave too much untouched – success would be their worst enemy. If the judicial form changes, but the substance of decision-making remains the same, they will have made the worse, not the best, of a bad job. Admittedly, a transformation in argumentative style might produce greater candour, but it has no necessary implications for the results reached. Arguing that candour is not all that it is democratically or morally cracked up to be, some contend that revealing the Wizard's authority as illegitimate is more likely to result in a redoubling of belief than in a feeling of liberation.[30] Yet, rather than conclude that the very process of rule by the judiciary in a liberal democracy be abandoned, such court-watchers seem committed to advocating a continuing exercise in judicial disingenuity, stamped with the validating imprimatur of academic approval. For them, on the other side of candour lies deceit and connivance.

This leads to the second major objection to Trakman's thesis. There is no guarantee at all that if judges were capable of genuinely grasping and implementing the dialogic ethic, they would reach progressive decisions. Indeed, Trakman's evidence is all to the contrary. Even if 'at their best, judges will construct thoughtful propositions based on reasonably informed suppositions,'[31] nothing necessarily follows about the progressive or reactionary nature of the ensuing decisions: a dialogic or relational approach to rights-talk is no more exempt from the indeterminacy critique than any other ethic. Trakman retains an almost naïve faith that argumentative style is more important than the arguer's identity. He implicitly assumes that which he chastises in others. Judges decide as they presently do in large part because of their normative instincts and political assumptions. Although the unveiling of these assumptions might spur greater reflection and motivate an occasional change of heart, most judges will validate and ratify their informing visions; they decide as they do because of, not in spite of, their instincts and assumptions.

Unless accompanied by substantial reconstruction of socioeconomic conditions, Trakman's conversational conversions will not alone usher in a fresh era of egalitarian justice. Without such substantive reform, they will bring only judicial chatter to the political table rather than establish a democratic dialogue that might throw over the present table of political commitments. Contrary to Trakman's speculation, for instance, the adoption of his preferred style of communal conversations in cases like *Morgentaler* will not automatically lead to a constitutional state of affairs that is solicitous of women's rights to control their own reproductive lives. As Margaret Atwood chillingly demonstrates in *A Handmaid's Tale*, the communal ethics of a select few, no matter how thoroughly ground out in the pestle of social dialogue, will not necessarily work to the advantage of all women: the dystopian Gilead is likely to be as much Trakman's legitimate offspring as Gilead's utopian sibling.[32] Trakman assumes that which his analysis clearly prohibits – that the form of reasoning is something that can always transcend and transform the substantive values of the reasoners. While it can contribute to that transformation, it cannot guarantee or underwrite it.

Ultimately, Trakman falls into the same trap that ensnares those modern formalists, like Ronald Dworkin and David Beatty, from which he wishes to disassociate himself. Instead of projecting adjudication as a matter of principle, he wants so much for it to be a process of empathic encounter. Although he condemns the judges for their attachment to abstract and discredited principles, he is content to believe in the transformative potential of courts and to portray the Supreme Court as an 'institution that calls some issues from the battleground of power politics to the forum of [solidarity]. It holds out the promise that the deepest, most fundamental conflicts between individuals and society will once, someplace, finally, become questions of justice.'[33] But it is just answers that are required, not pregnant questions of good intent. Unless and until there is a change in the ideological identity of society's decision-makers, the answers given to the 'deepest, most fundamental conflicts' will remain all too familiar and all too questionable. It is not increased empathy that is required, but a substantive reordering of empathic responses. Trakman ignores these historical facts and political realities at his own and society's peril.

Furthermore, Trakman's well-intentioned moves might obstruct any real progress in such a restructuring by obstructing or reducing the political pressure on other institutions more qualified and suited to effecting such substantive change. Although Trakman-like pragmatists might combine a transformation of adjudication with a proliferation of democratic dialogue in other institutional sites and practices, the continued attachment to courts as the best and primary forum for such engagements ultimately defeats itself. Jurisprudential good intentions pave the road to judicial tyranny. To use the courts as a venue for transformative action would require more disruptive and activist tactics than pragmatists seem prepared to countenance. The gamble that judges will take seriously the idea of dialogic constitutionalism and act upon the vocal challenge of previously excluded perspectives rather than use it as one more device to reinforce and legitimate the illusion of a privileged reality and vision of justice cannot be justified. Democracy unqualified prefers to debunk the Wizard than to attempt a wishful re-education in high-tech magic.[34]

The truncated dialogue of adjudication will always be dominated by lawyers and operate within a framework of institutional coercion and normative violence. As such, it is a caricature of democratic dialogue in which the dumb spend too much time knocking on the door of the deaf. Ordinary people do not take part in constitutional litigation and, therefore, never have the democratic opportunity to speak for themselves. It is almost perverse to liken judicial review to a dialogue or debate between citizens and the state about the reasonableness of government action.[35] If there is any debate, it is between different branches of government: citizens' complaints only provide an occasion for a discussion in which those citizens can only listen hopefully and can only speak episodically in the high-priced words of an arcane legal vocabulary. Democracy demands that citizens be more than eavesdroppers at the doors of power.

Lawyers and judges, as an elite class, embody a particular vision of society: they are predominantly white, European, male, heterosexual, and middle-class. Unless the sociocultural identity and political backgrounds of those appointed to judicial office dramatically shift, the law will remain 'a body of practices observed and ideas received over time by a caste of lawyers.'[36] To change this situation requires not only the agential endeavour of recruiting more representative judicial personnel, but also the structural challenge of transforming existing social and economic conditions. Presumably, the compulsion to make the judiciary more representative by appointing more women and minorities implicitly recognizes that identity is more important than argument. Despite the laudability of this objective, these representatives will come from the lawyers' ranks and speak in the law's idiolect; therefore, a truly representative judiciary in terms of social and economic status will remain a contradiction in democratic terms. The appointment of a truly diverse judiciary can only occur after a dramatic change in the political structure and substance of society. Such a change would make the need for an activist judiciary no longer obvious or compelling. This conclusion reinforces the more general observation that judicial activity and interpretation largely, although not exclusively, depend on the larger economic and political forces at play in society.

In adopting this critical stance, I am not a 'disappointed absolutist'[37] – one who clings to the belief in the need for formalist reasoning at the same time that she or he denies its possible realization. I do believe that a sustained engagement in meaningful conversation can advance the democratic cause; there is not a Hobson's choice between episodic judicial dialogue or endless shouting matches. Like the pragmatists,[38] I do not reject the possibility of reasoned argument, but the possibility that it can be rational in the sense of Right or Final. Practical reasoning is a necessary and desirable practice, but no democratic mandate requires the courts to be the most important institutional site for such practices: locus affects focus and interests shape identity. Law does the same for practical reason as philosophy does for reasoning at large; it attempts to turn it into a falsely privileged mode of discourse. If courts are to remain near the nub of democratic decision-making, the role and representation of the jury would need to be greatly expanded. As an occasion for democratic devolution, jury empowerment would bring a neglected challenge to the aristocratic instincts of legal professionalism and might invigorate the richness of dialogic debates. After all, law involves the lives of society's citizens and is much too important to be left to lawyers alone. Moreover, by withdrawing the fate of the polity from the clutches of lawyers, it might become possible for citizens to overcome the dispiriting belief that unless there is something large, powerful, and ahistorical on their side to support their claims – like the law or Coraf – they need not assert their right to govern themselves.[39] A revitalized jury system is one way to relieve political disempowerment and democratic ennui.

Instead of increasing efforts to make the courts more democratic, it would be preferable to expend civic energy in proliferating the extra-curial sites and situations for the democratic practices of engaged deliberation and genuine participation of economic equals. In this way, people might better develop the political sensibilities worthy of the truly democratic citizen: 'a sense of the contingency of their language of moral deliberation, and thus of their consciences, and thus of their community.'[40] An institutional possibility that might meet this challenge is the establishment of a centrally funded, but locally based series of justice commissions that would combine the best of royal commissions, private corporations, human rights agencies, and jury-enhanced courts. With a rotating and activist board of citizens and community groups, it could have the power and resources to investigate civic abuses on its own motion, facilitate the articulation of diverse viewpoints, make decisions, implement them through structural remedies, and monitor their efficacy. Along with a more democratic system of education, it might be possible to effect difficult change that did not have everyone's agreement, but did have everyone's respect. Democratic involvement could begin to mediate and mollify the antagonism between private interest and public benefit at the same time that it recognized the civic need to keep them contingently separate.

DOING THE RIGHT(S) THING?

Rights-talk still remains the preferred and familiar program of legal action for achieving social justice. Notwithstanding the dismal history of efforts to effect social change through the courts, contemporary activists are unable to resist the allure of rights-talk and still tend to look to the courts as the preferred forum of transformation. The appeal of the eighteenth-century 'rights of man' has been that they seem to 'provide *groups* who claim a better condition for themselves on *special* grounds – for instance as women, blacks or workers – with a *universal* justification for doing so, which makes it difficult for other people who accept the idea of such rights to resist the claim in principle.'[41] Yet, whatever the ambition and intentions of those who still cling to such a liberal program, it is not equal to the task of effecting social justice in a postmodern world. The very reasons that gave rise to rights-talk's original appeal have become the source of its contemporary failing as a program for progressive change – its universalistic pretensions, unyielding individualism, social insensitivity, and pervasive ahistoricality. Rights-talk has not only failed to deliver the progressive goods, but its vision of the good life is deeply flawed.[42] Moreover, its proponents have failed to show that the courts' handling of rights litigation has met the exacting standards of constitutional legitimacy, social justice, and instrumental efficacy: it cannot claim to be a purely objective exercise in legal justification, to supply the necessary level of operational determinacy or to result consistently in progressive contributions to political life.

The claim that law is always and inescapably political has profound implications for all lawyers and theorists. As well as undermining the mainstream jurisprudential project and its conceptions of law and lawyering, it obliges radical theorists to take seriously the legal process as a formative constituent of social life and as an important arena for political struggle. This does not mean a lemming-like rush into the courts or an unconditional embrace of the 'Rule of Law': these responses are more suited to the born-again jurisprudential zealot than the progressive sceptic. The belief that there will be a complete absence of law or a positivistic form of democratic law in a transformed world is a dangerous fantasy. A transformative view of law demands more than a facile pouring of new wine into the old institutional bottles of liberal formalism or a mere change in the personnel of the state. It requires a critical understanding of the political nature of legal structures, their instrumental limitations, and their resistance to accommodating change. In short, a constitutive theory of law, infused by a sense of historical indeterminacy and political contingency, can be conducive to the ambitions of progressive lawyering and can best guard against 'the slide into reformism or cynicism.'[43] Visionary imaginings must combine with concrete realities to create a political form of legal practice. Then, and only then, can engagement with and through law effect a substantive way of social living in which people can be less alien to their better selves and more able to shape their own collective destiny. Liberal legalism is not the way to go.

Nevertheless, while I am an unapologetic advocate of unmodified democracy, I do recognize that I am not writing in a sociopolitical vacuum and that Canada has already made a constitutional commitment to an entrenched bill of rights. Unlike in the United Kingdom and South Africa, the political debate in Canada is not about whether to introduce constitutional change by way of rights-talk, but how to put an institutional discourse of rights-talk to progressive ends and effect. Consequently, although the thesis of this book has been how the theory and practice of rights-talk betrays the cause of democracy, I concede that it might not be possible to ignore entirely constitutional litigation in a society that is already pervaded by rights-talk. While a wholesale resort to rights litigation as a schematic process for substantial social renovation is a fundamental error, the critical challenge is to move beyond such political stereotypes and their one-dimensional narratives for transformative action. The choice is *not* between a wholesale adoption or outright rejection of rights-talk as a vehicle for progressive change. While there is no 'outside' from which to work, there may be occasional strategic advantage in making 'inside' resort to the courts in the struggle to advance the project of progressive justice.

Many Marxists have fallen into the trap of positing the choice as between a wholesale adoption or outright rejection of rights-talk; they have allowed progressive debate over rights to be so polarized. Some have refused to be seduced by such expedient compromises and insist that rights-talk, whether as a categoric system of political practice or as a contingent strategy of radical intervention, can never be conducive to social and economic revolution. However, in the same way that it is no longer possible to invoke 'material interests' or 'class analysis' as a decisive ploy in political argument, forswearing engagement in any rights litigation at all is not a realistic or responsible tactic.[44] Like the abstract instincts of liberalism, the reductionist politics of class struggle fail to respect sufficiently differences of race, gender, and sexuality in its totalizing march to social justice. It falls victim to the same kind of universalistic judgment that afflicts liberal legalism in its all-or-nothing embrace of rights-talk as a political and legal way of life.

Taking seriously E.P. Thompson's invocation of the Rule of Law as a 'universal human good,'[45] other radical critics have advocated that rights-talk is not incompatible with socialism and must be adopted into the program of democratic socialism, albeit in a less transcendental and more historicized form.[46] Dazzled by the institutional allure of rights-talk, they go beyond occasional strategic resort to rights litigation and throw their lot in with rights-talk as an integral part of any transformed legal and political state of affairs. Yet this approach shaves the difference between liberal and socialist democracy too thin; it sacrifices lasting change for quick fixes. It is even more naïve than liberals, like Trakman, in its expectations for judicial support and motivation. Little serious consideration is given to the real risk that the courts and lawyers will become the primary movers and shakers in society and actually manage to squeeze the life out of any progressive initiative. As such, traditional leftist or liberal interpretations cannot effectively map the fragmented and diverse terrain of modern society, nor can such theoretical projections provide a viable or effective plan of transformative action. In the same way that rights-talk is not always emancipatory and empowering, it is not always diversionary and co-optive. To 'do the right thing' is a fluctuating and unfinished duty that is always fraught with risk: it is not a blanket willingness (or refusal) to 'do the rights thing.'[47]

Rather than dwell on rights-talk's failings and indulge in a cynical smugness, it is more helpful to offer constructive suggestions for action. As Rome burns, it does little credit to anyone to stand idly by and take comfort in pointing out that the city's fire-fighters are using oil in the mistaken belief that it is water. Accordingly, progressive scholars must look for better and different ways to empower disadvantaged groups. In effecting such a proposal, two approaches must be taken. The first step is to raise the critical consciousness of lawyers by disabusing them of their ingrained habit of resorting to the courts as the transformative forum of choice. They must become more sensitive to the debilitating effect of the extended involvement of courts in civic life. In postmodern terms, lawyers must appreciate the social limitations and historical constraints of rights-talk. Second, progressive lawyers must develop a posture of 'strategic scepticism' toward the efficacy of even limited use of litigation in the struggle for social justice. To direct the have-nots to the courts as a matter of course is, in a pertinent manner of speaking, to throw good money after bad.

The key objective for those devoted to improving the lot of the oppressed and downtrodden is to determine what substantive changes will best achieve that objective, how those measures can best be implemented, and which institutions can best carry through on that agenda. While the details and priorities of a progressive politics must be the continuing subject of healthy debate and respectful disagreement, there must also be a willingness to utilize a diversity of strategies to effect progressive change and to resort to a variety of institutional sites. However, it is important that such tactical calculations be sensitive to the prevailing realities of social power and economic ordering. The history of social struggle suggests strongly that the prospect of significant social change through litigation is, as Jackson J. so colourfully put it, 'a teasing illusion like a munificent bequest in a pauper's will.'[48]

Those committed to serious social change must remember that what is important is not the effect of a particular instance or series of constitutional litigation, but the very existence of the whole adjudicative process as a privileged mode of social action. In short, constitutional litigation and adjudication are special social activities that do not so much cause or condition, but are constitutive of, extant social conditions: 'It is not so much that the court is the natural expression of popular justice, but rather that its historical function is to ensnare it, control it and to strangle it, by re-inscribing it within institutions which are typical of a state apparatus.'[49] To participate in the litigation process as lawyer or litigant, however radical the claim or cause, is to be engaged *within* existing social relations; litigation may hinder social change and entrench the dominion of the established order. As such, it is dangerously naïve and overly romantic to contend that court-enforced rights can, will, or should be the preferred medium for social activists. It is a self-serving conceit for lawyers to encourage the continued use of litigation as a constructive and viable route to social justice. The language of the law has so often been and continues to be the language of the poor's subjection and misery. Not only is it difficult, as a practical and instrumental matter, to challenge subordination within and through the very institutions that subordinate people, but there is also the political and ideological grip that judicial discourse places on its participants: 'The legal forms we use set limits on what we can imagine as practical outcomes.'[50]

Nevertheless, while it is crucial not to exaggerate the contributions of the courts, it is equally important not to overstate the 'democratic' qualities of representative institutions or to deny entirely the possibility that legal forums might occasionally contribute to transformative struggle. Lawyers are not always and only 'the goon squad of the ruling class.'[51] As the pervasive conversational idiom of modern society, it is hard not to participate in the stylized conversation of rights-talk in any attempt to challenge existing arrangements and to improve the lot of ordinary people. But to join that conversation imposes a great risk of being co-opted and becoming vulnerable to take over. Nevertheless, the fear of co-optation must not lead to paralysis. It is not impossible or imprudent to adopt the use of traditional rights litigation as a limited strategy in the radical practice of law: the categoric denial of rights-talk is almost as bad as its categoric embrace. Between addiction and abstinence lies the considerable expanse of mindful moderation. It is this ample space that the progressive lawyer must exploit.

In efforts to transform law and society, a sensitivity to the contingent possibilities of any particular moment in social history is important. A close attention to contextual detail is vital. In particular historical conditions and social circumstances, rights-talk might not be entirely disutile. However, its use must be informed, guarded, and clear-headed; there is no room for romantic attachment. Like a sharp knife, it must be used with a caution that comes with the realization that it can so easily harm as well as do the bidding of its user. Some of the appropriate questions to ask about rights are posed by Elizabeth Schneider:

> Does the use of legal struggle generally and rights discourse in particular help to build a social movement? Does articulating a right advance political organizing and assist in political education? Can a right be articulated in a way that is consistent with the politics of an issue and that helps redefine it? Does the transformation of political insight into legal argumentation capture the political visions that underlie the movement? Does the use of rights keep us in touch with or divert us from consideration of and struggle around the hard questions of political choice and strategy?[52]

Ultimately, any gain through litigation will serve to lend popular credence to the legal system as a legitimate arena for successful transformative activism. To engender respect for any rights gained and to ensure their effective enforcement, it will be necessary to instil a general reverence for the courts as a whole.[53] While such a strategy might allow small advances to be made, it will actually defer and inhibit the kind of profound changes necessary for truly progressive transformation: minor improvements are the obstacles, not the precursors to major innovation. Moreover, small victories carry their own considerable price tag. Being abstract and potentially universalistic, rights-talk has no necessary political content and application; rights-talk is a site for struggle and occupation, not a completed project. Consequently, any right that is achieved cannot be controlled in its precise definition or utilization. It can be ambushed and held hostage by non-progressive lawyers and turned to the advantage of their own (privileged) clientele. Indeed, this is exactly what has happened in Canada. In the first three years after the introduction of the Charter of

Rights and Freedom's equality provision, there were approximately 600 court decisions, of which 44 decisions, or 7 per cent, involved sexual equality.[54] Most alarmingly, only 7 of these cases were initiated by or on behalf of women; the other 37 decisions were based on claims by men. Moreover, while obvious and important gains have been made through Charter litigation, they have tended to expand notions of due process and natural justice; they have not strengthened the arm of the oppressed to challenge or dislodge the elite brokers of established power.[55]

On the basis that established interests have greater access to courts and greater normative rapport with judges, the likelihood of systemic defeat being snatched from the jaws of a rights victory is not small. The corporate take-over of the Charter's protection of speech and religion is a stunning example in point.[56] Not only have corporations been able to reap considerable substantive protection, they have also managed to revise the rhetorical agenda so that their interests receive primary doctrinal consideration. The courts act cautiously when corporate concerns are implicated and, even when dealing with non-corporate issues, they succeed in underlining the centrality of corporate concerns to the constitutional paradigm. How else is it possible to understand a judicial mind-set that refuses to see that commercial advertising by Southam Newspapers and begging by panhandlers are basically the same thing? It is only the economic status of each that distinguishes them. Clearly, rights-talk is the kind of constitutional conversation to be avoided wherever and whenever possible. In direct contrast to prevailing views, the instincts of progressive lawyers must be against resort to litigation.

Imbued with an appropriate sense of critical consciousness, progressive lawyers should develop a self-conscious program of strategic scepticism. Such a program would include more the cultivation of a particular mind-set and the refinement of various tactical techniques than the establishment of a manifesto of litigable claims. The core idea is to act in a guerilla-like way – within a broad set of progressive objectives – to seize the possibilities of any contingent moment in order to achieve judicial decisions that heighten the status quo's contradictions and open up space for lasting political action. It is imperative in pursuing such legal tactics that lawyers do not become intoxicated by the spirit of their own rhetorical excesses. To take the reasoning of the judges seriously is to validate once again the very institution that is to be subverted: it is to fall victim to the contagion of traditional jurisprudence in which law thrives as a rational enterprise of abstract politics. The progressive lawyer must forsake such comforting platitudes and remember that 'the best we can do, as lawyers, is to raise consciousness about the way law and its functionaries have helped create a hegemony in which the inequality in our polity is made to look natural.'[57]

The situation that best exemplifies the benefits and risks of 'strategic scepticism' is the abortion litigation. The victory in *Morgentaler*[58] brought bright rays of progressive sunshine into the long and drab wintry days of constitutional litigation. Yet it must not be forgotten what is being celebrated and why it occurred. While it is undoubtedly true that the Supreme Court's decisions offer a public occasion for civic instruction,[59] the best democratic lessons are invariably overlooked or ignored. Indeed, *Morgentaler* and its aftermath might well be viewed as a national seminar in the contested efficacy of constitutional litigation and judicial review as forms of political activism. Some of the lessons to be learned include: the questionable instrumentality of judicial decisions in social change, the continuing capacity of judges for vacillation, the inhospitability of rights-talk to progressive claims, the need for disruptive litigation tactics, and the dangers of litigation success.

The first thing to be noted is that *Morgentaler* was not the victory that pro-choice supporters wanted it to be or the defeat that the anti-abortionists feared that it would be. The decision of the Supreme Court was no more (and no less) than another move in the social drama of political change. Indeed, much remained unchanged in the social reality of abortion: the availability and rate of abortions stayed constant. Before and after the decision, women in Toronto could get an abortion in almost all circumstances, whereas women in Prince Edward Island could not get an abortion in almost any circumstances. Of course, those who could afford to travel and pay for medical services did better than those who could not. As such, *Morgentaler* allowed the social forces in play to continue in effect; it did not start or accelerate the trend. The greatest impact has not been on the amount of abortions performed, but on the number of illegal abortions that occur; the Supreme Court's decision brought abortion out of the criminal shadows into the public light of day. Nevertheless, while this fact is to be applauded, the decision in *Morgentaler* did little to reduce continuing local obstacles to abortion: a constitutional prohibition on criminalization is far removed from a positive right to an abortion in a safe and accessible setting.[60]

The worst implication to be drawn by lawyers from *Morgentaler* would be to believe that by making the correct arguments and by following the same doctrinal logic, it will be possible to consolidate gains made or achieve further successes. To do this would be to take too seriously the transformative power of abstract reasoning and to endow the legal process with a spurious legitimacy. It remains true that in a political culture that grants an increasingly significant place to litigation and where rights-talk possesses a special resonance, claims phrased in the rhetoric of rights might be less easily rejected and might act as a catalyst for the mobilization of popular struggle. As such, it might be feasible and successful on occasion to point out the frequency with which contemporary society fails to live up to its own expectations. Nevertheless, in general, it will only be by maintaining a thoroughgoing scepticism to such talismanic tendencies and by recognizing the strategic significance of such litigation in particular socioeconomic circumstances that the viability of any resorts by progressive lawyers to the courts can be sustained.[61]

The greatest danger of a rights litigation strategy is that it might succeed occasionally, but often enough to warrant continued faith in its efficacy as the chosen venue for progressive struggle. The attempt to make a silk purse of social justice out of the pig's ear of constitutional jurisprudence becomes too easily a waste of radical zeal. With any apparent success, it is vital not to forget that adjudicative success (or failure) only marks the end of one phase of struggle and the beginning of another. It is not a triumph (or a defeat) unless the legal currency can be converted into a negotiable instrument for real social change. Most importantly, when a legal success is achieved, it must be remembered what is being celebrated: it is not the institution of the Supreme Court or the process of constitutional adjudication. To fête the institution or the process is to pave the way for long-term disaster. For when the institution or the process produces a decision that is hostile to progressive interests or overrules an earlier supportive decision, that decision will be endowed with the imprimatur of political legitimacy. Ironically, this will have been achieved because of, and not in spite of, the activists' efforts.

What ought to be celebrated about *Morgentaler* is the substance of the decision itself and its potential concrete effects. Another bench on another day might use the cover of the Charter to smite, not protect the interests that won on that day.[62] It is crucial to acknowledge that success was not due to lawyers or constitutional charters, but came about through the political force of committed women coming together and working together. It was a triumph of popular will that made it possible for the Supreme Court to decide as it did in *Morgentaler*. Whether

Morgentaler will be eviscerated or envigorated will also be decided by the ideological dynamics of public action and most definitely not by the immanent rationality of constitutional law. That a majority of judges had the foresight and the courage in 1989 to heed the democratic call for gender justice is a cause for jubilation. But *Morgentaler* ought not to be a rallying call for constitutional enchantment: one swallow does not a progressive summer make.

Of course, the fact is that many of the disadvantaged and disenfranchised are not accorded the privilege of choosing the institutional site or rhetorical conditions of their struggle for social transformation. Nevertheless, this is not as significant or as debilitating as first might be thought. The first step to enlightenment is the recognition that there is no available 'outside' from which to engage in transformative action: all struggle is already situated within the mechanisms that are to be resisted and reworked. Struggle must commence from where we are and with the historical problems and possibilities of the present. The only available strategy is to develop legal tactics that politicize and disrupt the courts in the process of using them for litigation.[63] The challenge is to engage in law and, at the same time, to delegitimate it by eschewing abstract notions of justice and rights in favour of concrete challenges.

As well as perpetuating the idea that justice comes from a judicial act of noblesse oblige rather than being a product forged at the anvil of social struggle, a dependence on litigation struggles over rights will dissipate much valuable energy that could be better used elsewhere. Direct citizen involvement is always to be preferred to constitutional litigation. At the heart of any progressive campaign for social justice, there must be a firm commitment to the development of popular coalitions so that the disenfranchised can become part of their own empowerment. If a true democracy is to be the goal, it must be effected by means that are themselves thoroughly democratic in nature. For instance, in responding to the plight of the homeless, those very people can be involved as paid consultants and workers in the planning and (re)building of affordable housing and public amenities so that once such homes are created, they might be able to pay their way in their cooperative management and maintenance.

The shift from less of an individual-centred and rights-based approach to more of a group-based and power-oriented program will facilitate this ambition. In this way, it might become possible to ' recognize and accommodate the political importance of process over legal goals and build links with communities whose perspectives' are not usually or easily represented in the jejune practices of constitutional litigation.[64] Apart from abjuring the tendency toward litigation, the lawyer has an important role to play in such a program. While it will involve a reorientation of what is traditionally understood to be the primary skills of lawyering, a revised legal practice will still call upon many of the peculiar talents of lawyers for sophisticated organization and sound planning. The model of the good corporate lawyer can be appropriated and given a community-based twist. In facilitating the establishment of community institutions, lawyers can enhance the cooperative's capacity to make informed decisions about its own development and activities; they can nurture a democratic culture and organizational structure that meet the needs and wishes of its members.[65] In this way, the lawyer becomes a public part of the civic community rather than a private adversary of it.

Chastised by critics for its rigidity, the law has learned to bend more and to cope better with contradiction. Formalism has proved to have unexpectedly durable and adaptable qualities. Indeed, the rhetorical life of contemporary law may be the intense experience of its own contradictory logic.[66] At best, the courts and, therefore, constitutional litigation can never be more than a surgical aid to an ailing political system. The more appropriate progressive response is to treat the cause of the malaise rather than its symptoms by working to democratize better the political process. Continued resort to the courts to resolve political issues reinforces the undemocratic view that the political and representative forums are inappropriate and ineffective; it will become an unfortunate self-fulfilling prophecy. The vast energies and resources of lawyers are better deployed in legislative reform than in ingenious litigation: lawyers are the only real long-term beneficiaries of the present obsession with courts. Paradoxically, the best way to push courts and litigators out of the social action is for political activists and progressive lawyers to pull themselves away. Without constitutional litigation to envigorate it, the judicial process might wither away as the leading institutional organ for social policy-making. As a matter of contingent wisdom, it is a definite case of less being more. Rights only work for those who are already privileged. To others, they are a travesty of justice. It is change, not its promise, that is needed.

THE DEMOCRATIC GAZE

As Baum's chastened Wizard observes, the Emerald City's residents had worn the green spectacles for so long that most of them had forgotten that they had them on and actually believed that it was an emerald city. As the ambitions and achievements of the pragmatists show, such bedazzlement is still widespread in the jurisprudential community. Moreover, if Canadians continue to close their eyes and minds to what is going on around them, they will run a risk similar to that of the Emerald City's denizens. But their fate will be less optimistic and more debilitating: Dorothy's route does not likely run through Ottawa. Nor are the trappings of judicial power as tacky or transparent. The majestic allure of legal wizardry seems to remain as effective and sturdy as ever.

Yet, while noble in intent and ambition, the dubious dream of judicial integrity has proved unrealizable and has become the nightmare of democratic politics. Although the new patois of rights-talk is offered as an invigorating tonic for an ailing democracy, its long-term effect will be to increase popular dependence on elitist practices and to induce an even deeper lethargy in the body politic. In a world of incorrigible indeterminacy and decisional fallibility, there is no escape from the fact that someone must take responsibility for life's difficult and often painful decisions. Someone, indeed, must be trusted with final authority. But that responsibility and authority must reside in the people, not their judicial usurpers. Contrary to what Madam Justice McLachlin of the Supreme Court of Canada concludes, there is substantial cause to 'be dismayed by the inescapable marriage of fallibility and finality in the judicial function.'[67] The only offspring of such a union can be an illegitimate judocracy.

Scholars like Leon Trakman and Jennifer Nedelsky dispel some of the conventional confusion on judicial legitimacy and help citizens to see the democratic errors of our judicial ways. For this, they deserve sincere praise and genuine support. But they still persist in encouraging the use of institutional glasses, albeit of a less opaque but still roseate variety. To believe that judges have any better chance of avoiding both the illusion of certainty (elevating reason above sentiment) and the fear of despotism (raising sentiment above reason) is itself to fall victim to scholarly wizardry – allowing theoretical desire to cloud practical judgment. The pursuit of pragmatic reasoning and, most importantly, the consequences for its lack of success must be entrusted to citizens. As Trakman so cogently reminds us, democracy is not about right answers, but the opportunity for everyone to seek answers to the right questions for themselves. When it comes to the issue of continuing judical power and legitimacy, the unimpeded democratic gaze is what is most needed to put our civic lives into clearer and more progressive focus. Rights-talk can never be more than an occasional and risky distraction.

7

Talking the Good Life: From Rights-Talk to Democratic Conversation

Any legal or political theory is a theory about community. It is nonsensical to talk of law or politics outside of a social context or to discuss a social framework separate from its law and politics. Law, politics, and societies are inextricably linked; each helps to define and constitute the others. By striving to provide an account of the terms and conditions of collective and individual life in a social group, the legal or political theorist cannot avoid confronting the abiding and central conundrum of human existence: What is the proper and best way to live? How are we to live together? Any legal or political theory worth its normative salt addresses these questions directly and attempts to offer cogent answers. Consequently, a primary and inescapable issue for political and legal theory is not whether an idea of 'the good life' is relevant to the theoretical project, but what that idea is to consist of and what weight it is to have in thinking about and criticizing legal and political practice.

In spite of their traditional denials to the contrary, even liberals are engaged in the enterprise of formulating and defending a viable conception of 'the good life.' It is not so much that liberalism operates without a substantive theory, but that it depends upon an implicit understanding that communal well-being is best achieved and preserved through the institutional entrenchment of rights-talk. Some modern liberals recognize this and consider the attempt to define liberalism through its opposition to community-based theories of law and politics to be ill-advised: it contributes to its perceived moral indifference and weakens its political appeal. For instance, John Rawls has recently suggested that 'the right and the good are complementary and the priority of right does not deny this.'[1] Similarly, Ronald Dworkin has begun to make an explicit defence of liberalism as 'a special form of community.'[2] Yet this reference to the vocabulary of social solidarity does not represent any fundamental change in liberal theory or politics; the packaging may have altered, but the product remains the same. At best, modern liberalism adopts a very 'thin' idea of community; the concern with individual autonomy still overrides any obligation to secure the common good.

In this chapter, I want to begin the theoretical work on a much larger project. It is a task that attracts and frustrates that radical branch of contemporary scholarship that is devoted to the cause of social liberation: the development and defence of a critical theory and transformative program that can effect a shift from the reneged promise of liberal rights-talk to the untried possibilities of dialogic democracy. The central challenge is to wrest legal theory and practice from the paralysing grip of a jaded liberalism without falling into the suffocating embrace of a rejuvenated communitarianism; there are very real problems with how the shared norms of civic virtue can operate as discriminatory principles of inclusion and exclusion. My general intention is to examine the circumstances, causes, and consequences of the liberals' half-hearted appeal to communitarian rhetoric. In its place, I sketch the outlines of an uncompromising account of the democratic state and its revised version of citizenship. To focus and concretize this initial enquiry, I will concentrate on how it might be possible to transform the practice and theory of 'free speech' in line with a more democratic vision of social justice. In short, I want to propose a way to move from liberal chatter to democratic conversation in the service of progressive politics.

TOWARD DIALOGIC DEMOCRACY

In recent years, a number of scholars have begun to abandon the liberal paradigm of legal and political theory and to take seriously the idea of community as a constitutive and regulative ideal.[3] These communitarian critics are challenging liberals at all levels – metaphysical, ontological, normative, and practical – of inquiry and justification. They combine to reject the core values and assumptions of the liberal credo: the primacy of private values over public virtues, the celebration of the independent individual as the source and standard of normative worth, and the collectivity's alleged neutrality between competing conceptions of the Good.[4] By contrast to liberals, communitarians emphasize civic virtue over universal rights, situated citizens over abstract individuals, and public connectedness over personal autonomy. They do not seek to reconcile the different interests of private persons, but to transcend them in the search for a common ground and civic unity through a virtuous public life. Self-interest is juxtaposed to communal virtue, and the locus of moral authority moves from the subjective life to the republican polity itself. In sum, the modernist individual is replaced by the mature citizen. Instead of collapsing the barrier between public and private life, the public sphere would become the nursery for private action and responsibility.

Although liberal rights theorists traditionally concede that 'a society devoted to [a liberal vision of law and justice] may pay a price ... in the communitarian spirit that too much concern with law is supposed to cripple,'[5] they now seem to be having second thoughts about the dispensability of this 'communitarian spirit.' Indeed, some writers present a liberal constitution of legal rights as the epitome of the political community in which moral legitimacy is not secured through social contracting, but is anchored in group obligations for mutual well-being. They contend that members of a *genuine* political community are governed by a common set of principles that constitute social justice. Following Dworkin's lead, some Canadian legal writers propose an account of law that blends traditional social practices with principles of justice to establish a just community. This is not a full-blown collectivism or an argument that individuals are socially constructed and have social obligations. It is the much more modest and secondary claim that certain shared interests are not reducible to individual entitlements and that they can be weighed against rights.[6] However, the attempt to use communitarian rhetoric in the service of liberal ideals is disingenuous. A liberal community is little more than an aggregate of self-interested individuals who band together to facilitate the pursuit of their own life projects – a relation of strategic convenience and opportunism rather than mutual commitment and support. Stripped of its solidaristic rhetoric, it amounts to the very Lockean social contract of the conditional kind that such liberals are at pains to discredit and disclaim.

Even if this communitarian reworking is taken seriously, it is a profoundly elitist and undemocratic vision of social life. Under the ostensibly liberating tutelage of legal principle, there functions a subtle regime of oppression. Despite paying lip-service to the participatory nature of democratic debate, a communitarian liberalism is about accepting and assuming political obligations and not about participating in the making of them. Rationality and expertise are the political order of the day: judges are elevated to the rank of moral prophets and philosopher monarchs. For citizens, politics becomes a spectator sport and the stunted character of public discourse confirms Rousseau's dictum that without robust debate and active citizens, there is nothing but debased slaves from the judicial and juristic rulers on down.[7] In contrast to liberal views, a community worthy of its name is not based on a set of abstract commitments to universal principles, but is grounded in the experience of interpersonal relations and its ties. It is more of an emotional and shared existence than a disembodied and cognitive enterprise of rule by judicial proconsuls. Individuals are products of their social contexts, not ahistorical entities of given preferences. As such, people must be encouraged to participate in and revise the social context through which their preferences are cultivated and questioned. As Richard Rorty so wonderfully put it, 'persons have dignity not as internal luminescences, but because they share in contrast-effects.'[8] Politics is legitimated by participation, not principle.

Liberals of all stripes exhibit a profound antipathy for common consciousness among citizens. Politics becomes nothing more than a lackey for private interest. Pluralism and relativism are constitutionally mandated because there can be no genuine public interests. The result is an aggregate of individuals secure in their abstract rights and liberties but divorced from each other. This, of course, is entirely predictable given the background theory of personality that underlies contemporary liberal accounts of politics. The common starting point of these accounts is a fictitious choosing self, stripped of almost all its particularity. This abstract self belongs to no particular family or community, has no set of allegiances or commitments, and possesses no substantive life plan. Although liberalism fêtes the individual and celebrates personal freedom, it recommends a set of social organizing principles that rests on a pessimistic notion of human personality. By depicting individuals as indifferent to others, it establishes an ephemeral lifestyle that stifles the ameliorating potential in them and surrenders political reform to the limiting vision of the self-absorbed. In a liberal regime, individuals become exiles in their own society, only united in their separateness and self-interestedness. As such, the dominant motif of liberal society is its tendency to anomie; individuals drift with no communal connections.

The difficulty with this individualistic ideology is that it ignores and suppresses actual human experience. Individuals are located in history, within a context of allegiances. They are not abstract or bloodless, but are in part constituted by their social context. To divorce individuals from this structure of allegiances is to rob them of the 'railings to which [individuals] can cling as they walk into the mist of their social lives.'[9] A Dworkinian form of politics stunts the possibility of developing a set of shared ends and values, a precondition to the emergence of a genuine populist democratic practice. By developing a moral sense and practical experience of community, individuals will be better able to contribute to the growth of a shared set of values and institutions in accordance with which social life could not be organized. Persons might come to be respected as themselves and not simply as rights-holders. In this way, society could develop a modus vivendi that encourages caring and sharing and actualizes the possibility for meaningful connection with others.

Although communitarianism provides a better theoretical framework for a discussion of 'the good life,' there are very real practical risks that its insistence on shared values might overwhelm important differences between citizens. Consequently, neither responsible liberalism nor strict communitarianism provides a viable program for transforming and reconstituting reality: liberalism protects abstract rights without regard to the actual quality of their availability or exercise, and communitarianism focuses on the substance of community values without sufficient concern for the individual's role in the community. Whereas liberal freedom requires each person to be a conscript in a continual state of social war, communitarian virtue becomes an enforced solidarity in which failure to identify completely with others is treated as an insurgent act of civic treason. Any genuine alternative of political thinking and practice must steer clear of the extremes of liberalism and communitarianism by recognizing that the self is neither absolutely opposed to community nor completely determined by community. The idea of dialogic democracy is such an alternative. It can reconcile the tension between the extremes by recognizing that social life 'consists of connectedness and autonomy, love and hate, toleration of others and anger at their differences from an ever-changing "us".'[10]

A genuine commitment to an unadulterated democratic practice will represent the most powerful institutional alternative to the liberal society of rights-talk. Instead of giving ontological priority to individual interest, participatory democracy enables people to appreciate and rework the profound and sensitive dialectical tension between self and others; it enhances the opportunities for the continuous negotiation of the multiple interplay between the unique and the individual, and the common and the communal. It is an engaged, not an abstract, rapprochement between particular and general concerns; it looks to the relation as much as the relators. Because participatory politics is regenerative, experiential, and empowering, democratic arrangements also meet the challenge of historical contingency. They respect its imperative but do not become enslaved to it; the possibility and importance of normative discourse is retained and invigorated.

In order to give some theoretical substantiation and practical bite to this general discussion, I will situate my critique in the contested terrain of 'free speech.' As seems fitting, the debate over free speech is the most heated and intense on the academic and political agenda. The topical problems of pornography, hate literature, election campaign financing, commercial advertising, and freedom of information attest not only to the importance of these exchanges but also to the confusion and indirection of the reigning theories. Like moths drawn to the light, legal theorists have been irresistibly attracted to the bright beacon of free speech. The challenge and ambition is as worthy as it is important: to ensure democracy's fragile flame is kept aglow so that its ennobling light can suffuse and enhance the practices and possibilities of social and political life. However, like their lepidopteran counterparts, most writers on free speech have found its attraction to be fatal to their intellectual ambitions. Despite a plethora of different approaches, they have been unable to solve its mysteries or harness its potential.

In tempting fate and tackling the perplexing problem of free speech, it is necessary to engage in a thorough critique of the existing understandings of free speech in a liberal society. After demonstrating their ideological instability and limited operational efficacy, I will suggest an alternative way of thinking about free speech and achieving a truly democratic politics. Throughout the essay, my aim is to understand better the present so as to make attempts at transformation more informed and viable – 'how little do we know that which we are, / How less what we may be.'[11] In pursuing this tack, I will be guided by the coordinates of power and value: the need to ensure that everyone can participate as equals in the constitutive dialogue of democratic politics and an accompanying concern with the substantive worth of the ensuing debate. Mindful that the quality of the dialogue is as important as its quantity, I will offer a rudimentary analysis of 'commercial speech.' The limited aim of that inquiry is to show that there are convincing and concrete recommendations entailed and required by my general theory of democratic dialogism; the gap between the feminist critique of Dale Spender and the control of shopping centres or the semiotic insights of Umberto Eco and the regulation of television advertising can be bridged by the dialogic theory itself. Moreover, within such a political commitment, the courts are an inappropriate agency with which to entrust the democratic responsibility of creating and protecting dialogic practices: judges are not the guardians of democratic politics, but some of its primary usurpers.

FREEING SPEECH

In all its different threads and strands,[12] the contemporary tapestry of free speech draws on a very inadequate set of premises and assumptions; it has an impoverished view of human personality and language and, most importantly, of the crucial relation between the two. As part of the more general liberal theory of freedom, the approach to free speech is premised on a social world comprising an aggregation of distinct individuals with a set of pre-social preferences and values. Social interaction provides opportunities to satisfy better their given preferences and to achieve a desirable level of *self*-fulfilment: shared values are a possible product of a just society, but not a condition for its existence.[13] Within liberal society, language is understood as a neutral medium that is available to all and that stands independently of the ideas and world it is intended to convey or depict; it is the letter carrier delivering a letter or the librarian handing out a book.[14] In its various renderings, the liberal objective is to facilitate this intellectual economy of exchange and to enhance individual choice and self-determination. Consequently, the pillars of liberal free speech are the private individual with ' different and indeed incommensurable and irreconcilable conceptions of the good'[15] and the transparency of language as a public medium through which to communicate them.

Apart from the naïve failure of most scholars to recognize its scope for domination, the liberal view fails to take language seriously and presents a falsely dichotomous view of the world. For the modern liberal, the challenge is to steer a middle course between the extreme images of an heroic Rodinesque individual and an overbearing Stalinesque state; people must stand free and alone or else risk being enslaved to a hostile community. Emancipation is suspended in the space between a public instrumentalism and an esoteric privatism. Of course, liberal theory ceaselessly vacillates in this posture and is forever seeking to mediate the competing influences of the government as a threat to and guarantor of individual freedom. Unfortunately, while discursive socialization or indoctrination is almost inevitable, it is not uniquely attributable to the actions of the government. Power is not the sole preserve of the government, but is distributed among an elite corporate sector. To check the abuse of dialogic power, there must be a critical shift of analysis from its sources and quantity to its consequences and quality.[16]

For instance, liberals seem to adopt simultaneously the contradictory position that language can be a neutral conduit in which speakers can fully and freely express themselves and also that language can be a potent vehicle for the indoctrination of some speakers by others. Yet the particular stance adopted will usually depend upon the identity of the speaker. When spoken by self-possessed individuals, language will be considered a transparent medium; when uttered by government, it will more often be treated as a suspect tool. The reality is more nuanced and less polarized. Whereas government is occasionally the voice of the muted many, the monied voices of the voluble few often speak in the language of dissemblance. In its own lumbering fashion, of course, liberalism is struggling to come to terms with the non-essential nature of language and its potential for both education and obfuscation. But, by adopting their particular stance, liberals are unable to grasp the dialectical and dialogic nature of individual identity and social action. Social reality, language, and intentionality converge and conflict in mutually sustaining and transforming patterns.

Language is not a transparency through which the world is observed or a catalogue of labels to be attached velcro-like to the appropriate contents of the world. There is no form of pure communication that merely represents instead of creating. The world is within the language and the language within the world. Language is a social medium. It shapes society and its individuals as they work to reshape it. No one is free to describe the world as they wish; they are always and already constrained by the prevailing ways of speaking. As such, discourse is as much constitutive of society, both personal and collective, as it is constituted by that society. It is a cultural and political artefact of the first order 'in the sense that it serves to constitute an authority structure.'[17] The world cannot speak for itself; it must be spoken for. Social reality is constantly being negotiated and constructed, renegotiated and reconstructed. Language is not a system of static symbols, but a form of social action and history making. To acquire and exercise a language is to engage in the most profound of political acts. As much feminist literature shows, to name the world is to control it.[18] Law manages to impose a largely masculinist construction on social life and thereby silences and marginalizes alternative ways of understanding and being in the world. As a particular mode of authoritative discourse, law inscribes its intrinsic values on the world.[19]

A particular villain of the liberal piece is the cherished and foundational distinction between public and private action. A pseudo-Blackstonian set of individual rights is imagined that must be protected, preserved, and promoted. An injustice occurs when the state, or someone acting through or on behalf of the government, interferes with or fails to protect such entitlements; there is little empirical or ideological analysis into the actual quality of those rights and their exercise. Instead, the courts engage in an analytical inquiry as to whether the government was involved or not. If it was, remedial intervention through the courts is warranted; if not, those affected must lobby for political reparations. The emphasis is upon whether the impugned act can be identified with the formal attributes of governmental authority and not upon whether it has actually inhibited or damaged the interests of particular citizens. Pedigree and form are the standards for evaluating impermissible behaviour rather than effect and substance. However, this public/private distinction is indefensible as a descriptive or prescriptive claim.[20] Government is implicated in all activity that occurs within its territorial jurisdiction. Its claim to sovereignty means that an active decision not to intervene and regulate, or mere inaction, is as much governmental responsibility as an active decision to do so. It is never a question of whether government should intervene, but when and how it should regulate the affairs of its constituent citizens.

The century-old efforts by American courts to administer this central, but illusory, public/private distinction are predictably troubled and troubling. Two examples will have to suffice. It is widely acknowledged that 'so far as the Constitution goes, a private person may engage in any discrimination he wants.'[21] Constitutional imperatives only apply to state actions. In free-speech doctrine, this has led to two pressing questions: the extent to which the state can refuse to make its own facilities available to the public for speech purposes (when can the state act as a private body?) and the extent to which private persons must allow their property to be used by the public for speech purposes (when must a private person be treated like the state?). In the first instance, while the courts have held that traditional forums like streets and parks are available for speech purposes,[22] they have tried to develop a 'public forum' doctrine that gives limited access to public property where the exercise of speech rights is compatible with normal activity at normal times.[23] The resulting doctrine is a bewildering amalgam of half-distinctions and semi-similarities: courts gravitate between generous and narrow interpretations of so-called public forums.[24]

The difficulty has primarily flowed from the courts' insistence that 'the [government], no less than a private owner of property, has power to preserve the property under its control for use to which it is lawfully dedicated.'[25] This means, of course, that the government's obligations depend upon what the powers of a private property owner are. As the relevant doctrine shows, this turns into a circular argument. The powers of private property owners are determined by the extent to which property is being used for public purposes or not; government property being used for non-public purposes can be regulated in line with the powers of private property owners. In short, each is defined and determined in terms of the other. Doctrinal intelligibility and determinacy are perennially elusive: knowledge of the availability of public property for speech activities is conditional on the unavailability of private property for speech activities, which is itself dependent on the availability of public property and vice versa. Definitional closure is only attainable, even temporarily, by constant acts of dissemblance and obfuscation.

Despite the American courts' vaunted reverence for the protection of speech rights, they have only tended to enforce them outside private property: it 'would be an unwarranted infringement of property rights to require them to yield to the exercise of first amendment rights.'[26] Nevertheless, in some circumstances, private property has been treated as being publicly held and, therefore, amenable to the exercise of speech rights. This, of course, does not dispose of the constitutional question, but redirects attention to those considerations that are relevant in the 'public' sphere. As expected though, the public/private distinction has proved thoroughly unequal to the task either as a general analytical tool or as an ideological screen. As with the 'public forum' doctrine, the courts have vacillated in their willingness to turn private property into public property. This is especially evident in dealing with shopping centres, where the confusion of legal doctrine is regularly reaffirmed in futile efforts by the courts to whip it into intelligible or determinate shape.[27]

Rather than grasp the political nettle by discarding the public/private distinction, the courts continue to reach substantive answers by asking analytical questions. Seemingly blind to American doctrine's congenital incoherence, Canadian courts seem almost enthusiastic to emulate their southern neighbours' judicial efforts. In the leading case of *Dolphin Delivery*, the Supreme Court accepted that picketing could be a protected form of expression, but held that private employers fell outside the reach of the Charter.[28] Further, even where government property is involved, the courts contrive to engage in an American-style balancing process under cover of the Charter's section 1.[29] However, whichever analytical approach is followed, social facts intrude on such a conceptual fantasy. For instance, it takes little reflection to realize that the opportunity to use shopping centres to distribute information or ideas is a more effective exercise of speech than standing on a street corner. It is a relatively inexpensive way of reaching large numbers of people, and the prohibition of such access works an unequal disadvantage to the poor: the wealthy can avail themselves of other, arguably more intrusive media – beaming TV messages directly into people's homes. Also, it must be remembered that government property is the only property to which many people can get access. Consequently, any curtailment of speech activities on such property has a disproportionately negative impact on the poor and their capacity to engage in public debate.[30]

THE LIBERAL IMPASSE

Modern scholars are belatedly becoming aware of the shortcomings of liberal theorizing. In particular, they have found it hard to ignore the all-too-cozy relation between politics and economics; franchise and finance are seen to be increasingly mutually dependent and reinforcing. The libertarian Tradition was developed to act as a citizen's shield against the slings and arrows of state censorship, especially those that were targeted at the content of certain speech. Yet, in a modern, high-tech world in which the paradigmatic speaker is MTV rather than the street-corner orator, any continued reliance on that outmoded Tradition will not only fail to protect democratic politics, but runs the considerable risk of impairing it. Each citizen's medieval shield offers little defence against the expensive and communicative subtleties of technological weaponry: the journey from the soapbox to the VCR has altered much on the sociocultural landscape. Contemporary conditions require the development and deployment of a collective laser. The pressing problem for modern liberals is to explain and justify under what circumstances the state is obliged or entitled to regulate the activities of particular speakers.

A progressive effort to move beyond the Free Speech Tradition while remaining within the liberal paradigm is made by Owen Fiss.[31] Advocating and defending a more interventionist role for the state, he maintains that the Free Speech Tradition is unsuited to the challenging conditions of the contemporary world. In particular, it can no longer deliver on its central promise 'to further democracy by protecting collective self-determination.'[32] Fiss recognizes that the threat to free speech comes as much from large private corporations as it does from public agencies. Accordingly, he recommends a more active role for the state in combating this threat and in engendering the quality of public debate that is so vital to the practice and preservation of democratic politics; he asks not whether the state has a role to play, but what that role should be. In this regard, Fiss's work deserves commendation and support. However, although he provides a convincing explanation of why the state should and must be involved in actively nurturing free speech, he is unable to offer any plausible or convincing account of how the state can or should perform that task.

In reaching this impasse, Fiss's thought beautifully captures the plight of modern liberalism. Although he recognizes the democratic failure of modern politics and constitutional doctrine, his ideological commitments prevent him from following through on his critique and developing a constructive program for democratic renewal. Modern liberals' vision is limited by their impoverished notion of the state and its relation to the citizenry and by their being handcuffed from generating any substantive visions of the social good. Disenchanted with the conservatism of a classical Lockean liberalism, they crave a more socially sensitive set of political principles that can recognize the mutual dependence of people and the social inequalities of contemporary society. But, unwilling to relinquish entirely their commitment to the core values of the liberal credo – the primacy of private values over public virtues, the celebration of the individual as the source and standard of normative worth, and the collectivity's neutrality between competing conceptions of the good – they can only make expedient and temporary resort to the programs and principles of a more truly civic and progressive politics. In short, progressive liberals cannot get to their intended democratic destination from their traditional starting place.

By focusing more on the structure of social arrangements than on the action of particular individuals, Fiss wants to shift critical attention away from 'the frustration of would-be speakers' and toward 'the quality of public debate.'[33] Within such a structural scheme, the government would cease to be the worst enemy of free speech, but would become, at least on occasion, its best friend. Instead of leaving politics to the capital caprices of a market economy, Fiss would permit and sometimes require the state to correct and chastise it; the market would become the butler of democracy and not its master. The denial of expressive autonomy to the loud few would be adequately compensated by the broader benefits to the presently silenced many. Instead of allowing the invisible hand of the market to orchestrate the social symphony (cacophony?), the democratic arm of the state would assume the communal baton. In short, Fiss wants to turn around the American Supreme Court's standard view that 'the concept that government may restrict the speech of some elements of our society in order to enhance the relative voice of others is wholly foreign to the First Amendment.'[34]

The impetus for much of Fiss's work comes from a genuine desire to rectify this state of sociolegal affairs and to guarantee that people possess real, and not simply abstract, freedom and equality.[35] He is insistent that by ignoring the pervasive impact of private power on individual citizens and concentrating on abuses of public power, constitutional lawyers contrive to insulate vast sectors of the social hierarchy from official scrutiny and eradication. The constructive consequence of Fiss's critique is the recommendation that constitutional norms apply to all facets of American life; private bureaucracies must not be allowed to hold the democratic community to political ransom. Yet Fiss's effort at reconstruction reveals the limits and failings of the liberal vision of democratic politics. It lacks an adequate or satisfactory social theory; it fails to acknowledge or understand the extent to which individuals are deeply formed and shaped by their social milieu. Although the boundaries are less analytically sharp and more historically permeable than was traditionally conceded, the distinction between the public and private spheres remains at the heart of the liberal understanding of social life.

For liberals, talking about the possibility of a private self that stands, in some essential and constitutive sense, independent of its social and historical circumstances is both achievable and desirable. Indeed, it is the chief idea that gives meaning and point to the liberal project. Yet they fail to appreciate the full implications of their attachments and proposals; they prove too much for their own liberal good. Without some notional sphere of private autonomy to be preserved from the intrusions of others, whether it be the government or other entities, the constitutional protection of rights and freedoms through judicial review is drained of meaning and legitimacy. They are thrown onto the horns of a painful dilemma. Unless they develop a substantive vision of distributive justice, no template will exist against which to measure the social value of any particular act or state of affairs. Without such a measure, there is only a desultory *ad-hockery*. However, if such a vision is developed, they will have abandoned their self-confessed commitment to liberalism and its neutrality toward substantive theories of communal good.[36]

For instance, in the archetypal dispute between the person who wants to use property to speak, distribute pamphlets, or picket and the property owner who wants to exclude such activities, liberals resort to the spurious rhetoric of individual rights. Yet, lacking the mythical support of a public/private distinction, any efforts to reach coherent or convincing resolutions of competing claims by individuals become impossible without addressing the deep and disturbing normative difficulties that such disputes raise. Rights-talk only masks these choices; it cannot resolve them. The competing claims of speaker and property owner can be framed in terms of rights, but their resolution will always depend upon an inextricable combination of constitutional principle and political power. A serious effort to confront this difficult conjunction demands a thorough reassessment of society's deepest commitments and operative assumptions. While these questions do not lend themselves to easy answers under *any* theory or practice of social justice, liberalism provides no theoretical framework for even understanding, let alone resolving, distributional issues of this kind. It requires the very conception of substantive good that it so proudly eschews, but so badly needs.

No amount of tinkering with the liberal project will suffice in completing this substantive undertaking: it is the very liberal structure of social practice and organization that prevents a successful resolution of the free-speech problem. Although there is much trumpeting to the contrary, democracy has always been optional to a liberal scheme of democratic governance rather than its precondition and raison d'être.[37] Each person is primarily a rights-holder; his or her identity as a member of a social group and as a citizen in a common and democratic enterprise is secondary. However, notwithstanding liberals' protestations, it is only by recognizing the need to nourish a genuine experience of shared commitments and mutual understandings – the very antithesis of liberal values – that theorists could make good on liberalism's critical promise. Paradoxically, it would seem that liberals must abandon liberalism if they want to meet successfully the modern challenge that liberalism has set for itself.

COMMERCIAL SPEECH

The debate over the constitutionality of restricting commercial speech has long occupied the energy and imagination of American jurists.[38] More importantly, it is a paradigmatic example of the fatal failings of the liberal approach to free speech and liberals' insistence on entrusting its protection to the courts. The issue received its first contribution from the Supreme Court of Canada under the Charter of Rights in the complicated and volatile case of *Ford* v. *Quebec*.[39] This involved a challenge by shopkeepers to Quebec legislation that required all signs and advertising to be in French only. The Supreme Court struck down the legislation as offending the Charter's guarantee that 'everyone has ... freedom of thought, belief, opinion and expression.' However, it held that under the limiting provision of section 1, it would be acceptable to require that all signs be in French, albeit not exclusively so, and that French be more prominent than any other language. The province refused to accept this apparent compromise. It legislated that all outside signs must be in French only, but that bilingual signs would be acceptable inside premises. Quebec exercised its right under section 33 of the Charter to exempt the legislation from constitutional scrutiny.

The Supreme Court recognized as a general principle that language was not merely a medium of expression: it was a 'means by which a people may express its cultural identity [and] by which the individual expresses his or her personal identity and sense of individuality.'[40] Explicitly following American jurisprudence, the court concluded that as commercial speech 'plays a significant role in enabling individuals to make informed economic choices, an important aspect of individual self-fulfillment and personal autonomy,' it deserved constitutional protection.[41] As such, *Ford* offers an excellent focus for the deconstructive critique of liberal democracy and its limited reconstructive and transformative potential. The matters alluded to by the Court – the constitutive character of language and the importance of informed choice – are indeed crucial elements in a democratic society and must be treated with solicitous attention. Yet, for these very same reasons, commercial speech is thoroughly undeserving of constitutional protection and should be democratically regulated. By according it a privileged status in the public discourse of democratic society, courts jeopardize the likelihood of informed choice and the enhancement of individual identity and encourage the dilution of language as a form of social action. It must be recognized that the *quality* of public discourse intimately shapes individual choice, as well as the shared meanings that protect people from that manipulation of language or expose them to its worst abuses.

A famous Bill no doubt captured the spirit of the sixteenth century: 'All the world's a stage, / And all the men and women merely players.'[42] But, today, a different Bill has become the contemporary bard – the billboard. All the world of the late twentieth century is an advertisement and all the men and women merely consumers in the sprawling marketplace; life mimics advertisements. It is not simply that there is a barrage of information and images on how we should look, act, eat, and think, but that advertising represents a cumulative projection of a particular definition of reality and vision of 'the good life': 'Pepsi – The Choice of A New Generation' or 'Nike – Just Do It.' Advertising does not so much concern the product being marketed as the moulding of the product's targeted consumer in the advertisers' image; it is not what is right about the product, but what is wrong with the buyer.[43]

The effect of such a commercially saturated atmosphere is to trivialize and impoverish democratic politics. Public discourse becomes hostage to economics and begins to dance to, instead of call, the economic tune: it is thoroughly infiltrated by the economic mind-set and attuned to its interests. People think of themselves primarily as consumers rather than citizens. The middle-class weaknesses of ostentation and envy are exploited; Yuppiedom becomes its own political credo and lifestyle. Under the aegis of advertising, electoral politics is eviscerated and reduced to a hollow spectacle; form triumphs over substance by converting it into its own empty reflection. As the package has become more significant than the product, so politicians' images are more important than their ideas. Campaigns are designed to exude credibility in which postures of leadership are mistaken for leadership. Rhetoric replaces vision and slogans act as a surrogate for debate; there is no real discussion as to the substantive merits of any proposed program. As in advertisements, so in politics: the glib not only succeed over the good, but the medium ensures that only the photogenic take part. The message (and the massage) is the medium.[44]

For the most part, commercial speech comes from corporations; and the current legal system protects corporate commercial speech through the fictions that corporations are people and that corporations are private. People speak, corporations do not; they are the artificial mouthpieces of accumulated power.[45] Through the sanctioning by *Ford* and its predecessors of the idea that economic fictions are rights-carrying entities at least as deserving of protection and concern as human beings, law constitutes a particular social and normative reality. Under the aegis of the public/private distinction, corporations are treated as private actors, separate from and in opposition to the state.[46] The major effects of this traditional way of thinking are twofold. By treating corporations separate from the state, it overlooks the important influence that corporations exert over government policy and the economy through lobbying, campaign financing, agency capture, media control, shared personnel, and economic pressure. Also, by positing corporations as having a similar status as citizens, it ignores the exercise of enormous power by corporations over the lives of citizens. From McDonald's to General Motors and Sears to MTV, corporations are primary loci for socioeconomic decisions and policy-making. Each effect combines to insulate corporations from democratic regulation, ensuring that large sections of the ruling elite will remain beyond the reach of popular control and the grasp of electoral accountability. Corporations are the favoured and bastard offspring of liberals' attachment to the public/private distinction.

In a social world in which the connection between commerce and communication is particularly intimate, the continued privileged status granted to corporate bodies by the state makes the state responsible for the disproportionate impact of corporate speech on social life and politics. Commercial speech is more about commerce than it is about speech and more about profits than people. While the wealthy are as democratically worthy of a political hearing as any other, their views are undeserving of any greater airing; the challenge is to limit rather than underwrite the impact of economic equality on public debate. The state cannot claim that its refusal to regulate is a neutral act. Corporations are creatures of the state and any redistributive consequences attributable to corporate activity implicate the state. It is only very rarely that corporations will act as agents of social liberation. Through corporations' willingness and ability to monopolize the technology of influence, the state is inextricably involved in the distribution of social power and the quality of political debate. It is not only a major player in the crucial game of influence-peddling, but its success or failure affects the lives of the many citizens on whose behalf it plays. The state and its citizens are bound to lose if the state persists in pretending it is only an umpire or spectator.

The overwhelming presence and volume of corporate expression in contemporary society means that the Supreme Court's reasoning in *Ford* effectively constitutionalizes the corporate strategy to (re)constitute life in the impoverished image of the commercial imagination.[47] If economic choices are so important, why would advertising be left to the discretion of those who stand to benefit most from a partial disclosure of information? Any putative 'right to know' is surely better policed by the citizenry than by its potential transgressors. Moreover, if the speech privilege is said to include the right not to speak as well as to speak freely, the implications for commercial communication by manufacturers and entrepreneurs are enormous. They will be empowered to resist all but the most modest and uncontroversial requests for the publication of basic production information.

Commercial speech, in the sense of disseminating information about products, is not a bad thing per se. A large quantity and high quality of such advertising will likely be a vital feature of a democratic society and economy. The crucial issue is who or what is to regulate and monitor such activity – the citizenry and consumers at large, through various legislative measures and regulative agencies, or the commercial sector of the economy in the name of the market? A commitment to dialogue has an obvious and clear preference: the regulation of commercial speech must be placed firmly in the hands of the democratic process and not placed beyond their reach by the courts in the name of consitutional wisdom. The argument for reduced protection through a lower level of judicial scrutiny is only a small but insufficient concession.[48] This approach still gives corporations an unwarranted insulation from democratic regulation. The force of my proposal is not necessarily to ban commercial speech but to give it no special weight in democratic calculations of social justice. To do otherwise is to elevate the pursuit of profit to a much more dignified status than it deserves and to give the views of the wealthy too great a say in public affairs.

Of course, to deny constitutional protection to corporations does not dispense entirely with the problem of commercial speech: monied persons as well as corporations can advertise.[49] Furthermore, it is insufficient to target the type of speech as well as the identity of the speaker: the attempt to draw such distinctions is as futile as it is impractical. The only viable solution – and one that is demanded by both ideological and strategic considerations – is to abandon the whole endeavour to grant a spurious constitutional privilege to particular rights, including and especially those to free speech. Without such a bold step, the commitment to attaining a truly substantive practice of democratic politics will be stillborn; corporations will devise strategies to circumvent more limited arrangements.

These conclusions are likely anathema to the liberal establishment, but they are essential to the move toward an egalitarian democracy. The constitutional protection of commercial speech and speech generally through the institution of judicial review frustrates rather than enhances democratic dialogue, individual freedom, and social enrichment. It threatens to realize a state of affairs in which corporate 'tyrants indulge in monologues over millions of solitudes.'[50] Information is a two-edged sword, and more is not always better; quality is more important than quantity. In today's social world, it is the commercial dilution of public discourse to a distracting and anodyne patter that is as much a threat as Big Brother. Citizens are choking on a commercial glut of inconsequential information rather than starving on a constrained diet of official misinformation. It is only necessary to ration the supply of ideas and facts when people still retain the crucial capacity to be selective and care enough to exercise it. The most effective censorship occurs through the dulling or trivialization of that cognitive process of discrimination.[51] By granting constitutional immunity to commercial speech, we hasten this demise of democratic politics and place social justice at the behest of corporate boardrooms and other foyers of private power.

DEMOCRATIC DIALOGUE

What would a non-liberal theory look like? What is the alternative to a liberal approach to free speech? Unfortunately, the position of the 'left' on free speech has never been entirely satisfactory. Too often, it has allowed liberals to take the high ground and presented its own position as a vulnerable combination of moral ambivalence and political naïvety. By countenancing a dangerous romance with state regulation, it has raised the Orwellian spectre of enforced dogma and official conformity. Good intentions have proved insufficient to bridge the gap between democratic ideals and practical realities. The major difficulty has been the willingness to accept the liberal account of the problem to be solved and to work within its limiting framework: liberal start points inevitably lead to liberal end results. Before the left can offer a viable theory of free speech, it must vacate the liberal territory and rethink the problem from the ground up: the nature of 'freedom' and 'speech' must be constructed afresh. In short, if there were a different and better understanding of the mutually constituting dialectic between the 'individual' and discourse, there would be a different and better understanding of free speech and the conditions for its realization.

The world, and our ideas about it, take on meaning within historically specific modes of communication. Language is not an echo of Being or the trace of a universal metaphysic. A society's resources for conversation determine not only the knowledge at its disposal, but also its very ways of knowing. Consequently, the need to understand dialogue – the discursive interactions between individuals – as the crucible of social action in which individuals mutually constitute and reconstitute themselves and others is paramount. If it is accepted that dialogue is both the producer and product of interacting individuals, it becomes apparent that the challenge is twofold: to ensure that the quality of that dialogue is sufficiently open and fluid so that people might confront each other in the routine practices of daily life as equal participants and, also, that it is sufficiently shared and certain to protect people from its unscrupulous manipulation. It is only by establishing such conditions of face-to-face intimacy and engaging in such dialogic encounters that we will reach and share satisfactory knowledge and truths. Moreover, to establish a dialogic community, the prevailing circumstances of social power will have to be recognized and rectified; conversation is inimical to hierarchy.

Insofar as we live by a telos, it will not be found in History, The Human Condition, or Rights-Talk, but will be created and criticized in our shared efforts at mutual understanding and debate. Meaning and normative standards will be available and real, but will hold no claim to universal validity. A society constitutes its own conception of rational argument rather than uncovers an independent criterion of rationality. Appropriately, conversation offers no objective foundations. Instead, participants are bound by their acceptance of the contingent, yet real, status of their own conversation and their shared commitment to respect its dynamic. Criticism can be intelligible, engaged, constructive, and authoritative: 'We are not left with a nothingness, but with our affirmative ability to speak about human things in a human voice.'[52] We define and transform others as we ourselves are reciprocally defined and transformed by others. There is a profound connection between conversation and who we, as participants in that conversation, are and can be. Indeed, by its very nature, true dialogue is always critical and challenging. The vision of a dialogic community – 'mutual understanding, respect, a willingness to listen and to risk one's opinions and prejudices, a mutual seeking of the correctness of what is said'[53] – is not abstract or disembodied, but can give concrete guidance to our practical lives. It will, for example, oblige and empower people to wrest control of responsible decision-making from the technical experts, like lawyers and bureaucrats.

Such a dialectical view of the relations between language, social action, and individual intentionality implies a shift in attention from individuals to the circumstances of their dialogic and constitutive interactions. Conversation and connection become important and valuable in themselves and not simply as a means to the personal end of self-expression: they are the pith and substance of social life. Of course, in the same way that it must not be overvalued, the liberal campaign for free speech ought not to be undervalued; its solicitude for the interests of individual speakers against unwarranted state interference is of great significance. However, a continued resort to the precepts and foundational premises of rights-talk can only have reactionary effects and results. Even those, like Trakman and Nedelsky, who want to interpret rights as tools to express and strengthen community fail to appreciate fully the extent to which rights-talk is a confining, individualistic, and one-dimensional mode of dialogic engagement.[54] Legal adjudication is a truncated conversation that assumes a correct hermeneutic and operates within an institutional framework of coercive and normative violence.

An alternative concern with the establishment of a dialogic community focuses as much on the interactive conditions of human development as on the interacting individuals. This permits the individualistic notion of freedom of speech to be replaced by a more solidaristic understanding in which freedom becomes a facilitation and mediation of engaged conversations. A progressive vision of community eschews a debilitating anomie and a chilling sameness. It explores and inhabits the neglected spaces of intersubjective relations. By thinking about and understanding our personal and social lives as complex and overlapping accumulations of such relations, we might be better able to effect a proper accomplishment of the democratic ideal. An acceptance of intersubjectivity helps us to come to terms with our vulnerability to and dependence on others as well as our commitment to and responsibility for others. When the individual self is viewed as constituted in and through its intersubjective connections, the notions of autonomy and solidarity can be better and differently understood: criticism and commitment, innovation and connection can be mutually supported. At the heart of this enterprise is the understanding that self-definition is a function of intersubjective experience; it is the relation and not the relating entities that should be protected and nurtured. As Carol Gilligan puts it, it is vital to posit 'a world comprised of relationships rather than of people standing alone, a world that coheres through human connection.'[55]

Advocacy of this dialogic politics will prompt obvious comparisons to the liberal projects of Jurgen Habermas's 'ideal-speech situation' and Richard Rorty's 'continuing conversation of mankind.'[56] Yet there are very significant differences between my position and theirs. While they both are concerned with making good on the commitment to democracy and emphasizing the dialogic nature of political wisdom, they remain cramped within a too modernist frame of mind and fail to overcome the liberal limitations of their operative premises. For instance, Habermas is a transcendental rationalist who looks to ground historical conversation in a *consensus gentium* and to establish enduring principles for public policy formation. His 'ideal speech situation' is intended to foster 'communicative competence' and 'intersubjective universalization' so that a discursive ethic can justify a liberal way of living. However, as Rorty shows, this is much too abstract and ahistorical. Habermas is still in thrall to a discredited foundationalist metaphysics and the false prophets of philosophical Truths.

Adopting a rigorously antifoundationalist stance, Rorty strives for 'an expanding repertoire of alternative descriptions rather than The One Right Description' and celebrates the refusal 'to play by the rules of someone else's final vocabulary.'[57] Notwithstanding this, he remains more a liberal than a democrat. Although his radical philosophy sets him apart from Habermas, his liberal politics keep him squarely within the same political tradition. Rorty seeks 'to retain Enlightenment liberalism while dropping Enlightenment rationalism.'[58] His commitment to democracy is conditional and circumscribed; the scope and depth of democratic governance is only warranted and supported in proportion to its capacity to enhance private autonomy and individual liberty. Although Rorty contends that philosophy must become more democratic, he ultimately concludes that democracy must remain in the service of liberalism. In short, Rorty puts the history back into philosophy, only to leave the politics out of history. He attempts to produce an apolitical vision of history in the name of an historicist philosophy. His failure to appreciate adequately the grubby, materialistic, and collective conditions under which individual efforts at self-realization take place makes Rorty's notion of political struggle too clinical, intellectual, and individualistic.

In contrast to both Rorty and Habermas, I envisage a much greater contextualization of conversation so that actual people speak in specific historical circumstances, address the politics of their socioeconomic situation, and give tangible meaning to democracy in their own lives. Dialogic democracy follows through on the imperative of contingency and, in nurturing 'an expanding repertoire of alternative descriptions rather than The One Right Description,' gives appropriate weight to material circumstances that constrain and inform efforts at discursive redescription and civic transformation. Democratic conversation is not outside of power relations, but is constitutive of them: it is never possible to 'get outside ouselves and view the world from nowhere within it.'[59] Similarly, rationality is a product of dialogue, not a precondition for it, and reasoning is a collaborative endeavour, not a solitary reflection. The test of a conversation's intrinsic validity and normative force is that it be as uncoerced and as free as it can be in light of the fact that any conversation is made possible and compromised by the social conditions and historical circumstances in which it takes place.

Within such an understanding of dialogic democracy, people are recognized as being socially situated, but not socially saturated. Freedom is no longer associated with a lack of constraint. There is never a situation of 'no constraints,' only an historical dialectic of openings and closing: the issue is which constraints, not whether some or none. The individual does not precede social encounters, but takes on substance within them. Freedom does not stand in opposition to community, but only exists within communities. Social worth and self-esteem are embedded in and nourished by affective affiliations: 'solidarity is the social side of love.'[60] To live in a community is not to experience life as a forced march in strict formation; that is one conception of community, but it is not the only or best one. In place of order, rank, and stability, there must be a fluid, participatory, and egalitarian vision of community in which conflict and disagreement are facilitative of its enduring value.[61] Such a vision will embrace difference as a celebration of individuality and avoid a stultifying levelling that legislates a homogeneous 'other' against which people are encouraged to define and measure themselves.

A NEW STATE OF AFFAIRS

Liberalism is a failure; it cannot pass conceptual, social, legal, or political muster. A continued reliance on its intellectual assumptions and ideological prescriptions is indefensible.[62] Liberal institutions and instincts neither promote equality nor engender respect for it. Furthermore, they limit the process and agenda of politics to the furtherance of private self-interest. The challenge is to replace liberalism with a substantive vision of social justice that is capable of responding to the vast inequalities of economic and political power that liberalism and its disciples permit and, through their theoretical intransigence, condone. The immediate need is to conceive of individuals, relations with others, and freedom in different ways. People are not isolated and self-contained units that stand ontologically free of their social settings. The fact is that the contemporary image of individuals as self-interested competitors in the human race is a product of existing social structures and their supporting liberal ethos. Yet, whatever the rhetoric, the reality is that society is made up of a thick web of interdependent relations. Although many currently seem content to deny its extent, the fate of each person is intimately and inexorably tied to that of others. Rather than allow this dependency to be abused in circumstances of social inequality, the task is to establish the best conditions to nurture a more cooperative ethic and a greater sense of responsibility for the lives of others. Social justice must look to the lived concerns of everyone and not simply the abstract claims of the few.

If steps to effect significant social change or legal reform are to stand any chance of success, traditional perspectives must be abandoned and a new way of theorizing about the state developed. An alternative and competing conception of the state is offered by Marxism. Marxists share the same antipathy to the modern state as liberals, but for very different reasons. If liberalism was a rebellion against despotic rulers, Marxism was a revolution against the despotism of want.[63] Its adherents not only maintain that there is a strong connection between economic position and political power, but insist that the latter is slave to the former; those who can pay the government piper call the political tune. Domination occurs because the means of economic production are unequally distributed and controlled. This allows the economic exploitation of the many by the few in the name of economic competition and under the approval of democratic rule. Moreover, the whole legal regime in which economic activity takes place is established and supervised by those who control the productive conditions of life: 'Legal relations as well as forms of the State are to be grasped neither from themselves nor from the so-called general development of the human mind, but have their roots in the material conditions of life.'[64] Accordingly, in order to ensure full human emancipation, Marxism calls for the complete abolition of the state. Democratization of the state is only a way station on the Marxist road to the collapse of politics.[65]

Although it offers a powerful and appealing corrective to the naïvety of its liberal counterpart, this traditional Marxism fails to offer a fully convincing account of power in modern Canadian society.[66] Although liberalism has no concept of society as system or structure, Marxism has a marked tendency to offer explanations that are too systemically sweeping and one-dimensional in scope and content. While 'class' is a valuable analytic device, it cannot bear the normative weight that is traditionally placed upon it. This weakness is particularly apparent in its representation of the modern state as a monolithic structure of centralized and univocal authority. Like liberals, Marxists accept the privileging of the sovereign state over other modes of political power. By so doing, they ignore the localized contexts of power relations and (mis)understand politics. Their truncated framework of analysis depoliticizes much that is important to the study of oppression and the means for its eradication. Furthermore, the shortcomings of Marxist critique jeopardize the details of any program of political action.[67]

Both liberalism and Marxism have an impoverished notion of the state. Each views it as an instrument rather than as a structure; it is cast as a discrete institutional actor within a larger universe of social life. Whereas liberalism sees the state as the prime origin of power and law as a servile mode of disembodied reason, Marxism views the state as a convenient conduit for economic power that is constituted elsewhere and law as its enabling logic. If liberalism has an overly naïve view of state authority, Marxism has a too cynical one. Both are unrealistic because they persist in treating the state as being entirely synonymous and co-terminous with government. The government is neither independent of private power nor completely subservient to it; it has its own interests and is infiltrated by those of economic elites. The government is one part, albeit an important one, of a much larger entity that constitutes the state. In the vernacular of government, 'society consists of a constellation of governments, rather than an association of individuals held together by a single government.'[68]

But more than that, the state is not an institution or set of organizations; it is a site and a structure for the creation or exercise of power. While power is a universal fact of social life, its location and constitution are contingent. Relying on coercive imposition and manufactured consent, it consists of all the practical activities and theoretical imagery that establish and sustain the whole institutional framework and experience of power. In contemporary society, powerlessness is a condition of disabled consciousness and not only a situation of coercive deprivation. The state is as much an ethos as it is an establishment. To describe only the organizations and bodies that coalesce to constitute the state – government departments, Crown corporations, multinational corporations, trade unions, sporting clubs, churches, schools, Girl Guides, and the like – is to omit the crucial and invisible force field of power that animates and brings them into being; it is to mistake the carapace for the whole of the turtle. At the heart of power lies the productive medium of beliefs, truths, and knowledge. Accordingly, the state is not a universal pattern of fixed relations, but a dynamic regime of political struggle that encompasses and oppresses citizens as it constitutes and contains them.

The history and terrain of oppression in contemporary Canadian society is much too varied, dynamic, and complex to fit into a single empirical pattern or theoretical framework. What is needed is a less reductionist theory of politics that understands the distribution and exercise of power in a much more multifaceted, heterogeneous, and ubiquitous way. It will be one in which the state is not so much a solution, but the problem; not so much a source of social relations, but an expression of their contingent organization; not so much a unified set of social arrangements, but a site for a struggle over them; and not so much a solid and centralized phenomenon, but a fluid and diffuse network of confrontations. Such a theory will not only facilitate a more cogent and instructive critique of prevailing circumstances, but will recommend a more suitable and effective set of concrete proposals for changing society in a way that best avoids the possibility of reproducing today's deep and problematic structural faults.[69] Such measures will recognize that neither central planning nor an unregulated market is possible or desirable, even though each represents and fulfils important aspirations of the social individual. A move beyond the New Right and Old Left stand-off is desperately needed.[70]

The unique or abiding hallmark of the state, cannot be affixed to any particular land of kind of activity, nor can it be identified by the formal attributes of the actor or agency. The state is all the institutions, processes, values, and truths that gel to deprive individual citizens of control over their own identity and destiny. This means that from the perspective of powerlessness, there is no reason or point in trying to theorize about the special characteristics of governmental versus non-governmental behaviour or authority. From the citizens' viewpoint, it is nonsensical to attempt to distinguish between the forces of their oppression in this way; theirs is an experience of too much impersonal control by the state and too little personal control over it. The technical niceties of whether it is Texaco or Ontario Hydro, the Toronto Board of Education or a separate school board, the police or Burns Security that is abusing its power are of little consequence or moment to the alienated citizen.

For instance, at a time when privatization is much the rage, it is misguided to determine the liabilities and responsibilities of an organization in line with its putative public or private status.[71] Two good examples are the corporate histories of Canadair and de Havilland. Canadair was created during World War II as a Crown corporation to build military aircraft, but it was sold in 1947 to General Dynamics Corporation, the largest beneficiary of American military procurement contracts. The corporation was returned to the Canadian government in the early 1970s and resold to Bombardier Inc. in 1986. Similarly, de Havilland was a Canadian subsidiary of the British aircraft manufacturer, Hawker Siddeley; the federal government bought it to save jobs. Along with Canadair and some other government corporations, it was rolled into the Canada Development Investment Corporation in 1982. Boeing Corporation bought de Havilland in 1985.[72] It is patently ridiculous and unfair to make the control and regulation of these bodies dependent on the peripatetic identities of their owners. Their impact on employees, neighbours, surrounding communities, and individual citizens is almost unaffected by their formal legal and corporate status.

THE FOURTH ESTATE

The theoretical and practical challenge is not to eradicate power, but to redistribute it and bring it to popular heel. By only paying lip-service to democracy, modern Canadian society mutes its ethical imperatives and stymies its subversive possibilities. The fact that bureaucracy is an almost indispensible feature of modern life does not mean that it cannot be opened up to democratic politics. The belief that change in this direction is not possible itself makes change less likely to occur. There must be a reaffirmation of the idea that people can simultaneously be ruled and be free, but only if they rule themselves.[73] Democracy is not a system of governance or a set of political institutions; it is the kind of society in which power is not possessed by self-styled experts, but is held by the citizens who are affected by its exercise. Instead of insulating the state from popular control, it is necessary to put economics in the service of politics and to repoliticize all parts of the state's operation. The task is to integrate all citizens in their social and political powers so that they become active participants in the institutions that profoundly contribute to the shaping of their very identities and the creating of the environment in which they live out their lives.

A particularly telling example of the power of corporations and their scope for democratic intervention is provided by the media. The historical promise of mass media to extend dialogue and collective consciousness has been partly fulfilled and partly reneged on. As presently constituted, the fourth estate of the realm is dominated by the oligarchic operations of huge corporations. Most corporations' primary raison d'être is not disseminating news or providing entertainment, but making money and accumulating capital. Even the CBC has to function as an effective commercial undertaking. Moreover, not only are media corporations considered to be beyond the scope of legitimate government regulation, but they are accorded special constitutional privileges. The advent of a modern high-tech world has meant that control over the channels of mass communication is the basis for broader control; politics has become more a visual spectacle than a substantive debate. In such circumstances, the abdication of such power to private interest is folly. If information is the life-blood of contemporary society, large corporations are allowed to regulate the pulse of the body politic in accordance with the dictates of economic logic. It is naïve to think that in any society, no matter how democratic, the media will cease to wield huge power. However, the challenge is not to dissipate that power, but to place it in the service of democratic politics and under popular control. In effecting a democratic reform, no particular weight must be placed on the distinction between private and public bodies; the CBC, the *Globe and Mail*, and the Midland *Times* would be regulated by the reference to the substantive impact of their actions on public debate and the extent to which they were already democratically controlled. As Alexander Solzhenitsyn put it:

> The press can both stimulate public opinion and miseducate it ... Hastiness and superficiality are the psychic disease of the 20th century, and more than anywhere else this disease is reflected in the press ... The press has become the greatest power within the Western countries, more powerful than the legislature,

the executive, and the judiciary. One would then like to ask: By what law has it been elected and to whom is it responsible?[74]

By rethinking and reorienting free speech on these revised democratic premises, it becomes possible to go beyond the predictable and stereotyped terms of contemporary debate. A concern for dialogic authenticity cuts across a Dworkinian deontological preoccupation with speaker autonomy and a Meiklejohnian functional concentration on audience interests.[75] While both concerns are important and must be respected by any progressive proposal for change, a reliance on either as the exclusive regulative ideal is ultimately self-defeating. Dialogue turns us away from liberal notions of individual freedom, whether singly or aggregately expressed, and points us toward the democratic activities of associational individuals. When the stale ethical vocabulary of means and ends is abandoned, the formal conditions for conversational encounters can begin to embody and inculcate a substantive relationship between interlocutors that is important in and for itself. Within such a dialogic community, freedom would not be understood as a splendid but desolate isolation in which a right to soliloquize might be the extent of freedom, nor as a state-enforced conformity in which the right to hear another's monologue might exhaust freedom. In contrast, the regulative ideal of dialogue incorporates both a right to hear, to be heard, and to be answered. It establishes and maintains the social conditions for open-ended, continuing, and meaningful conversations in which people engage as equals. In place of the traditional reliance on individual rights to free speech, there might exist a set of social processes to facilitate open discourse.

Although a reliance on dialogue is richly suggestive in reorganizing the doctrine and practice of 'free speech,' it is important that it not be treated as an abstract ideal from which a series of pat positions on the traditional range of hard cases can be logically extrapolated. However, in contrast to the pseudo-exchanges of a liberal democratic republic,[76] dialogue generates and reinforces its own ethic. It not only offers a substantive measure for judging the quality of political life, it also provides the means by which to bridge the normative gap between general ideals and practical application. Conversation is the embodiment of the procedural and substantive goals that a democratic society can aspire to and achieve; it improves and strengthens itself through constant practice and usage. One crucial consequence of such a dialogic understanding will be a reordering of the hard cases to be confronted and resolved. There are no final or right answers, but only different options whose exercise and appropriateness will depend upon the particular problem and its socioeconomic context.

A commitment to 'democratic conversation' requires a changing and changeable mix of interventions and abstentions. It eschews sweeping statements about, for instance, whether any collectively sanctioned interference in media activities is desirable. While a mandated entitlement of public access to large-scale media outlets might be necessary, the universal availability of access to fringe publications would be self-defeating. Access by the powerful to the small presses of the relatively powerless threatens to replicate the existing imbalance and to stymie the development of a diversely democratic culture. Moreover, a concern for dialogue obliges us to reconsider the meaning and operation of 'censorship.' It forces an acknowledgment that harm results not simply from the silencing of certain voices, but also in allowing certain voices to dominate and operate a virtual monologue. A fully developed 'dialogic entitlement' would combine active steps to bring in previously stilled voices and positive moves to shut down stentorian voices.[77] In all cases, there would be a realistic appreciation of the dialogic forum being limited and finite in its economic and discursive dimensions. The response that 'the answer to bad speech is more speech' is limited and simplistic. Dialogue demands more than the existence of speech somewhere by someone, but a realistic opportunity to have that speech heard and, preferably, responded to by others.

Democratic conversation requires an abandonment of the public/private distinction. This does not mean that everything becomes public and individuals lose all sense of privacy or personal autonomy. The problem that the distinction is intended to address remains central to the critical enterprise. What its abandonment does mean is that we will have to decide democratically on those moments and activities when society at large should devolve full power and authority to individuals and establish a space in which they are immune from collective interference. This will not be a collective abdication of responsibility for the fate of others, but will represent a constructive affirmation of the need for everyone to be involved in providing a positive and empowering freedom for each citizen. Nor will this devolution be a once-and-for-all reckoning, but a continuing and evolving responsibility to rework and realign these publicly created and sustained occasions of privacy. It is as much a problem to obliterate the distinction as it is to reify it. The challenge is to demystify the distinction and recognize its artefactual character and liberatory potential; we must put it in service to democratic ideals rather than be servants to its counterfeit authority.

For instance, threats to the democratic ideal come from many different sources. At times, government will be the problem and a strong and 'private' media will be the solution; the *Spycatcher* débâcle in England and the law lords' pathetic ruling is an obvious example.[78] At other times, the media will be the problem and government regulation will be the solution; the *Gay Alliance* affair and the Supreme Court's pusillanimous judgment immediately spring to mind.[79] What is demanded is a self-conscious blend of 'private' and 'public' initiatives rather than an unthinking and uncompromising allegiance to one at the expense of the other. Such a substantive and perpetual undertaking is the strength and not the weakness of democratic politics. The state ought not to be in opposition to the citizenry, but must become an institutional venue through which citizens struggle to achieve a common good. In a democracy, there is more than dialogue between the state and its citizens. When government speaks, it ought to be the reverberated outcome of the democratic conversation between citizens.

A NEW CITIZEN

To complement a revised understanding of the state, there must be a revitalized practice of citizenship. Although such an idea has a rich and distinguished past, its contemporary significance and potential have largely been overshadowed by rights-talk, which has hijacked citizenship and made it subservient to its own civic ambitions. In the liberal almanac, citizenship is little more than 'the right to have rights.'[80] This is the abasement of citizenship, not its apotheosis. If there is to be a serious effort to move away from rights-talk's 'dialogue of despair'[81] to democracy's conversation of hope, the rights-holder must give way to the citizen in the political scheme of things. Of course, the kind of citizens that people can be is affected by the kind of society and community in which they live. However, an enhanced idea and practice of citizenship can begin to transform the society and community in which people live so that they view themselves as participants in a larger civic project and see others as not only threats to their own freedom and fulfilment. Citizenship is more a social and engaged activity than an individual and isolated status.

Citizenship allows people to inhabit the contested terrain between individual rights and communal Right by colonizing it in the name of democracy. Neither individualistic nor communitarian, a democratic theory and practice of citizenship recognizes that any vision of 'the good life' is always provisional and contingent. There is no fixed or final version of what amounts to the best way to live: the good life is to be found in the details of living, socially and privately, which must be reworked and renegotiated constantly. Whereas liberals put representative democracy in the service of private values and Marxists imagine that direct democracy will bring an end to politics, citizens accept that the relation between public virtue and private values is open to revisable articulation and that the attraction of democracy is its promise to keep politics always open and fluid. As such, citizenship under radical democracy is not committed to a common good, but is an engaged practice of civility in which the common good is always up for consideration and conversion. For the democratic citizen, a good life consists in the public-spirited engagement with others over the shape and substance of 'the good life.'

Liberal rights-talk has made a vital contribution to the emancipation of people from restrictions on their ability to play a full and equal part in society and to have real control over their own lives: the French and American revolutions at the end of the eighteenth century are historic reminders of its genuine liberatory instincts. Nevertheless, the modern embrace of liberalism only serves to sustain 'a frightened kind of politics'[82] in which there is a fear of the state (but a continuing attachment to courts) and a distrust of popular views (but a glorification of individual preferences). The vocabulary and voice of rights-talk are no longer up to the task of instituting an authentic practice of democratic citizenship. Rights-talk lacks the necessary discursive resources and versatility through which to appreciate the multiplicity of human connections and to craft a progressive vision of social justice: its flat and simplistic idiom is unsuited to the complexity and challenges of modern politics. For instance, within the terms of liberal discourse, there is no relevant distinction between citizens who are cross-burning members of the Ku Klux Klan and citizens who campaign against such racist activities. Indeed, the antiracist campaigners can be construed as being illiberal and acting unjustly in their efforts to inhibit the free speech of the racists. Rights-talk's inability to deal with this issue in a nuanced and subtle way is testament to its impoverishment and unsuitability as a favoured style of political discourse. There is no means through which to judge the exercise of a particular right as better or worse without resort to something other than rights-talk.

In contrast, within a democratic dialogue of citizenship, it is possible to integrate rights-talk within a much broader and deeper conversational context. As such, rights-talk would not be beyond political exchange, but would be brought under its bailiwick. Crucially, this would allow the notion of 'responsibility' to occupy a similar role in the democratic conscience as rights presently does. Whereas rights-holders exist in an abstract realm of optional interactions with anonymous others, the citizen is located at a historical time and in a local place where personal and social living are situated in a web of connections between real people – some who are known and others who are not, some who are liked and others who are not. It would mean that in exercising their rights and making claims, people would have to take into account their responsibilities to others, particularly those less fortunate and more vulnerable than themselves. Actions and practices would have to be evaluated in the sociohistorical context of the democratic community: the particular mix of rights and responsibilities will always be reconfigurable in light of contingent concerns. For instance, while this might mean the banning of certain racist speech, it would not follow that the threat of racial hurt will always be enough to silence all manner of racist speech: the practical resolution of particular difficulties is more important than the generation of universalizable principles.

The pressing and persistent challenge would not be how best to maximize personal autonomy and individual entitlement, but how best to incorporate such values with the equally important virtues of social solidarity and the acknowledgment of difference. While citizenship emphasizes a sense of belonging and connection, it respects the fact that different groups of citizens can have different concerns and interests. Solidarity is not sameness and union is not unity: difference is what people have in common.[83] A major item on the political agenda of the democratic state will be the need to accommodate diversity and plurality without disaggregating to such an extent that the citizens are not acting as a civic community. In place of rights-talk's willingness to go along with a me/them mentality, civic citizenship and the participatory state encourage a me/we involvement: it understands that the fate of each of us is unavoidably tied to the fate of all of us and that the self and the collectivity are not antagonistic entities, but complementary components of a political community.

Where rights-talk is abstract, democratic conversation is engaged; where rights-talk is individualistic, democratic conversation is civic; where rights-talk is legalistic, democratic conversation is popular; where rights-talk is myopic, democratic conversation is visionary; where rights-talk is anemic, democratic conversation is full-blooded; where rights-talk is absolute, democratic conversation is contingent; where rights-talk is exclusionary, democratic conversation is inclusionary; where rights-talk is narrow, democratic conversation is expansive; and where rights-talk is blunt, democratic conversation is nuanced. Moreover, while indeterminacy is fatal to the operation and validity of rights-talk, democratic conversation places indeterminacy at the heart of its practice. In an important sense, democratic conversation's opportunity is found in rights-talk's failing. Today's rights-holders must be prepared to take that chance for tomorrow's citizens.

LASTING WORDS

The bitter irony of democracy's stunted practice is that it has been brought about and justified in the name of greater individual freedom. Whatever its good intentions, liberalism has been ambushed by the privileged and political debate has begun to be held to corporate ransom. The attached advertisements testify to the moral bankruptcy of free speech's liberal tradition. While each of them illustrates the corrupting and controlling influence of corporate power, the fact is that the censorious actions of Pepsi and the radio stations are clearly justified by that very same tradition of free speech that the advertisers seek to invoke against them. Under a liberal understanding, Pepsi and the radio stations are merely exercising their constitutional freedom to choose when to speak and what to say. Similarly, the Anti-Censorship Project and the Molson Workers come to be treated as being themselves in the business of censorship and the curtailment of free speech. Such a state of affairs is to be deplored.

To counter this degradation of the democratic ideal, there must be asserted a collective commitment to the enhancement of dialogue as the activity par excellence through which people constitute and reconstitute themselves. A thoroughgoing discussion of 'free speech' is an important place to begin. This especially includes the belated acceptance that its resolution is not a technical matter of legal principle, but an ideological struggle over the kind of society and individuals that people want to be. As such, it cannot be entrusted to the participants in the judicial forum. Furthermore, although talk alone will not set the world to rights and wholesale socioeconomic redistribution will be necessary, a commitment to democratic dialogue is as good a place as any from which to com-

THE GREAT CANADIAN

FREE SPEECH TASTE TEST

PICK THE SCRIPT THAT BEST SUITS YOUR TASTE FOR FREE SPEECH

A

HOST: Hel-lo. Hel-lo. Welcome to another episode of You Bet Your Life: the show that make us face up to real life situations — whether we like it or not... Today's contestant is Molson Toronto brewery worker Wayne Workman.

WORKMAN: Hi.

HOST: His lovely wife Gwen, and their boy Billy.

GWEN: Hello.

HOST: Today's skill-testing question is: What is more important to Molson Breweries? Is it re-cycling beer bottles or re-cycling beer workers?

(Buzzer)

Sorry, times up. The answer is... BEER BOTTLES.

WORKMAN: But, I've worked for them for years...

HOST: Sorry.

GWEN: We need both our salaries to make ends meet.

HOST: Too bad. Besides, the severance, will tide you over.

WORKMAN: Screw the severance. I want work. I need work. How'm I s'posed to live without work? They've got lots of work. Why not give me one of those other jobs ...

ANNOUNCER: Molson workers only want what they already had — a job. No handouts, buyouts or payoffs. Just a job.

Support the Molson workers. Don't buy Molson's, Coors, Fosters or Miller beers. Help us make Molson recycle beer workers — not just beer bottles... Paid for by Local 304 Brewery Workers.

THIS IS THE SCRIPT FOR A RADIO COMMERCIAL SUBMITTED TO 15 ONTARIO STATIONS BY LOCAL 304, BREWERY WORKERS (NUPGE)

B

HOST: [illegible]

WORKMAN: [illegible]

HOST: [illegible]

GWEN: [illegible]

HOST: [illegible]

(Buzzer)

[illegible]

WORKMAN: [illegible]

HOST: [illegible]

GWEN: [illegible]

HOST: [illegible]

WORKMAN: [illegible]

ANNOUNCER: [illegible]

THIS IS THE SCRIPT FAVOURED BY ALL BUT TWO OF THOSE STATIONS.

☐ CHECK THE ONE THAT SUITS YOUR TASTE FOR FREE SPEECH BEST ☐

Local 304 Brewery Workers,
238 Jane St., Toronto, Ont.

SEND YOUR VOTE TO

John Carroll, Molson Breweries,
3300 Bloor St., W., Toronto, Ont. M8X 2X7

SUPPORT THE MOLSON WORKERS

DON'T BUY Molson, Coors, Foster or Miller beers.

Help us make Molson recycle beer workers...not just beer bottles.

Boycott Pepsi!

The Exxon of The Soft Drinks Industry

by Richard Yao, Esq.

On March 24, the Exxon oil tanker *Valdez*, manned by an alcoholic captain, spilled over 10 million gallons of oil into the waters of Prince William Sound, Alaska, wreaking incalculable damage to the surrounding marine life and ecosystem.

But a week or so earlier, Pepsi was guilty of something just as reprehensible. Surrendering to blatant Fundamentalist censorship pressure, Pepsi pulled Madonna's TV ad. Just as Exxon did not think much about destroying our ecosystem, Pepsi did not think twice about selling our First Amendment birthright. This needs to be condemned just as strongly as Exxon's giant oil spill.

Surprise. Wayne Calloway, Pepsi's chairman, is also on Exxon's Board. And Exxon's previous Chairman and CEO is on Pepsi's all-powerful Executive Committee. Mr. Exxon himself is one of the people who really run Pepsi.

~~EXXON~~ ~~PEPSI~~

"Saturday Night Live." "Married...with Children." The TV movie "Roe v. Wade." TV advertisers have pulled out of these and other programs because of threats from militant Fundamentalists who want to control what you watch in the privacy of your own home. In this context, Pepsi's surrender is as chilling as that of the giant bookstore chains succumbing to the threats of the Ayatollah Khomeini in the Salman Rushdie controversy.

This is why we have called for a grassroots boycott of Pepsi. We need to send corporations like Pepsi a clear message: profits and expediency must not have priority over our First Amendment birthright. So while you're tearing up your Exxon credit card, remember to boycott Pepsi! You can help us by *immediately* sending out the coupons below.

To: Pepsico, Inc./Chairman Wayne Calloway
Purchase, N.Y. 10577 [and call: (914) 253-2000]

☐ I'm boycotting Pepsi to protest your surrender to Fundamentalist extremists on the Madonna ad.

Signature ____________________

To: Richard Yao, FA Anti-Censorship Project
P.O. Box 20324, Greeley Sq. Station
New York, N.Y. 10001-9994

☐ I agree with you. We need to send Pepsi—and the Fundamentalist censors—a message!

☐ To help pay for this ad, here's my tax-deductible gift of:

____ $50 ____ $100 ____ $250 ____ $500 ____ (other).

Name ____________ Street ____________

City ____________ State ______ Zip ______ Phone ____________

Richard Yao *is the Director of the FA Anti-Censorship Project which has fought censorship attempts against Scorsese's "Last Temptation of Christ" and Rushdie's "Satanic Verses." Yao has been described by Martin Scorsese as being "in the forefront of the fight against censorship." His call for a boycott against Pepsi has been featured by the Wall Street Journal, L.A. Times, Liz Smith, MTV and scores of radio stations around the country.*

mence that daunting but vital task. Dialogue is not simply a precondition for the building of the good community, but is an integral part of the democratic good life.

It would take another book to pursue the implications of 'democratic dialogue' and to demonstrate its transformative potential. Accordingly, the limited aim of this chapter has been to expose the general shortcomings of liberal theory that both inform and ultimately invalidate the continuing debate over commercial speech. Although I have run the risk of imitating the moth and liberal scholars, I hope that by approaching free speech from a different angle and imagining a different light, I will avoid their fate. Unfortunately, Fiss and other liberals are in greater danger. They remain trapped within the limited horizons that demarcate the liberal vision of democratic politics. They can only begin to imagine the political possibilities that a less individualistic and more civic ideal of constitutionalism can afford. With the courage of their egalitarian convictions, they need do no more (and no less) than confront their own 'faint-hearted[ness]'[84] and walk out into the open spaces of democratic politics where the liberal is only one kind of democrat and the democrat is not only one kind of liberal.

In a community committed to democratic dialogue, corporations and other institutions will have to be stopped from talking *at* people. Instead, people will have to be encouraged to talk *with* one another. In working toward the social and material conditions for such conversation, much will have to be confronted and altered that is inimical to a truly just and egalitarian society. In so doing, people will learn that conversation and debate are not only some of the great pleasures of the good life, but that they are also its necessities. As Michael Ignatieff so passionately and pertinently writes:

> We need justice, we need liberty, and we need as much solidarity as can be reconciled with justice and liberty. But we also need, as much as anything else, language adequate to the times we live in ... Our needs are made of words: they come to us in speech, and they can die for lack of expression. Without a public language to help us find our own words, our needs will dry up in silence ... Without the light of language, we risk becoming strangers to our better selves.[85]

8

In Waiting

Not in Utopia, – subterranean fields, –
Or some secreted island, Heaven knows where!
But in the very world, which is the world
Of all of us, – the place where, in the end,
We find our happiness, or not at all!
– William Wordsworth[1]

The human capacity to dream is irrepressible. And this is no bad thing. No matter how often old dreams die, new dreams spring up in their place. Once people lose the will to dream, they succumb too easily to a debilitating fatalism in which they see their lot as one to be endured rather than improved. But, while giving up on dreaming entirely is to submit to despair, to live entirely in a world of dreams is to mistake fantasy for reality. This is the dubious achievement of most Canadian judges and scholars, particularly those who are in thrall to Coraf and its ideal realization. Yet, if these same lawyers are to abandon such fantasies, they must have the courage and commitment to dream afresh and imagine a less gloomy and more optimistic future for Canadians. The fact that 'the old is dying and the new has not yet been born' ought to be an opportunity to be seized, not a predicament to be rued.[2] The liberal society of constitutional rights-talk must give way to a democratic society of civic conversation.

DEMOCRATIC ACTION

In spite of an occasional lapse into Estragonic despondency, constitutional lawyers and legal scholars manage to hold on to a seemingly indefatigable Vladimiric optimism about the impending arrival of Coraf and the merit of rights-talk. No matter how many decisions betray their confident expectation or how few critics share their sanguine conviction, they stand firm in their cherished 'hope that the applause will begin shortly and continue for a long time to come.'[3] But, while their dogged single-mindedness is admirable, constitutional lawyers' credulity and short-sightedness are surely suspect; their good faith is misplaced. While judges are committed by oath to make the best of a bad job, jurists have no such excuse: they should affirm to speak democratic truths to official power. Down, but never defeatist, the traditional scholarly endeavour is a romantic consolation that must in reality be seen not so much as a high-minded pilgrimage of patient hopefulness, but as a disingenuous exercise in civic futility. It is true that Coraf might well come, but the more pertinent question is whether it is worth waiting for. Indeed, it may be that waiting is our communal destiny and despair: Coraf might merely be the collective consciousness of the conservative denizens of the moment, a kind of grim Pozzo in judicial attire. Nevertheless, there will be no redeeming Day of Judgment, but only the conspicuously less-than-divine (Thurs)days of judgment in Ottawa.

Waiting for Coraf is not so much living as an alibi or pretext for living. 'Keeping our appointment' is not enough and only serves to kindle further hope when none is warranted. To cling to a dream of deliverance is only a form of existential denial. Confronted by the stark evidence of accumulated disappointments, people resort to the kind of day-dreaming that does little more than ensure that they will become further mired in a cheerless politics of resignation. By endlessly waiting for Coraf, lawyers place people themselves *in waiting*; this powerlessness inculcates a servile and sycophantic attitude. Such a practised posture of dependence is anathema to the democratic spirit. It is infinitely better to run the unfamiliar risks of genuinely popular rule than to succumb to the commonplace security of distant authority. Moreover, the hope of future salvation hides people's deeper lack of faith in themselves. All that people need wait for is for themselves to seize the difficult but diverse opportunities to transform themselves and the social world around them.

Of course, as an historical artefact, rights-talk has played a positive role in the social struggle for democratic empowerment and retains obvious normative strengths, such as the value of privacy, distrust of bureaucracy, and worth of rational justification.[4] However, rights-talk overthrew the divine right of kings, clergy, and aristocracy only to replace it with the sovereignty of the abstract individual – God in more philosophical and less theological uniform. It has not effected the democratic transformation that its proponents promise or continue to believe in. In place of the civic lightness of liberal being that rights-talk induces, those committed to social change will want to talk about ways to nurture the kind of democratic conversation that can tap into the historical well-springs of citizens' social experience. In this way, it might be possible to develop a genuine sense of solidarity that respects difference and allows everyone to partake in the fortunes, good and bad, of the community. The rights-talk of liberal legalism has had its day and must now be abandoned.

People should not be misled into thinking or believing that the achievements of rights-talk are the product of reason alone. Its aspirations are not brought to fruition in the scholarly study, but struggled for in the streets of history. Ideas must combine with a concrete context in order to derive and express meaning. Power and knowledge are inextricably linked and mutually reinforcing; each implies the possibilities and parameters of the other. The struggle for social justice has been waged and won by the powerful who also had knowledge enough to frame their claims in the rationalistic rhetoric of rights. The military force of the barons who obtained concessions from King John in the Magna Carta of 1215 and the propertied classes who engineered the Glorious Revolution of 1641 have been replaced by the economic might of multinational corporations. Although the precise tactics may be different, the general stratagem remains the same – they curb the power of the state (and the people) by expressing their own claims to power in the legal discourse of liberal rights. For those committed to real social change, the challenge is to see through the charade of rights-talk and to bring about a democratic devoluton of the institutional resources and opportunities for civic conversation. Direct steps must be taken to empower and liberate the silenced and marginalized. There must be talk and action; angst is not enough.

T.S. Eliot notwithstanding, lawyers and intellectuals commit the greatest treason when they succumb to the belief that the rightness of the reason is always more important than the usefulness of the deed.[5] The privileged and their legal spokespersons quibble about reasons in a way that the disenfranchised and disadvantaged find an indulgent distraction: actions and results not only speak louder than reasons, but they often disclose the real reasons and meanings behind the actions. Acceptance of this insight does not deny a role for intellectual activity in the struggle for social transformation; it does suggest a more modest understanding of the power of ideas and, therefore, intellectuals' own sense of political importance. Criticism must become an instrument of struggle rather than a reactive reflection on that struggle.[6] Popular action has won more freedom and justice than has the publication of a book or the judgment of a court. Insofar as pamphlets and judgments contribute to political change, they do so in a more subordinate way than lawyers, liberals, or (some) radicals think. Those who march in the streets or parade in the malls are in the vanguard of social change: the well-placed Reebok has more power than the finely turned legal opinion.

When the French took to the barricades in the summer of 1789, they sent shock waves through history that are still being felt all over the world. They did not storm the Bastille as an act performed in the name of Truth or Reason, but as a defiant struggle on behalf of freedom and justice. The desire for *Liberté, Egalité, Fraternité* often manifested itself in the excesses of bloody revolution and bitter revenge. That epochal occasion demonstrated that people need not endure history as irresistible fate, but can seize it and turn destiny to popular advantage. It was the courage and commitment of ordinary people, not philosophers or lawyers alone, that made the improbable possible. The inarticulate gave expression to a romantic longing whose poetic embodiment continues to reverberate in the modern political consciousness. Similiarly, when people take to the streets of Johannesburg, Prague, Beijing, Moscow, Timisoara, Frankfurt, or Los Angeles, they are rarely motivated by any particular or perfected plans for social renovation. Such uprisings are more often sparked by some local and relatively minor act of official injustice or bureaucratic crassness; they tend to be instinctive, spontaneous, and unpredictable in their timing and intensity. Moreover, if they are committed to act in the name of anything, it is the vague but noble desire for human dignity or a stark belief that 'enough is enough.' People do not give their lives for academic musings, nor do revolutions await the final theoretical nod from the ivory tower.

POSTMODERN PROMPTINGS

For some, this humbling of intellectual activity pays too high a price in its devaluation of transformative relevance. Joel Handler laments that such a postmodern perspective cannot deliver the political goods: it will not be able to confront and confound fully the oppressive workings of elite institutions. His fear is that it will result in left politics being steered down a political blind alley in which transformative energies will be exhausted in obsessive and paralysing odysseys in self-discovery: liberal capitalism will have reasserted itself courtesy of its postmodern antagonist, and bourgeois hegemony will persist. He is particularly troubled that 'without a positive theory of institutions, postmodernism cannot come to grips with institutionally-based power.'[7] In short, the contention is that postmodernism will only engender a politics of quietism and irresponsibility that will be long on personal angst and short on social solidarity. Indeed, targeting my earlier work, he is adamant that such an approach to legal theorizing and political advocacy is intellectually mistaken and ideologically disastrous:

> It seems to me that if postmodernism is to seriously challenge the ideological hegemony of liberal capitalism, it must come with an alternative vision, a vision of the economy and of the polity that will complement its vision of community. Allan Hutchinson calls his postmodern book, *Dwelling on the Threshold*. That concedes the field.[8]

In this book I have tried to show that, far from conceding the field, this is the best way that those committed to progressive change can occupy the field and begin to challenge 'the ideological hegemony of liberal capitalism.' If more vision is needed, there is nothing in the postmodern tack that I have taken that prevents the exercise of visionary faculties. Indeed, it allows such reconstructive insights to take flight; it is traditional liberal theorizing that clips the wings of the political imagination in the service of rights-talk's hegemonic projection. Nevertheless, this book is careful not to pursue *one* 'alternative vision of economy and community.' In line with its democratic and pluralistic instincts, my postmodern critique rejects a belief in any single or accurate vision of community or social justice; a deconstructive critique must not be allowed to become the last refuge of an foundationalist scoundrel. There is no place for an enforced orthodoxy or rigid conformity, for 'a just society is not a society that has adopted just laws, once and for all, rather it is a society where the question of justice remains constantly open.'[9] Rejecting comprehensive programs and universal positions, the postmodern critic must attend to local and contingent circumstances of claims to knowledge and to the situated places from which people speak and act.

Those lawyers and scholars who are committed to progressive action in a postmodern world must resist the temptation to seek theoretical closure and practical dogma. They must decline the familiar litany of easy answers in favour of a more challenging slate of better and different questions: 'We have learned the answers, all the answers: it is the question that we do not know.'[10] Closure is always contrived, frequently arbitrary, and usually conducive to established power relations. Obsessed with elucidating right and final answers, progressive scholars often forget that the agenda of questions to be answered is constantly changing. Within the traditional Corafian mode of political and legal theorizing, justice becomes a matter of revelation and progress consists of a slow march to a promised land that is always around the next historical bend. In a postmodern world, living is more immediate and engaged.

While my critique rejects the metaphysical privileging of grand theory and meta-narratives, like liberal legalism's rights-talk, it most certainly does not deny the worth of social, historical, or political theorizing. Provided that it is suitably provisional, revisable, and contextual, such theorizing is at the heart of a transformative political praxis. In rejecting History, it does not ignore the lessons of history and, in rejecting Telos, it does not ignore the value of criticism. As all claims are located within a dynamic set of social practices, there is an insistence that all theorizing pay attention to the structural circumstances of that social milieu and, in particular, to appreciating its own embeddedness in such historical contexts. Critical insight is a prelude to transformative action. Understood in this way, a postmodern perspective neither craves to provide an integrated or finished program for political action nor recoils from the task of struggling toward an enhanced social solidarity and experience of justice. Instead, it points to a renewed engagement and sustained challenge to existing historical conditions. Truth, individuality, agency, and collective action are problematized, not to discard them from the radical vocabulary of progressive politics, but to render them more immediately transformable and politically useful. In contrast, rights-talk reduces people to walk-on characters in an unfolding drama rather than active citizens in their own struggle to define and achieve emancipation.

Accordingly, any theoretically sophisticated or satisfactory account of law and politics must grapple with the extant protocols of power and, in making any proposal for transformative change, must recognize its own revisable and experimental character. Exemplified in the radical work of Cornel West, a postmodern politics of radical democracy 'promotes a critical temper and democratic faith without making criticism a fetish or democracy an idol.'[11] By moving beyond the debilitating politics of abstraction and ahistoricality, such praxis looks to create personal meaning and social knowledge in the situated particulars of embedded experience. The ambition is not to fix an all-encompassing Truth or Justice in a distant metaphysical realm, but to pay constant attention to the multiple truths and contextual details of engaged living.[12] Of course, being political, that process will always be open and fluid; meaning will always be provisional and revisable. Moreover, by using rich accounts and critical readings of historical experience to promote political knowledge and action, that politics will always be contestable: politics itself can never be a privileged ground for anything.

Liberal critics and constitutional scholars are right in thinking that my constructive proposals cannot guarantee a politics that will be uniformly progressive or whose practice will be consistently effective. But to think otherwise is to continue in the belief that the establishment of foundational truths is possible and could ground a radical political praxis. The felt need that people have for such solid ground under their metaphysical feet is an effect of traditional theory's mistaken insistence that, once fixed, Truth, History, Rights, or Dialogue will guide and insulate action from error. Disabused of such foundationalist yearnings, people will begin to understand that politics is inside, not outside, History's suzerainty. A program of progressive politics must constantly be negotiated and renegotiated. Consequently, while unmodified democracy implies a progressive politics, it does not necessarily lead to one. What is progressive can never be determined in advance or in the abstract; such assessment can only be made with an attention to the local conditions and prevailing exigencies of the situation. All that the critic can do is open spaces for action and increase opportunities for transformation, but it cannot fill those spaces. Whether these openings become holes to fall down or climb out of is left to those minded to act. Citizenship in a postmodern polity is not a received status, but is a continuing responsibility to make the best of the situation for oneself and others.

All that a postmodern mentality can do is to show that power is never apart from reason: logic and ambiguity, authority and arbitrariness, and universality and contingency are implicated in each other. Leaving the risks and responsibility of reconstruction with real people in real situations, what is good politics or best for the community will always remain contestable. There is no guarantee against tyranny – *nothing* can deliver us from that. While there must be talk of a dawn of egalitarianism, there are many who still live in the dusk of oppression.[13] No theoretical standpoint alone can ensure that the long night's journey into light can be accomplished without struggle, mistakes, and further pain. The challenge and trick for radical critics is to nurture and develop those talents and sensibilities that will attune them better to the nuances and vulnerabilities of structural settings and local contexts. Relieved of the anxiety to craft solutions that are somehow apt for all times and places, they can concentrate on the pressing problems of contemporary Canadian society and experiment with interventions that can best address the prevailing institutional structures of power.

A TRAGIC FARCE

To make good on this democratic imperative to view social institutions 'as experiments in cooperation rather than as attempts to embody a universal and ahistorical order,'[14] it is crucial to abandon the historical infatuation with liberal rights-talk and replace it with a renewed dedication to unmodified democracy as the institutional and substantive setting par excellence for politics as experiment. This radical realization offers the best way to enhance and transform civic conversation. However, strong democracy is not put forward as a candidate to replace liberalism as Canada's natural self-image: postmodernism eschews the belief in any single or accurate historical vision of community. Instead, I champion unreconstructed democracy because it provides the least-worst match with the non-foundationalist project for a truly pluralist polity and ensures that transformative struggle will change social conditions as well as the way we talk about them. Democracy's political dynamism provides the best available complement to historical contingency. In a truly democratic polity, citizenship is not about subservience to a legalistic vision of rights-society, but involves face-to-face, localized confrontations in conditions of economic equality that most promote personal empowerment and social solidarity. Everyone, not only intellectuals and lawyers, will have the opportunity to experiment as dramatists, actors, and critics. At bottom, the realization of radical democracy is probably a dream. But, like the best of dreams, it is an ironic awakening to life's poetic possibilities.

At the end of Beckett's *Waiting For Godot*, Estragon and Vladimir make a feeble effort at hanging themselves. Too incompetent to even commit suicide, they seem unable to finish any course of action that they contemplate:

VLADIMIR
We'll hang ourselves tomorrow. (*Pause.*) Unless Godot comes.
ESTRAGON
And if he comes?
VLADIMIR
We'll be saved.
...
ESTRAGON
Well? Shall we go?
VLADIMIR
Pull on your trousers.
ESTRAGON
What?
VLADIMIR
Pull on your trousers.
ESTRAGON
You want me to pull off my trousers?
VLADIMIR
Pull ON your trousers.
ESTRAGON
(*realizing his trousers are down*). True.
He pulls up his trousers.
VLADIMIR
Well? Shall we go?
ESTRAGON
Yes, let's go.
They do not move.

In this ending, Beckett suggests life is spent in a tragicomic series of distractions and evasions that reduce the dynamic possibilities of living to a static farce in which Nothing happens. Any hint of resolve is immediately dissipated by the tramps' inaction; indecision and procrastination are their defining characteristics. Estragon and Vladimir's ingenuity is exhausted in their almost pathological need to shirk the burden of freedom and responsibility. As much as anything else, Beckett's masterpiece signifies the paralysis of the imagination. In jurisprudential terms, it represents the prosaic triumph of legalistic discourse over poetic promise of democratic politics. Trapped in a precarious purgatory between the unfulfilled hope of formalist salvation and the compulsive fear of nihilistic damnation, the legal vaudevillians are left to act out an ideological drama on an institutional stage that does neither themselves nor Canada's citizens any justice. With their trousers on or off, the legal rhetoricians of rights-talk are a sad sight to behold. Waiting For Coraf is a farce with the air of tragedy that should evoke only hollow peals of tragic laughter: its legal performance has far outlasted its democratic run.

While Beckett has much to tell about Canada's constitutional predicament, he has little to offer by way of inspiration for its amelioration. Another Irish iconoclast, the equally uncompromising and hard-edged Sinéad O'Connor, can fulfil that task better. She declares that any successful attempt at transformation will take a bold combination of serenity, courage, and wisdom – the serenity to accept that which cannot be changed, the courage to change that which can, and the wisdom to know the difference.[15] Waiting For Coraf is a serene act that is neither courageous nor wise. Indeed, it is the last thing that needs to be done. The realization of a fully functioning democracy will take all the courage, wisdom, and serenity that can be mustered.

Notes

CHAPTER 1 WAITING FOR CORAF: LIBERALISM AND THE CHARTER

1 S. Beckett, *Waiting for Godot* (London: Faber and Faber 1954), 51b.
2 D. Laframboise, 'The Future of Public Administration in Canada,' *Canadian Journal of Public Administration* 25 (1982), 510.
3 Beckett, supra note 1, 40a.
4 Ibid. 44a and 12b.
5 Even the most pragmatic of constitutional commentators affirm 'repeated acts of faith' that law 'has both boundaries and moral significance not wholly reducible to, although never independent of, the ends for which it is deployed.' L. Tribe, *Constitutional Choices* (Cambridge: Harvard University Press 1985), 4.
6 See D. Boorstin, 'The Perils of Indwelling Law,' in R.P Wolff (ed.) *The Rule of Law* (New York: Harper & Row 1971), 78–9.
7 O.W. Holmes Jr., *The Common Law* (Boston: Little, Brown 1881), 1.
8 R. Dworkin, *Law's Empire* (Cambridge: Belknap Press 1986), 407 and 400.
9 See E.P. Thompson, *Whigs and Hunters* (London: Allen Lane 1975).
10 L. Fuller, *The Morality of Law* (New Haven: Yale University Press 1969), 210.
11 H.L.A. Hart, *The Concept of Law* (Oxford: Clarendon Press 1961), 206.
12 For a broader historical and political introduction to these events, see A. Hutchinson and P. Monahan, 'Democracy and The Rule of Law,' in A. Hutchinson and P. Monahan (eds.) *The Rule of Law: Ideal or Ideology?* (Toronto: Carswell 1987), 97–123.
13 See infra chs. 3 and 6.
14 E. Gerry, *The Records of the Federal Convention of 1787*, M. Farrand ed. (New Haven: Yale University Press 1937) vol. 1, 48. Roger Sherman's

response was to the democratic point. Bills of rights were 'mere paper protection'; 'the only real security that you can have for all your important rights must be in the nature of your government ... If you are about to trust your liberties with people whom it is necessary to bind by stipulation ... your stipulation is not even worth the trouble of writing.' 'Letters of a Countryman, November 22, 1787' reprinted in P. Ford (ed.), *Essays on the Constitution of the United States* (Port Washington, NY: Kennikat Press 1910), 220.

15 *Osborn* v. *Bank of the United States*, 22 US 738 at 866 (1824). See E. Corwin, *The 'Higher Law' Background of American Constitutional Law* (Ithaca, NY: Cornell University Press 1965).

16 H.L.A. Hart, *Essays on Bentham* (Oxford: Clarendon Press 1982), 79.

17 *The Law of the Constitution* (London: Macmillan 1885), 46.

18 See *The Road to Serfdom* (Chicago: University of Chicago Press 1946), *The Constitution of Liberty* (Chicago: University of Chicago Press 1960), and *The Political Ideal of the Rule of Law* (Cairo: 1955).

19 J. Rawls, *A Theory of Justice* (Cambridge: Belknap Press 1971), 13.

20 For a fuller account of this liberal rivalry and its deeper theoretical underpinnings, see A. Hutchinson and P. Monahan, 'The "Rights" Stuff: Roberto Unger and Beyond,' *Texas Law Review* 62 (1984), 1477, 1479–91.

21 See John Hart Ely, *Democracy and Distrust* (Cambridge, MA: Harvard University Press 1980), 67 ('We may rant until we're blue in the face that legislatures aren't wholly democratic, but that isn't going to make courts more democratic than legislatures').

22 R. Dworkin, *A Matter of Principle* (Cambridge: Harvard University Press 1985), 31.

23 *Law's Empire* (Cambridge: Belknap Press 1986), 211.

24 Dworkin, supra note 22, 32.

25 *Reconstructing American Law* (Cambridge, MA: Harvard University Press 1984), 110.

26 D. Wrong, *American and Canadian Viewpoints* (1955) 3, as quoted in *Southern Exposure: Canadian Perspectives on the United States*, D. Flaherty, ed. (Toronto: McGraw-Hill 1986).

27 This process was much more complex and less idealized than many commentators would have people believe. See infra.

28 See *Entick* v. *Carrington* (1765), 95 ER 807, and *Roncarelli* v. *Duplessis*, [1959] SCR 121.

29 See *Alberta Press*, [1938] SCR 100, and *Switzman* v. *Elbling*, [1957] SCR 285.

30 See *Co-operative Committee on Japanese-Canadians* v. *A-G for Canada*, [1947] AC 87.

31 See P. Hogg, *Constitutional Law of Canada* (3rd ed.) (Toronto: Carswell 1992), 779–91, and I. Greene, *The Charter of Rights* (Toronto: Lorimer 1989), 23–36.

32 *House of Commons Debates* (10 May 1985), 4611.

33 See infra ch. 6.

34 *Re Motor Vehicle Act*, [1985] 2 SCR 486 at 497 per Lamer J.

35 B. Magee, 'Sandcastles and The Search for Certainty,' *Listener* 99 (1978), 576, 570. For a summary of this broader jurisprudential challenge in Canada, see A. Hutchinson, 'Crits and Cricket' in R. Devlin (ed.), *Canadian Perspectives on Legal Theory* (Toronto: Emond Montgomery 1990), 181.

36 R. Bourne, *The Radical Will* (O. Hansen ed.) (New York: Urizen Books 1977), 483. See M. Walzer, *The Company of Critics: Social Criticism and Political Commitment in the Twentieth Century* (New York: Basic Books 1988), 41, and J. Merod, *The Political Responsibility of the Critic* (Ithaca, NY: Cornell University Press 1987).

37 M. Kundera, *The Book of Laughter and Forgetting* (New York: Penguin Books 1980), 237.

38 Beckett, supra note 1, 15b and 13b.

39 Ibid. 18a, 51a, 50b, and 58b.

40 See H. Berman, 'The Origins of Western Legal Science,' *Harvard Law Review* 90 (1977), 894, and J.C. Smith and D. Weisstub, *The Western Idea of Law* (Toronto: Osgoode Hall Law School, York University 1981).

41 M. Foucault, *Madness and Civilization* (London: Tavistock 1967), x.

42 By 'politics' I do not simply mean conflicts over the exercise and control of government power; this is only a subspecies of a larger genus. I use the term to refer to the conflict over all the terms and conditions – social, economic, institutional, passionate, and whatever – of our collective and individual lives. See R.M. Unger, *Social Theory: Its Situation and Its Task* (Cambridge, MA: Cambridge University Press 1987), 10. Also, by 'law' I do not mean all phenomena that can be considered legal; my focus is more restricted. While I encompass law as an analytical category and practical activity, my enquiry is largely about the work of courts and lawyers, whether they are dealing with the common law, statutes, or constitutional norms. This essay makes no claims about the work of legislatures or constitutional conferences. Accordingly, my concern is with the relation between the larger world of politics and the smaller sphere of doctrinal development.

43 See I. Duchacek, *Power Maps: Comparative Politics of Constitution* (Santa Barbara, CA: ABC-Clio 1973), 3. For other leading works in this genre, see C.J. Friedrich, *Constitutional Government and Democracy* (Waltham, MA:

Blaisdell 1968) and C. McIlwain, *Constitutionalism: Ancient and Modern* (Ithaca, NY: Cornell University Press 1940).

44 R. Romanow, J. Whyte, and H. Leeson, *Canada Notwithstanding: The Making of the Constitution* (Toronto: Carswell 1984), 218.

45 See D. Milne, *The New Canadian Constitution* (Toronto: Lorimer 1982); M. Mandel, *The Charter of Rights and the Legalization of Politics in Canada* (Toronto: Wall & Thompson 1989), 1–34; and P. Russell, *Constitutional Odyssey* (Toronto: University of Toronto Press 1992), 92–126.

46 Government of Canada 'Minutes of Proceedings and Evidence of the Special Committee of the Senate and the House of Commons on the Constitution' Issue 48 (1980–81), 110.

47 Section 33 has only been used successfully twice: once by the Saskatchewan government for back-to-work legislation and once by the Quebec government after the Supreme Court's decision on the sign laws. The latter occasion led to such constitutional and political turmoil that its already tenuous legitimate use is severely compromised. See Hogg, supra note 31, 891–901. For a debate on section 33's worth and efficacy, see J. Whyte, 'On Not Standing For Notwithstanding,' *Alberta Law Review* 28 (1990), 347, and P. Russell, 'Standing Up For Notwithstanding,' *Alberta Law Review* 29 (1991), 293.

48 F. Rodell *Woe Unto You, Lawyers!* (2d ed.) (New York: Berkley 1980), 65.

CHAPTER 2 INDETERMINATELY SPEAKING: FROM AXIOM TO ACTION

1 A. MacIntyre, *After Virtue: A Study in Moral Theory* (Notre Dame, IN: University of Notre Dame Press 1984), 69.

2 See G. Paton and D. Derham, *A Textbook of Jurisprudence* (4th ed.) (Oxford: Clarendon Press 1972), 403–25, and R. Dias, *Jurisprudence* (5th ed.) (London: Butterworths 1985).

3 See P. Hogg, *Canadian Constitutional Law* (3rd ed.) (Toronto: Carswell 1992), 832–4.

4 See *Edwards* v. *Attorney General for Canada*, [1930] AC 124. Another example is the status of children.

5 See infra ch. 4.

6 *R.* v. *Sullivan*, [1991] SCR 489.

7 P.W. Duff, 'The Personality of an Idol,' *Cambridge Law Journal* 3 (1927), 42, 44.

8 See *Re Layland* (1993), 104 DLR (4th) 214 (Ont. D. Ct.).

9 See *Salomon* v. *Salomon & Co.*, [1897] AC 22.

10 See *People's Pleasure Park Co.* v. *Rohleder* (1909), 61 S.E. Rep. 794.

11 See M. Horwitz, *The Transformation of American Law 1870–1960* (New York: Oxford University Press 1992), 65–108.

12 *Hunter* v. *Southam*, [1984] 2 SCR 145.

13 W. Stevens, 'From Chocura to Its Neighbours' in *The Palm at the End of the Mind* (New York: Random House 1974), 245.

14 See *Ford* v. *Quebec (Attorney-General)*, [1988] 2 SCR 712, and *Irwin Toy Ltd.* v. *Quebec (Attorney-General)*, [1989] 1 SCR 927.

15 *Irwin*, ibid. at 969 (quoting *Switzman* v. *Elbling*, [1957] SCR 285 at 306 per Rand J.).

16 Ibid. 979.

17 Ibid. 1003.

18 *R.* v. *Big M Drug Mart*, [1985] SCR 295.

19 See *Re Public Service Employees Relations Act*, [1987] 1 SCR 313, and *Professional Institute* v. *Northwest Territories*, [1990] 2 SCR 367. On this issue, see D. Beatty and P. Kennett, 'Striking Back,' *Canadian Bar Review* 67 (1988), 573.

20 See P. Singer, *Animal Rights* (Englewood Cliffs, NJ: Prentice-Hall 1982) and V. Pocar, 'Animal Rights: A Socio-legal Perspective,' *Journal of Law and Society* 19 (1992), 214.

21 C. Stone, *Should Trees Have Standing?* (Los Altos, CA: W. Kaufman 1973), 1, and L. Tribe, 'Ways Not to Think About Plastic Trees: New Foundations for Environmental Law,' *Yale Law Journal* 83 (1974), 1315.

22 See infra.

23 G. Gaus, *The Modern Liberal Theory of Man* (London: Croomhelm 1983), 3–4.

24 J. Rawls, *A Theory of Justice* (Cambridge: Belknap Press 1971). See also R. Nozick, *Anarchy, State and Utopia* (New York: Basic Books 1972) and R. Dworkin, *Taking Rights Seriously* (London: Duckworth 1979).

25 J.H. Ely, *Democracy and Distrust* (Cambridge: Harvard University Press 1982), 127.

26 See A. Hutchinson, 'Les Misérables Modernes,' *Canadian Review of Books* 1(3) (1992), 1.

27 See B. Laskin, 'An Inquiry into the Diefenbaker Bill of Rights,' *Canadian Bar Review* 37 (1959), 77, 82. For a critique of this vaunted neutrality, see infra ch. 3.

28 M. Price, 'A Question of Live and Let Smoke,' *Globe and Mail* (25 March 1992), A-16.

29 For an account of how the Charter's equality provision has been used, see infra ch. 7.

30 See *Phillips* v. *Social Assistance Appeal Board (N.S)* (1986), 76 NSR (2d) 240 (CA).

31 See F. Michelman, 'The Meaning of Legal Equality,' in *The Cambridge Lectures 1985* (Montreal: Éditions Y. Blais 1987), 85–102, and P. Westin, 'The Empty Idea of Equality,' *Harvard Law Review* 95 (1982).

32 An aberrational decision in this regard is *Kask* v. *Shimizu*, [1986] 4 WWR 154. MacDonald J. stated that 'one's sense of what is essential in a free and democratic society is violated if the state draws distinction between one person and another person or one group of persons and another group of persons on the basis of their wealth or poverty or their large or small income.' Ibid. 157.

33 [1989] 1 SCR 143.

34 Ibid. 164.

35 Ibid. 174–5.

36 *Nichomachean Ethics* Bk. V3, 1131 (W. Ross trans.) (New York: Random House 1925).

37 Supra note 33, 171.

38 See *Symes* v. *Canada*, [1993] 4 S.C.R. 695.

39 See *Re Labour Trilogy*, [1987] 1 SCR 313.

40 See *Re Lavinge*, [1991] 2 SCR 211.

41 O. Holmes, *Collected Legal Papers* (Magnolia, MA: Peter Smith 1921), 312.

42 See infra, ch. 4.

43 See A. Hutchinson and R. Maisey, 'Blurred Visions: The Politics of Civil Obligation,' in K. Cooper-Stephenson and E. Gibson (eds.) *Tort Theory* (North York, ON: Captus University Publications 1993), 276.

44 See *Gay Alliance Toward Equality* v. *Vancouver Sun*, [1979] SCR 435.

45 *Wheeler* v. *Leicester City Council*, [1985] 2 All ER 1106 (H.L.).

46 Ibid. 1112.

47 For a fuller discussion of these issues, see A. Hutchinson and M. Jones, 'Wheeler-Dealing: An Essay on Law, Politics and Speech,' *Journal of Law & Society* 15 (1988), 263.

48 [1990] 3 SCR 697.

49 Ibid. 733–4 and 755–7 per Dickson C.J.

50 Ibid. 804 per McLachlin J.

51 See *Re Ontario Separate School Funding*, [1987] 1 SCR 1148. Wilson J. does make an interesting attempt to theorize a relationship between the Charter and the earlier Constitution Act, 1867.

52 See *Ford* v. *Quebec (Attorney General)*, [1988] 2 SCR 712.

53 See *Société des Acadiens et du Nouveau-Brunswick Inc.* v. *Association of Parents for Fairness in Education, Grand Falls District, 50 Branch*, [1986] 1 SCR 549 at 566 per Dickson C.J.

54 *Re Ontario Human Rights Commission* v. *Simpson-Sears Ltd.*, [1985] 2 SCR 536.

55 See R. Dworkin, *Taking Rights Seriously* (London: Duckworth 1979) and *A Matter of Principle* (Cambridge: Harvard University Press 1984).

56 *Slaight Communications* v. *Davidson*, [1989] 1 SCR 1038 at 1056.

57 [1986] 2 SCR 713.

58 [1986] 2 SCR 573.

59 *R.* v. *Oakes* [1986] 1 SCR 103.

60 See A. Hutchinson, 'Determinacy and Democracy: An Essay on Legal Interpretation,' *University of Miami Law Journal* 43 (1989), 541.

61 *Irwin Toy Ltd.* v. *Quebec (Attorney-General)*, [1989] 1 SCR 927.

62 Ibid. 233.

63 Indeed, the Supreme Court itself has hedged over the meaning and application of *Oakes*. See G. La Forest, 'The Balancing of Interests under the Charter,' *National Journal of Constitutional Law* 1 (1993), 133.

64 See E. Weinrib, 'The Morgentaler Judgment: Constitutional Rights, Legislative Intent and Institutional Design,' *University of Toronto Law Journal* 42 (1992), 22.

65 See *R.* v. *Morgentaler*, [1988] 1 SCR 30; *Borowski* v. *Canada*, [1989] 1 SCR 342; and *Daigle* v. *Tremblay*, [1989] 2 SCR 530.

66 I want to make it clear that I believe that Bill C-43 was unjust and ought to have been struck down as unconstitutional. But it would be inconsistent and disingenuous of me to claim that this is unarguably demanded by the Charter. For a contrary view, see E. Weinrib, supra note 64 at 69–76. Furthermore, my claim is far from novel. Indeed, most writers concede that section 1 is fluid and imprecise. See, for example, R. Elliot, 'The Supreme Court of Canada and Section 1 – Erosion of the Common Front,' *Queen's Law Journal* 12 (1987), 277, and P. Chapman, 'The Politics of Judging: Section 1 of The Charter of Rights and Freedom,' *Osgoode Hall Law Journal* 24 (1986), 867.

67 *Morgentaler*, supra note 65, McIntyre J. and La Forest J. (dissenting) at 38. See also *Tremblay* v. *Daigle* (1989), 59 DLR (4th) 609 (QCA).

68 Ibid. *Daigle*, Bernier J. at 613, Nichols J. at 615, and LeBel J. at 638.

69 See, for example, the competing judgments in *Committee for The Commonwealth of Canada* v. *Canada*, [1991] 1 SCR 139. For an extensive study of this split, see D. Beatty *Talking Heads and the Supremes* (Toronto: Carswell 1990).

70 See for example, R. Dworkin, *Law's Empire* (Cambridge: Belknap Press 1986), 313–27.

71 See supra ch. 1.

CHAPTER 3 THE CRISIS OF LEGITIMACY: DAYDREAM BELIEVING

1 'Among School Children,' in *The Collected Poems of William Butler Yeats* (London: Macmillan 1940).
2 See A. Hutchinson, *Dwelling on the Threshold: Critical Essays on Modern Legal Thought* (Toronto: Carswell 1988), 261–93.
3 For a critique, see A. Hutchinson and P. Monahan, 'Democracy and the Rule of Law,' in A. Hutchinson and P. Monahan (eds.) *The Rule of Law: Ideal or Ideology?* (Toronto: Carswell 1987), 97–123.
4 F. Rabelais, *Gargantua and Pantagruel* (New York: AMS Press 1963), chs. 37–43.
5 F.S.C. Northrop, *The Complexity of Legal and Ethical Experience* (Boston: Little, Brown 1959), 6. According to Fuller, adjudication is a device that gives formal and institutional expression to a reasoned argument in human affairs. As such, it assumes a burden of rationality and objectivity not borne by other social processes; see 'The Forms and Limits of Adjudication,' *Harvard Law Review* 92 (1978), 353.
6 See *Re Motor Vehicle Reference*, [1985] 2 SCR 486 per Lamer J.
7 Learned Hand, 'Mr. Justice Cardozo,' *Harvard Law Review* 52 (1938), 361.
8 See E. Andrew, *Shylock's Rights: A Grammar of Lockian Claims* (Toronto: University of Toronto Press 1988), 14.
9 See A. Hutchinson and P. Monahan, 'The Unfolding Drama of American Legal Thought: Law, Politics and Critical Legal Scholars,' *Stanford Law Review* 34 (1984), 199, 202–8, and M. Tushnet, *Red, White and Blue: A Critical Analysis of Constitutional Law* (Cambridge: Harvard University Press 1988).
10 *Southern Pacific Co.* v. *Jensen*, 244 US 205, 222 (1917).
11 O. Fiss, 'Objectivity and Interpretation,' *Stanford Law Review* 34 (1982), 739, 745.
12 R. Dworkin, *A Matter of Principle* (1985), 527.
13 See, for example, P. Hogg, *Constitutional Law of Canada* (3rd ed.) (Toronto: Carswell 1992) and B. Slattery, 'A Theory of the Charter,' *Osgoode Hall Law Journal* 25 (1987), 701.
14 B. McLachlin, 'Of Power, Democracy and the Judiciary,' *Law Society Gazette* 25 (1991), 20.
15 Ibid. 21 and 27.
16 Ibid. 25.
17 D. Beatty, *Putting the Charter to Work* (Kingston, ON: McGill–Queen's University Press 1987), 53.
18 P. Monahan, *Politics and the Constitution* (Toronto: Carswell 1987). I am

more concerned here with judicial legitimacy generally, not the theoretical validity of communitarianism as a political program. See infra ch. 6.

19 See C. Taylor, 'Cross-Purposes: The Liberalism–Communitarianism Debate,' in N. Rosenblum ed., *Liberalism and the Moral Life* (Cambridge: Harvard University Press 1989), 159.

20 W. Kymlicka, *Liberalism, Community, and Culture* (Oxford: Clarendon Press 1989), 165.

21 See D. Beatty, *Putting the Charter to Work* (1987); 'Constitutional Conceits: The Coercive Authority of the Courts,' *University of Toronto Law Journal* 37 (1987), 183; *Talking Heads and the Supremes: The Canadian Production of Constitutional Review* (Toronto: Carswell 1990); and 'A Conservative's Court: The Politicization of Courts,' *University of Toronto Law Journal* 40 (1991), 15.

22 Ibid. *Talking Heads*, vi.

23 Ibid. ix.

24 Ibid. 'Constitutional Conceits ... ,' 19.

25 Ibid. 2, 15, and *Talking Heads*, vi, 15, 135.

26 This kind of formalist fundamentalism goes further than even someone like Robert Bork. Although he continues to argue that *Brown* v. *Board of Education*, 347 US 483 (1954) was wrongly decided, he concedes that it is now part of the American constitution and cannot be overruled. See R. Bork, *The Tempting of America: The Political Seduction of the Law* (New York: Free Press 1990), 74–84.

27 Beatty, supra note 21, *Charter to Work*, 54, 182, 186.

28 Ibid. 72.

29 Ibid. 5, 61, and *Talking Heads*, 25, 36.

30 *R.* v. *Oakes*, [1986] 1 SCR 103.

31 Beatty, supra note 21, *Talking Heads*, 263.

32 Ibid. vii, 113.

33 Ibid. 19–22, 80–3.

34 Ibid. 17.

35 Ibid. 22.

36 Ibid.

37 Ibid. 15.

38 See D. Cohen and A. Hutchinson, 'Of Persons and Property: The Politics of Legal Taxonomy,' *Dalhousie Law Journal* 21 (1990), 20.

39 The proof of any theoretical pudding is in the eating. See, for example, A. Hutchinson and A. Petter, 'Private Rights/Public Wrongs: The Liberal Lie of the Charter,' *University of Toronto Law Journal* 38 (1988), 278; A. Hutchinson, 'Mice under a Chair: Democracy, the Courts and the Administra-

tive State,' *University of Toronto Law Journal* 39 (1990), 374; and A. Hutchinson, 'Waiting For Coraf (or The Beatification of the Charter),' *University of Toronto Law Journal* 41 (1991), 332.

40 Beatty, supra note 21, *Talking Heads*, 72, and 'Constitutional Conceits,' 21–2.

41 R. Gordon, 'Law and Ideology,' *Tikkun* 3(1) (1988), 14, 15.

42 McLachlin, supra note 14, 26. So that there is no misunderstanding, I am obviously in favour of 'the Rule of Law' insofar as this is used to condemn acts of arbitrary government. But I am opposed to a version of the Rule of Law that incorporates a judicially enforced Charter of Rights. See Hutchinson and Monahan, supra note 3.

43 For a fuller account of constitutional visions, see infra ch. 4.

44 W. Conklin, *Images of a Constitution* (Toronto: University of Toronto Press 1989), 3. Conklin tends to talk about 'rationalism' rather than formalism, but I do not believe that this is of any great significance in terms of my critical claims.

45 Ibid. 74–81.

46 Ibid. 173–217.

47 Ibid. 219–35.

48 Ibid. 173–84.

49 Ibid. 186.

50 Ibid. 216.

51 Ibid. 218.

52 See M. Oakeshott, *Rationalism in Politics* (New York: Basic Book, 1962) and R. Unger, *Critical Legal Studies Movement* (Cambridge: Harvard University Press 1987), 1–20.

53 See D. Kennedy, 'Form and Substance in Private Law Adjudication,' *Harvard Law Review* 89 (1976), 1685.

54 Ibid. 7.

55 Ibid. 41.

56 Ibid. 63.

57 *Harrison* v. *Carswell*, [1976] SCR 200.

58 Conklin, supra note 42, 41–3.

59 Ibid. 45.

60 P. MacCormick, 'Party Capability Theory and Appellate Success in the Supreme Court of Canada,' *Canadian Journal of Political Science* 26 (1993), 523.

61 See *Hunter* v. *Southam Inc.*, [1984] 2 SCR 145; *Retail, Wholesale and Department Store Union, Local 580 et al.* v. *Dolphin Delivery Ltd.*, [1986] 2 SCR 573; and *Andrews* v. *Law Society of British Columbia*, [1989] 1 SCR 143.

62 Conklin, supra note 44, 256–9, 269–71.
63 See Hutchinson, supra note 2, 261–94.
64 Aristotle, *The Politics* (T.A. Sinclair and T.J. Saunders trans.) (Harmondsworth: Penguin 1981), 225.
65 Ibid. 226.
66 See Conklin, supra note 44.
67 See *Harrison* v. *Carswell*, supra note 57.

CHAPTER 4 AN ABSTRACTION OF VISION: A MISERABLE EXISTENCE

1 *The History of John Bull* (1712), ch 24, as quoted in *The Oxford Book of Quotations* (London: Oxford University Press 1953).
2 Dickson, 'Address to the Mid-Winter Meeting of the Canadian Bar Association' 2 February 1985, at 14.
3 It must be emphasized that this chapter deals with rights-talk as a categoric mode of analysis and does not speak to the vexing question of the value of using rights-talk in a strategic manner. See infra chap. 6.
4 M. Sandel, 'The Procedural Republic and the Unencumbered Self,' *Political Theory* 12 (1984), 81.
5 See E. Wolgast, *The Grammar of Justice* (Ithaca, NY: Cornell University Press 1987).
6 See D. Kennedy, 'Form and Substance in Private Law Adjudication,' *Harvard Law Review* 89 (1976), 1685.
7 See H. Steiner, *Justification and Social Vision in the Modern Tort Law of Accidents* (Madison: University of Wisconsin Press 1987).
8 See M. Oakeshott, *Rationalism in Politics* (New York: Basic Books 1962), 123–5, and R. Unger, *Critical Legal Studies Movement* (Cambridge: Harvard University Press 1987), 91–109.
9 See supra, ch. 1.
10 Aristotle, *Politics* (E. Barker ed.) (Harmondsworth: Penguin 1968).
11 'On the Jewish Question,' in *The Collected Works of Marx and Engels* (1976) vol. III, 160.
12 A. de Tocqueville, *Democracy in America* (J. Mayer ed.) (Garden City, NY: Doubleday 1969), vol. 2, 308.
13 See C. Lawrence, 'The Id, the Ego and Equal Protection: Reckoning with Unconscious Racism,' *Stanford Law Review* 39 (1987), 317.
14 See D. Bell, *And We Are Not Saved* (New York: Basic Books 1987); A. Freeman, 'Legitimizing Racial Discrimination through Antidiscrimination Law: A Critical Review of Supreme Court Doctrine,' *Minnesota Law Review* 62 (1978), 1049.

15 *Hunter* v. *Southam*, [1984] 2 SCR 145 at 159 per Dickson C.J. The problems with treating corporations as rights-holders are fully canvassed in ch. 2.

16 V. Hugo, *Les Misérables* (N. Denny trans.) (Harmondsworth: Penguin 1976), 639–40.

17 See T. O'Reilly-Fleming, *Down and Out in Canada: Homeless Canadians* (Toronto: Canadian Scholar's Press 1992). The situation is proportionately worse for the young, women, and people of colour. See W.J. Wilson, *The Truly Disadvantaged: The Inner City, the Underclass, and Public Policy* (Chicago: University of Chicago Press 1987).

18 See, for example, P. Siebert, 'Homeless People: Establishing Rights to Shelter,' *Law & Inequality* 4 (1986), 393, and C. Ladd, 'A Right to Shelter for the Homeless in New York State,' *New York University Law Review* 61 (1986), 272.

19 H. Hershkoff and A. Cohen, 'Begging to Differ: The First Amendment and the Right to Beg,' *Harvard Law Review* 104 (1991), 896.

20 Ibid. 915.

21 Hershkoff and Cohen, supra note 19, 910.

22 See R. Unger, *The Critical Legal Studies Movement* (1986), 15–22, 88–90.

23 See J. Fudge, 'The Effects of Entrenching a Bill of Rights upon Political Discourse,' *International Journal of the Sociology of Law* 17 (1989), 445.

24 Hershkoff and Cohen, supra note 19, 902, 910.

25 Ibid. 914.

26 Ibid. 900. They compound this difficulty by arguing that 'the beggar nonetheless feels himself at an advantage, because the more fortunate need him as an object of charity.' Ibid. This is surely a perverse inversion of moral hierarchy.

27 Hugo, supra note 16, 30.

28 F. Nietzsche, *Beyond Good and Evil* (W. Kaufmann ed.) (New York: Vintage Books 1966), 87.

29 Hershkoff and Cohen, supra note 19, 898, 912. It is tempting to propose a litigation strategy that strives to establish something like a right to private property. There are many interesting and suggestive proposals for such tactics. See, for example, J. Waldron, *The Right to Private Property* (Oxford: Clarendon Press 1988) and J. Singer, 'The Reliance Interest in Property,' *Stanford Law Review* 40 (1988), 611. However, the response of American courts to such claims has been less than encouraging. See *Dandridge* v. *Williams*, 397 US 471 (1970). Moreover, there are other more viable and less risky avenues of struggle open to progressive lawyers. Infra, pp. 264–75.

30 See F. Engels, *The Condition of the Working Class in England* (W.O. Henderson and W.H. Chaloner eds.) (Oxford: Blackwell 1958), 311.

31 Hershkoff and Cohen, supra note 19, 903.
32 D. Sayer, *The Violence of Abstraction: The Analytical Foundations of Historical Materialism* (Oxford: Blackwell 1987). Even most liberal theorists concede that to talk of 'moral agency' in conditions of abject poverty is nonsensical. See J. Rawls, *A Theory of Justice* (Cambridge: Belknap Press 1971), 202–9.
33 Hershkoff and Cohen, supra note 19, 912.
34 A. France, *The Red Lily* (W. Stephens trans.) (London: John Lane 1970), 91.
35 Marx and Engels, supra note 11, 164.
36 R. Unger, *Law in Modern Society* (New York: Free Press 1976), 206.
37 L.H. Tribe, *Abortion: The Clash of Absolutes* (New York: Norton 1990), 3 ('clash of absolutes, of life against liberty'); G. Steiner, *The Futility of Family Policy* (Washington, DC: Brookings Institution 1981), 51 ('the most intractable and most prominent of family policy issues'); and C.A. Mackinnon, *Feminism Unmodified: Discourses on Life and Law* (Cambridge: Harvard University Press 1987), 93–4 ('inextricable from sexuality ... [and] a life and death decision that women should be legally allowed to make').
38 S. Gavigan, 'Beyond Morgentaler: The Legal Regulation of Reproduction,' in J. Brodie, S. Gavigan, and J. Jenson (eds.) *The Politics of Abortion* (Toronto: Oxford University Press 1992), 135. See also B. Benderly, *Thinking About Abortion* (Garden City, NY: Dial Press 1984), 64.
39 I recognize that I am another man making another intervention into the abortion debate. My defence and justification is that I want to abandon the patriarchial discourse of rights-talk and clear a space so that women can work toward the articulation of a different discourse that is more attuned to their interests and aspirations. The role of men is to step aside, listen, and act upon the demands and desires of women. Of course, there is no one women's viewpoint on abortion and it would be folly to pretend that there is ever likely to be one.
40 See supra, ch. 3.
41 D. Greschner, 'Abortion and Democracy: A Critique of *Tremblay* v. *Daigle*,' *McGill Law Journal* 35 (1990), 633, 652. See also C. West, 'Jurisprudence and Gender,' *University of Chicago Law Review* 55 (1988), 1.
42 U. Le Guin, *Dancing at the Edge of the World* (New York: Perennial Library 1989), 156.
43 B.K. Rothman, *The Tentative Pregnancy: Prenatal Diagnosis and the Future of Motherhood* (New York: Viking 1986), 114.
44 See G. Corea, *The Mother Machine* (New York: Harper & Row 1985).
45 See E. Wolgast, *The Grammar of Justice* (Ithaca, NY: Cornell University Press 1987), 42–4. This is discussed further at infra.

46 See supra.
47 See R. Petchesky, *Abortion and Women's Choice: The State, Sexuality, and Reproductive Freedom* (New York: Longman 1984), 141–67.
48 *R.* v. *Morgentaler*, [1988] 1 SCR 161.
49 Ibid. 161, 171, 171, 173, and 173.
50 410 US 113 (1973).
51 Supra note 48, 183, 164, 164, and 164.
52 See infra, ch. 5.
53 *Harris* v. *McRae*, 448 US 297 at 316 (1980).
54 R. Copelon, 'Unpacking Patriarchy: Reproduction, Sexuality, Originalism, and Constitutional Change,' in J. Lobel (ed.) *A Less Than Perfect Union* (New York: Monthly Review Press 1988), 303.
55 E. Weinrib, 'The Morgentaler Decision: Constitutional Rights, Legislative Intention, and Institutional Design,' *University of Toronto Law Journal* 42 (1992), 22, 76.
56 See Petchesky, supra note 47, and Z. Eisenstein, *Feminism and Sexual Equality* (New York: Monthly Review Press 1984).
57 See J. Nedelsky, 'Reconceiving Autonomy: Sources, Thoughts and Possibilities,' in A. Hutchinson and L. Green (eds.) *Law and Community: The End of Individualism* (Toronto: Carswell 1989).
58 See B. Cossman, 'The Precarious Unity of Feminist Theory and Practice: The Praxis of Abortion,' *Toronto Faculty Law Review* 44 (1986), 85, and R. Colker, *Abortion and Dialogue* (Bloomington: University of Indiana Press 1992).
59 M. Atwood, *The Handmaid's Tale* (Toronto: McClelland & Stewart 1985), 83.
60 Supra note 48, 172.
61 *Daigle* v. *Tremblay*, [1989] 2 SCR 530.
62 For a theoretical introduction to the idea that everything is 'always already' interpreted, only capable of reinterpretation and never recoverable in its primal condition, see A. Hutchinson, *Dwelling on the Threshold* (Toronto: Carswell 1988), 11–22. The following account was put together from reports in the visual and text media. I am grateful to Lisa Fishbayn for her insightful work in compiling and collating these sources.
63 S. Milsom, 'A Pageant in Modern Dress,' *Yale Law Journal* 84 (1975), 1585.
64 For a fuller account of world-making through law, see A. Hutchinson and D. Cohen, 'Of Persons and Property: The Politics of Legal Taxonomy,' *Dalhousie Law Journal* 13 (1990), 20.
65 *Tremblay* v. *Daigle* (1989), 59 DLR (4th) 609 at 628 per LeBel J.A.

66 See supra note 61, 665.
67 Ibid. 650–1.
68 See Colker, supra note 58.
69 Supra note 65, 618 per Nicols J.A. (describing *Morgentaler* as a 'chance mishap').
70 Ibid. 612 per Bernier J.A.
71 Ibid. 613 per Bernier J.A.
72 Ibid. 613 per Bernier J.A., 615 per Nichols J.A., and 638 per LeBel J.A.
73 Ibid. 620–1 per Chouinard J.A.
74 Ibid. 638 per LeBel J.A. For an argument in favour of fetal rights, see B. Hovius, 'The Morgentaler Decisions: Parliament's Options,' *Canadian Family Law Quarterly* 3 (1988), 137.
75 Ibid. 613 per Bernier J.A.
76 For a sensitive account of this state of affairs, see L. Finley, 'Breaking Women's Silence in Law: The Dilemma of the Gendered Nature of Legal Reasoning,' *Notre Dame Law Review* 64 (1989), 886, 900–1.
77 Supra note 65, 614 per Bernier J.A.
78 For a legal analysis of the fetus in these terms, see M. McConnell, 'Sui Generis: The Legal Nature of the Fetus in Canada,' *Canadian Bar Review* 70 (1991), 548.
79 Supra note 65, 613 per Bernier J.A. See also, J. Diggins, 'Paternal Interest in the Abortion Decision: Does the Father Have a Say?', *University of Chicago Law Forum* (1989), 377. In *Borowski*, Martland had stated that 'the possibility of the husband bringing proceedings to attack the legislation [permitting therapeutic abortions] is illusory.' *Minister of Justice of Canada* v. *Borowski*, [1981] 2 SCR 575 at 597.
80 *Tremblay*, Ibid. 638 per LeBel J.A.
81 Ibid. 612 per Bernier J.A. In *Re Medhurst and Medhurst* (1984), 45 O.R. (2d) 575, Reid J. stated that 'it is difficult to think of anyone who could have an interest equal to that of the husband in the pregnancy of his wife.' Ibid.
82 Ibid. 613 per Bernier J.A.
83 See supra.
84 Ibid. 614 per Bernier J.A.
85 Ibid. 619 per Nichols J.A.
86 Supra note 59, 66.
87 In my view, Bentham conceded too much when he suggested that such nonsense could be supported even by stilts (though 'stilted' it undoubtedly is). See J. Bentham, 'Anarchical Fallacies,' in *The Works of Jeremy Bentham* (Edinburgh: W. Tait 1843), 501.

88 C. Pateman, 'Feminism and Democracy,' in G. Duncan (ed.) *Democratic Theory and Practice* (1983), 204.

89 See F. Olsen, 'The Family and the Market: A Study of Ideology and Legal Reform,' *Harvard Law Review* 96 (1983), 1497, 1578.

CHAPTER 5 THE STATE OF RIGHTS-TALK: PRIVATE RIGHTS AND PUBLIC WRONGS

1 S. Bowles and H. Gintis, *Democracy and Capitalism: Property, Community, and the Contradictions of Modern Social Thought xi* (New York: Basic Books 1987).

2 J. Dewey, *The Public and Its Problems* (Denver, CO: A. Swallon 1977), 8–9. A similar observation is made by Vining. See J. Vining, *Legal Identity: The Coming of Age of Public Law* (New Haven, CT: Yale University Press 1978), 181 ('The world envisioned by the legal mind has been even to our day one of castles upon hilltops'.)

3 This essay owes much to the earlier work of Paul Brest; see 'State Action and Liberal Theory: A Casenote on *Flagg Brothers* v. *Brooks*,' *University of Pennsylvania Law Review* 130 (1982), 1296. Although the American state action doctrine is universally condemned, it still plays a major role in contemporary judicial review; see *Lugar* v. *Edmondson Oil Co.*, 457 US 922 (1982). For a thorough survey of the law and the literature, see E. Chemerinsky 'Rethinking State Action,' *Northwestern University Law Review* 80 (1985), 503.

4 See S. Beck, 'Corporate Power and Public Policy,' in Consumer Protection, Environmental Law and Corporate Power, vol. 50, *Studies for Royal Commission on the Economic Union and Development Prospects for Canada* (Ottawa: Government of Canada 1985).

5 See H. Glasbeek 'The Corporate Social Responsibility – The Latest in Maginot Lines to Save Capitalism,' *Dalhousie Law Journal* 11 (1988), 363.

6 See J. Laux and M. Molot, *State Capitalism: Public Enterprise in Canada* (Ithaca, NY: Cornell University Press 1988).

7 See J. Fox and M. Ornstein, 'The Canadian State and Corporate Elites in the Post-War Period,' *Canadian Review of Sociology and Anthropology* 23(4) (1986), 481.

8 See M. Olsen, *The Logic of Collective Action* (Cambridge: Harvard University Press 1971).

9 See S. Beck, supra note 4, 183–93.

10 See M. Stokes, 'Company Law and Legal Theory,' in W. Twining (ed.) *Legal Theory and Common Law* (Oxford: Basil Blackwell 1986).

11 See Marx, 'On the Jewish Question,' in R. Tucker (ed.) *The Marx-Engels Reader* (New York: Norton 1972), 31–2.

12 C. Lindblom, *Politics and Markets* (New York: Basic Books 1977), 356.

13 *Retail, Wholesale and Department Store Union, Local 580* v. *Dolphin Delivery Ltd.*, [1986] 2 SCR 573.

14 Presumably by way of sop, the majority also held that picketing is a form of expression protected by the Charter. However, this view was qualified by the further holding that, had the Charter applied, the restriction in *Dolphin* would have constituted a 'reasonable limit' within the meaning of s. 1.

15 McIntyre J. tries to suggest that, although the Charter does not apply to the judiciary, the courts are 'bound by the Charter as they are bound by all law.' Here, however, he is using the word 'bound' in a particular sense to refer to the fact that the courts are required to apply the Charter in their judicial capacity as 'neutral arbiters.' Ibid. 600.

16 See P. Monahan, *Politics and the Constitution* (Toronto: Carswell 1987).

17 *Hunter* v. *Southam Inc.*, [1984] 2 SCR 145, at 156. See also *Regina* v. *Big M Drug Mart*, [1985] 1 SCR 295, at 336 ('freedom can primarily be characterized by the absence of coercion and constraint').

18 See A. Kronman and R. Posner, *The Economics of Contract Law* (Boston: Little, Brown 1979), 33.

19 See J. Finnis, *Natural Law and Natural Right* (Toronto: Clarendon Press 1980).

20 See H.L.A. Hart, *The Concept of Law* (Oxford: Clarendon Press 1961).

21 See R. Dworkin, *A Matter of Principle* (Cambridge: Harvard University Press 1984) and D. Beatty, supra ch. 3.

22 R. Bellamy, 'Defining Liberalism: Neutralist, Ethical or Political?' in R. Bellamy (ed.) *Liberalism and Recent Legal and Social Philosophy* (Stuttgart: F. Steiner 1984), 23.

23 *Race Relations Board* v. *Charter*, [1973] AC 868. The judgments are remarkable for their lack of any functional consideration of the issue, except for the dissenting judgment of Lord Morris. Ibid. 894.

24 *Racial Relations Board* v. *Applin*, [1975] AC 259 at 286 per Lord Simon. See also *Blathwayt* v. *Lord Cawley*, [1976] AC 397 at 426 per Lord Wilberforce ('private selection [has not] yet become a matter of public policy').

25 See *Race Relations Act* 1976, ss. 25 and 23(2).

26 See R. Hale, 'Coercion and Distribution in a Supposedly Non-Coercive State,' *Political Science Quarterly* 38 (1923), 470, and M. Cohen, 'Property and Sovereignty,' *Cornell Law Quarterly* 13 (1927), 8.

27 D. Kennedy, 'The Structure of Blackstone's Commentaries,' *Buffalo Law Review* 28 (1979), 205, 264.

28 See M. Horowitz, 'The History of the Public/Private Distinction,' *University of Pennsylvania Law Review* 130 (1982), 1423, 1426.
29 See, for example, P. Hogg, *Constitutional Law of Canada*, 835–50 (3rd. ed.) (Toronto: Carswell 1992); K. Swinton, 'Application of the Canadian Charter of Rights and Freedoms,' in W. Tarnopolsky and J. Beaudoin (eds.) *The Canadian Charter of Rights and Freedoms* (Toronto: Carswell 1982), 41; and J. Whyte, 'Is the Private Sector Affected by the Charter?' in L. Smith (ed.) *Righting the Balance: Canada's New Equality Rights* (Saskatoon, SK: Canadian Human Rights Reporter 1986).
30 Hogg, ibid. 850.
31 Whereas, in *R.* v. *Rahey*, [1987] 1 SCR 588, the Supreme Court held that the Charter did apply when a court order is issued on the court's own motion for a public purpose, in *British Columbia Government Employees' Union*, [1988] 2 SCR 214, it decided that it also applied when the government was a party to such an order.
32 (1986), 26 DLR (4th) 728 (Ont. C.A.).
33 See, for example, D. Gibson, *The Law of the Charter* (Toronto: Carswell 1986), 110–24; Y. de Montigny, 'Section 32 and Equality Rights,' in A. Bayefsky and M. Eberts (eds.) *Equality Rights and the Canadian Charter of Rights and Freedoms* (Toronto: Carswell 1985); and B. Slattery, 'Charter of Rights and Freedoms – Does It Bind Private Persons?' *Canadian Bar Review* 63 (1985), 148.
34 D. Beatty, 'Constitutional Conceits: The Coercive Authority of Courts,' *University of Toronto Law Journal* 40 (1991), 183, 190–1.
35 R. Dworkin, *Taking Rights Seriously* (London: Duckworth 1979), 127.
36 H. Lessard, 'The Idea of the "Private": A Discussion of State Action and Separate Sphere Ideology,' *Dalhousie Law Journal* 10 (1986), 107 at 120.
37 See *Lumley* v. *Gye* (1853), 118 ER 749. For a thorough account of the circumstances surrounding this case and its subsequent history, see F. Sayre, 'Inducing Breach of Contract,' *Harvard Law Review* 36 (1922), 663; H. Glasbeek, 'Lumley v. Gye – The Aftermath,' *Monash University Law Review* 1 (1975), 187; and J.A.G. Griffith, *The Politics of the Judiciary* (3rd ed.) (London: Fontana Press 1985), 53–82.
38 Supra note 13, 600.
39 See Hogg, supra note 29, 845.
40 See Whyte, supra note 29.
41 See Slattery, supra note 33, 157.
42 Supra note 32.
43 *Minister of Justice* v. *Borowski*, [1981] 2 SCR 575.
44 *Daigle* v. *Tremblay*, [1989] 2 SCR 530 at 564.

45 See *McKinney* v. *University of Guelph*, [1990] 3 SCR 229.
46 Ibid. 262 per La Forest J.
47 *Douglas College*, [1990] 3 SCR 570 at 584 per La Forest J.
48 See Hogg, supra note 29, 846.
49 See *Black* v. *Law Society of Alberta*, [1989] 1 SCR 591 and *R.* v. *Lerke* (1986), 25 DLR (4th) 403 (Alta. CA).
50 See *Hunter*, supra note 17.
51 See *Phillips* v. *Social Assistance Appeal Board* (1986), 76 NSR (2d) 240, affd. (1986), 27 DLR (4th) 156 (sub nom. *Re Phillips and Lynch*). Moroever, this would be true even if the Nova Scotia court had chosen the alternative remedy of extending benefits to single fathers. It still would have been open to the legislature to have lowered or eliminated the benefits paid to all recipients. Indeed, this is precisely what happened following a recent British Columbia ruling striking down regulations providing lower welfare rates for those under 26: see *Silano* v. *The Queen*, [1987] 5 WWR 739 (B.C.S.C.). The response of the provincial government was to offset increased payments to younger claimants by reducing general welfare rates. In other words, equality was achieved by lowering benefits for those over 26 who are the bulk of welfare recipients.
52 *Schachter* v. *Canada*, [1992] 2 SCR 679.
53 *Re New Brunswick Broadcasting Co. Ltd. and CRTC* (1984), 13 DLR (4th) 77 at 89.
54 *National Citizens' Coalition* v. *A.G. Canada* (1984), 11 DLR (4th) 481 (Alta. Q.B.).
55 *Ford* v. *Quebec*, [1988] 2 SCR 712.
56 Such a statutory prohibition would clearly be subject to Charter scrutiny. As McIntyre J. notes in *Dolphin*, supra note 13, 603, if there had been a statutory provision specifically outlawing secondary picketing 'the case would be on all fours with *Blainey* and, subject to s. 1 of the Charter, the statutory provision could be struck down.'
57 *Southern Pacific Co.* v. *Jensen*, 244 US 205 at 222 per Holmes J. (1917).
58 See A. Berle, 'Constitutional Limitations on Corporate Activity – Protection of Personal Rights from Invasion through Economic Power,' *University of Pennsylvania Law Review* 100 (1952), 933.
59 Supra note 17.
60 See, for example, *Andrews* v. *Law Society of B.C.*, [1989] 1 SCR 143 and *Wilson* v. *B.C. Medical Services Commission* (1988), 55 DLR (4th) 171 (B.C.C.A.).
61 See *The Labour Trilogy*, [1987] 1 SCR 313.
62 Ibid. 391 (emphasis added).

63 *P.I.P.S.C.* v. *Northwest Territories*, [1990] 2 SCR 367.
64 For an example of how the Charter may be used to undermine labour interests, see *Lavigne* v. *O.P.S.E.U.*, [1991] 2 SCR 211.
65 See *Labour Trilogy*, supra note 61.
66 See J. Nedelsky, 'Reconceiving Autonomy: Sources, Thoughts and Possibilities,' in A. Hutchinson and L. Green (eds.), *Law and Community: The End of Individualism* (Toronto: Carswell 1989).
67 See supra ch.4.
68 For an inspired attempt to move beyond liberal notions of procedural fairness toward a democratic style of participatory involvement, see J. Handler, *The Conditions of Discretion: Autonomy, Community, Bureaucracy* (New York: Russell Sage Foundation 1986).

CHAPTER 6 DOWN THE YELLOW BRICK ROAD: RIGHTS TALK BACK

1 L.F. Baum, *The Wizard of Oz* (Indianapolis: Bobbs-Merrill 1944).
2 B.N. Cardozo, *The Nature of the Judicial Process* (New Haven: Yale University Press 1921), 102. Oliver Wendell Holmes, Jr, originally introduced to jurisprudence the resort to pragmatism at the turn of the century. See T. Grey, 'Holmes and Legal Pragmatism,' *Stanford Law Review* 41 (1989), 787. For an attempt to survey and synthesize the pragmatic tradition, see R. Summers, *Instrumentalism and American Legal Theory* (Ithaca, NY: Cornell University Press 1982). For a general survey, see M. Brint and W. Weaver (eds.) *Pragmatism in Law and Society* (Boulder, CO: Westview Press 1991) and 'Symposium: The Renaissance of Pragmatism in American Legal Thought,' *Southern California Law Review* 63 (1990), 1569.
3 See R. Posner, *The Problems of Jurisprudence* (Cambridge: Harvard University Press 1990), 405.
4 B. Slattery, 'Are Constitutional Cases Political,' *Supreme Court Law Review* 11 (1989), 507, 515. In 1837, Francis Lieber noted that writing a book on legal reasoning was 'like a recipe of a cookery book.' See T. Perry (ed.) *The Life and Letters of Francis Lieber* (Boston: Osgood 1882), 116.
5 See 'Revolution without Foundation: The Grammar of Scepticism and Law,' *McGill Law Journal* 33 (1988), 451; 'The Jurisprudence of Despair,' *University of British Columbia Law Review* 23 (1989), 549; and 'Political World,' *Canadian Journal of Law and Jurisprudence* 3 (1990), 139.
6 'Revolution without Foundation: The Grammar of Scepticism and Law,' *McGill Law Journal* 33 (1988), 451, 475 [hereinafter referred to by page number in the text].
7 He also goes on to say that as well as having no ground on which to

stand, I have also managed to 'paint myself into an irrationalist corner' (484). To be without ground and painted in a corner seems to me a miraculous feat.

8 Langille charges that I 'misuse this potent source of inspiration, reading in skeptical conclusions which Wittgenstein would regard as nonsense' (453) and that such conclusions are 'deeply shallow' (456). Apart from the fact that I do not consider myself to be a disciple of the Wittgenstein creed, the irony of this assessment seems to be lost on Langille. Surely, a major lesson of Wittgenstein was that while meaning is not perennially elusive, a text (including his own) is more a site for the struggle between competing interpretations and not an occasion for the resolution of them.

Moreover, even if Langille's reading of Wittgenstein was somehow 'right,' in the sense that he said what Langille says he said, Langille is unclear how this itself advances, let alone successfully completes, the attempt to make sense of the interpretive act. He must go on to demonstrate that his interpretation of Wittgenstein is a useful and convincing account of legal language and its operation. Like some fundamentalist Christians or dogmatic Marxists, he seems to believe that if the Bible, the Communist Manifesto or, in Langille's case, the *Philosophical Investigations* said it, then it must be so. This is to engage in the error of 'pointing,' which Langille chastises sceptics for committing – 'to *criticize* one must argue political theory, not point it out' (504).

9 L. Wittgenstein, *Philosophical Investigations* (G.E.M. Anscombe trans.) (Oxford: Basil Blackwell 1953) para. 124.

10 See supra ch. 3 and A. Hutchinson, 'That's Just the Way It Is: Langille on Law,' *McGill Law Journal* 34 (1989), 145.

11 See D. Cornell, 'Institutionalization of Meaning, Recollective Imagination and the Potential for Transformative Legal Interpretation,' *University of Pennsylvania Law Review* 136 (1988), 1135, 1207. See also S. Fish, *Is There a Text in This Class?* (Cambridge: Harvard University Press 1980).

12 See J. Derrida, 'Signature Event Context,' *Glyph* 1 (1977), 172.

13 See D. Kennedy, 'Toward a Phenomenology of Adjudication,' in A. Hutchinson and P. Monahan (eds.), *The Rule of Law: Ideal or Ideology?* (Toronto: Carswell 1987).

14 See H.L.A. Hart, *The Concept of Law* (Oxford: Clarendon Press 1961).

15 See L. Wittgenstein, *Preliminary Studies for the 'Philosophical Investigations'* (2d ed.) (Oxford: Basil Blackwell 1969), 24.

16 On those values, see H. Arthurs, R. Weisman, and F. Zemans, 'The Canadian Legal Profession,' *American Bar Foundation Research Journal* (1986), 447, and J. Hagan, M. Huxter, and P. Parker, 'Class Structure and Legal

Practice: Inequality and Mobility among Toronto Lawyers,' *Law and Society Review* 22 (1988), 9.

17 See O. Fiss, 'Objectivity and Interpretation,' *Stanford Law Review* 34 (1982), 739, 755, and R. Dworkin, *Law's Empire* (Cambridge, Belknap Press 1986), 407.

18 See for example, D. Spender, *Man-Made Language* (London: Routledge and Kegan Paul 1980) and B. Hooks, *Yearning* (Toronto: Between the Lines 1993).

19 See *Brown* v. *Allen*, 344 US 443 at 540 per Jackson J. (1953).

20 P. Hacker, *Insight and Illusion* (Oxford: Clarendon Press 1986), 191.

21 The telling of an old joke seems appropriate here. A mathematician, philosopher, and lawyer apply for a university professorship. The mathematician is interviewed first and he is asked what two plus two equals. He provides an exhaustive and mind-numbing explanation of why the answer is four. The philosopher is asked the same question and she offers a lengthy disposition about it all depending on the base-system used. Finally, the lawyer is interviewed, and when asked the same question, is short and to the point: 'Tell me the answer you want and I'll argue that way.'

22 See *Reconceiving Rights as Relationships.* Unpublished ms. (1993), 2.

23 Ibid. 21.

24 Leon E. Trakman, *Reasoning with the Charter* (Toronto: Butterworths 1991).

25 Ibid. 173.

26 Ibid. 197.

27 Ibid. 5. On the Communitarian flirtation by recent articulations of liberal legalism, see supra ch. 3.

28 Ibid. 190.

29 Ibid. 170. A similar optimism is shared by Craig Scott and Patrick Macklem. See 'Constitutional Ropes of Sand or Justiciable Guarantees?: Social Rights in a New South African Constitution,' *University of Pennsylvania Law Review* 141 (1992), 1.

30 See S. Altman, 'Beyond Candor,' *Michigan Law Review* 89 (1991), 296.

31 Ibid. 169.

32 See M. Atwood, *The Handmaid's Tale* (Toronto: McClelland & Stewart 1985) and supra ch. 4.

33 R. Dworkin, *A Matter of Principle* (Cambridge: Harvard University Press 1985), 71.

34 For a more confident view that fears about the judiciary's incompetence are misplaced and overstated, see Scott and Macklem, supra note 29, 43–84.

35 See O. Fiss, 'Foreword: The Forms of Justice,' *Harvard Law Review* 93

(1978), 1. For a more sensitive suggestion to deploy judicial remedies as 'hints' in this constitutional dialogue, see N. Duclos and K. Roach, 'Constitutional Remedies as "Constitutional Hints": A Comment on Schachter,' *McGill Law Journal* 36 (1991), 1.

36 B. Simpson, 'The Common Law and Legal Theory' in W. Twining (ed.) *Legal Theory and Common Law* (Oxford: Basil Blackwell 1986), 20.

37 The term first appeared in H.L.A. Hart, *The Concept of Law* (1961), 135.

38 See for example, M. Michelman, 'Conceptions of Democracy in American Constitutional Argument: The Case of Pornography Regulation,' *Tennessee Law Review* 56 (1989), 291.

39 See R. Rorty, 'Feminism and Pragmatism,' *Michigan Quarterly Review* 30 (1991), 231, 254.

40 R. Rorty, *Contingency, Irony, and Solidarity* (Cambridge: Cambridge University Press 1989), 61.

41 E. Hobsbawm, *Workers: Worlds of Labour* (New York: Pantheon Books 1984), 303.

42 See J. Handler, 'Postmodernism, Protest and the New Social Movements,' *Law and Society Review* 26 (1992), 695, and J. Handler, *The Conditions of Discretion: Autonomy, Community, Bureaucracy* (New York: Russell Sage Foundation 1986), 190–200.

43 K. Klare, 'Law-Making as Praxis,' *Telos* 40 (1979), 135.

44 See M. Mandel, *The Charter of Rights and the Legalization of Politics in Canada* (1989); and J. Fudge and H. Glasbeek, 'The Politics of Rights: A Politics with Little Class,' *Social and Legal Studies* 1 (1992), 45.

45 E.P. Thompson, *Whigs and Hunters* (London: Allen Lane 1975), 265.

46 See A. Hunt and A. Bartholomew, 'What's Wrong with Rights?', *Law and Inequality* 9 (1991), 1, and C. Sypnowich, *The Concept of Socialist Law* (Oxford: Clarendon Press 1990).

47 For further discussions of this postmodern approach to lawyering, see A. Hutchinson, 'Doing the Rights Thing?: Toward a Postmodern Politics,' *Law and Society Review* 26 (1992), 773, and D. Herman, 'Beyond the Rights Debate,' *Social and Legal Studies* 2 (1993), 25.

48 *Edwards* v. *California*, 314 US 160 at 186 (1941). For a much fuller exploration and defence of these claims, see A. Hutchinson, 'Les Misérables Redux: Law and the Poor,' *California Interdisciplinary Law Journal* 2 (1993), 301, 326–31.

49 M. Foucault, *Power/Knowledge: Selected Interviews and Other Writings* (C. Gordon ed.) (Brighton: Harvester Press 1980), 1.

50 R. Gordon, 'Critical Legal Histories,' *Stanford Law Review* 36 (1984), 57, 111.

51 D. Price, 'Taking Rights Cynically: A Review of Critical Legal Studies,'

Cambridge Law Journal 48 (1989), 271. See also P. Macklem, 'Of Texts and Democratic Narratives,' *University of Toronto Law Journal* 41 (1991), 639.

52 E. Schneider, 'The Dialectic of Rights and Politics: Perspectives from the Women's Movement,' *New York University Law Review* 61 (1986), 589, 622–3.

53 See H. Glasbeek, 'Some Strategies for an Unlikely Task: The Progressive Use of Law,' *Ottawa Law Review* 21 (1989), 387, 396.

54 G. Brodsky and S. Day, *Canadian Charter Equality Rights for Women: One Step Forward or Two Steps Back?* (Ottawa: Canadian Advisory Council on the Status of Women 1989). Instead of being about the equality concerns of the disadvantaged, the equality provision has been used to deal with charges such as drunk driving and the manufacture of pop cans. See M. Mandel, *The Charter of Rights and the Legalization of Politics in Canada* (Toronto: Wall & Thompson 1989). Nevertheless, Brodsky and Day still believe that the problem has been primarily doctrinal. For a sceptical critique, see J. Fudge, 'The Public/Private Distinction: The Possibilities and Limitations to the Use of Charter Litigation in Further Feminist Struggles,' *Osgoode Hall Law Journal* 25 (1990), 485, and B. Cossman, 'Dancing in the Dark,' *Windsor Yearbook Access to Justice* 10 (1990), 223.

55 See H. Glasbeek and J. Fudge, supra note 44.

56 See infra ch. 7.

57 H. Glasbeek, supra note 53, 411.

58 *R.* v. *Morgentaler*, [1988] 1 SCR 161.

59 See Rostow, 'The Democratic Character of Judicial Review,' *Harvard Law Review* 66 (1952), 193, 208, and A. Bickel, *The Least Dangerous Branch: The Supreme Court at the Bar of Politics* (2nd ed.) (New Haven: Yale University Press 1986), 26.

60 For a fuller discussion of abortion, see supra ch. 4.

61 The record of the civil rights movements offers evidence of the limited successes (and substantial dangers) of obliging the political and legal establishment to honour its own half-hearted commitment to the universal dimension of rights-talk. See R. Delgado, 'The Ethereal Scholar: Does Critical Legal Studies Have What Minorities Want?', *Harvard Civil Rights–Civil Liberties Law Review* 22 (1987), 301, and K. Crenshaw, 'Race, Reform, and Retrenchment: Transformation and Legitimation in Anti Discrimination Law,' *Harvard Law Review* 101 (1988), 1331.

62 For an account of this possibility in the American context, see F. Olsen, 'Comment: Unravelling Compromise,' *Harvard Law Review* 103 (1989), 105.

63 For a power-oriented rather than rights-centred approach to law practice, see P. Gabel and P. Harris, 'Building Power and Breaking Images: Critical

Legal Theory and the Practice of Law,' *New York University Review of Law and Society* 11 (1983), 369, and C. Smart, 'Feminism and Law: Some Problems of Analysis and Strategy,' *International Journal of Sociology of Law* 14 (1989), 109.

64 S. Razack, *Canadian Feminism and the Law: The Women's Legal Education and Action Fund and the Pursuit of Equality* (Toronto: Second Story Feminist Press 1991), 57.

65 See E. Cahn and J. Cahn, 'The War on Poverty: A Civilian Perspective,' *Yale Law Journal* 73 (1964), 1317, and Slye, 'Community Institution Building,' *Villanova Law Review* 36 (1991), 1035.

66 See A. Hutchinson, 'Democracy and Determinacy: An Essay in Legal Interpretation,' *University of Miami Law Review* 43 (1989), 541.

67 'Of Power, Democracy and the Judiciary,' *Law Society's Gazette* 25 (1991), 20, 27.

CHAPTER 7 TALKING THE GOOD LIFE: FROM RIGHTS-TALK TO DEMOCRATIC CONVERSATION

1 J. Rawls, 'The Priority of Right and Ideas of the Good,' *Philosophy and Public Affairs* 17 (1988), 251, 252.

2 R. Dworkin, *Law's Empire* (Cambridge: Belknap Press 1986), 188 and, generally, 195–216.

3 See, for example, M. Sandel, *Liberalism and the Limits of Justice* (Cambridge: Cambridge University Press 1982); A. MacIntyre, *After Virtue* (2nd ed.) (Notre Dame, IN: University of Notre Dame Press 1986) and *Whose Justice? Which Rationality?* (Notre Dame University Press 1988); C. Taylor, *Philosophy and the Human Sciences* (Cambridge University Press 1985); and W. Kymlicka, *Liberalism, Community and Culture* (Oxford: Clarendon Press 1989).

4 See for example, J. Rawls, *A Theory of Justice* (Cambridge: Belknap Press 1970) 446–52; R. Dworkin, *A Matter of Principle* (Cambridge: Harvard University Press 1985), 181–204; and B. Ackerman, *Social Justice in the Liberal State* (New Haven: Yale University Press 1981) 3–30.

5 Dworkin, ibid. 32.

6 See, for example K. Mahoney, 'The Canadian Constitutional Approach to Freedom of Expression in Hate Propaganda and Pornography,' *Law and Contemporary Problems* 55 (1992), 83; and E. Boetzkes, 'Sex Selection and the Charter,' *Canadian Journal of Law and Jurisprudence* 7 (1994), 173.

7 J.J. Rousseau, *The Social Contract* (G. Cole trans.) (Chicago: H. Regnery 1950) Bk. II.

8 R. Rorty, 'Postmodernist Bourgeois Liberalism,' in R. Hollinger (ed.), *Hermeneutics and Praxis* (Notre Dame, IN: University of Notre Dame Press 1985), 218.

9 R. Dahrendorf, *Life Chances: Approaches to Social and Political Theory* (London: Weidenfeld and Nicolson 1979), 32.

10 M. Tushnet, *Red, White and Blue: A Critical Analysis of Constitutional Law* (Cambridge: Harvard University Press 1988), 318.

11 Lord Byron, *Don Juan* (Paris: Galignani 1824), c. xv, st. 99.

12 See E. Barendt, *Freedom of Speech* (Oxford: Clarendon Press 1985), 8–23.

13 See L. Tribe, *American Constitutional Law* (Westbury, NY: Foundation Press 1978), 578, and T. Emerson, *The System of Freedom of Expression* (New York: Random House 1979), 6–7. For a 'sophisticated' example of the preformed liberal individual, see R. Dworkin, *A Matter of Principle* (1984), 181–204.

14 See T. Hobbes, *Leviathan* (C.B. MacPherson ed.) (Harmondsworth: Penguin 1968), 101, and J. Locke, *An Essay Concerning Human Understanding* (A. Pringle-Pattison ed.) (London: Dent 1924), Bk. 3, ch. 2.

15 J. Rawls, 'The Basic Liberties and Their Priority,' in S. McMurrin (ed.) *Liberty, Equality and Law* (Salt Lake City: University of Utah Press 1987), 17.

16 See supra ch. 5.

17 J.G.A. Pocock, *Politics, Language and Time* (Chicago: University of Chicago Press 1973), 15. See also G. Peller, 'The Metaphysics of American Law,' *California Law Review* 73 (1985), 1181. This insight is not new, but the older view did not pursue the political implications of social construction through discourse. See B.L. Whorf, *Language, Thought and Reality* (J. Carroll ed.) (Cambridge, MA: MIT Press 1956).

18 See for example, D. Spender, *Man-Made Language* (London: Routledge and Kegan Paul 1982).

19 See L. Finley, 'Breaking Women's Silence – What Language Can We Use?', *Notre Dame Law Review* 64 (1989), 886.

20 See supra ch. 5.

21 *Minnick* v. *California Department of Corrections*, 452 US 105 at 128 per Stuart J. (1981).

22 *Hague* v. *C.I.O.*, 307 US 496 (1939).

23 See *Brown* v. *Louisiana*, 383 US 131 (1966).

24 See *United States Postal Service* v. *Council of Greenburgh Civic Ass'ns.*, 453 US 114 (1981); *Perry Education Assoc.* v. *Perry Local Educators' Assoc.*, 460 US 37 (1982); and *Cornelius* v. *NAACP Legal Defense and Education Fund*, 105 S. Ct. 3439 (1985). For a strong critique of these doctrinal develop-

ments and their earlier history, see L. Tribe, *Constitutional Choices* (Cambridge: Harvard University Press 1985), 204–10, and R. Cass, 'First Amendment Access to Government Facilities,' *Virginia Law Review* 65 (1979), 1287. For an account of how categories like 'public forum' and 'non-public forum' can be manipulated to serve differing objectives and interests, see C.T. Dienes, 'The Trashing of the Public Forum: Problems in First Amendment Analysis,' *George Washington Law Review* 55 (1986), 109.

25 *Adderley* v. *Florida*, 398 US 39 per Black J. (1966).

26 *Lloyd Corp.* v. *Tanner*, 407 US 551 at 567 (1972).

27 See *Marsh* v. *Alabama*, 326 US 501 (1946); *Food Employees Local 590* v. *Logan Valley Plaza*, 391 US 308 (1968); *Lloyd Corp.* v. *Tanner*, supra note 19; *Hudgens* v. *NLRB*, 424 US 507 (1976); and *Pruneyard Shopping Centre* v. *Robins*, 447 US 74 (1981). For a thoroughgoing critique of these cases, see D. Kairys 'Legal Reasoning' in D. Kairys, *The Politics of Law: A Progressive Critique* (New York: Pantheon Books 1982), 11–17.

28 See *Dolphin Delivery*, [1986] 2 SCR 573.

29 See *Committee for the Commonwealth of Canada* v. *The Queen in Right of Canada*, [1991] 1 SCR 139.

30 For a development of this theme, see A. Hutchinson and M. Jones, 'Wheeler-Dealing: An Essay on Law, Politics and Speech,' *Journal of Law and Society* 15 (1988), 263.

31 'Why the State?' *Harvard Law Review* 100 (1987), 781 (*'State'*), and 'Free Speech and Social Structure,' *Iowa Law Review* 71 (1986), 1405 (*'Speech'*).

32 *State*, ibid. 784.

33 Ibid. 786.

34 *Buckley* v. *Valeo*, 424 US 1 at 48–9. Fiss's suggestion that 'state regulation of speech is consistent with, *and may even by required by*, the first amendment' is surely a strategic rather than an historical claim. *State*, supra note 31, 783 (emphasis added).

35 See O. Fiss, 'Groups and the Equal Protection Clause,' *Journal of Philosophy and Public Affairs* 5 (1976), 107.

36 A related difficulty is that any move in this non-liberal direction would oblige its proponents to accept the impossibility of a neutral or objective mode of constitutional adjudication. Without clearly defined realms of public and private activity, the traditional knit of constitutional rights starts to unravel. Constitutional law will come to consist of claims about the appropriate allocation of state powers and social resources among citizens. In this revised understanding, neutrality ceases to be a plausible characteristic or attainable goal of judicial review. See supra ch. 3.

37 See A. Hutchinson and P. Monahan, 'Democracy and the Rule of Law,' in

A. Hutchinson and P. Monahan (eds.), *The Rule of Law: Ideal or Ideology?* (Toronto: Carswell 1987), 97.

38 See, for example, L. Tribe, *American Constitutional Law*, 890–904.

39 *Ford* v. *Quebec (Attorney-General)*, [1988] 2 SCR 712.

40 Ibid. 748.

41 Ibid. 767. See *Virginia State Board of Pharmacy* v. *Virginia Citizens Consumer Council*, 425 US 748 (1976) and *Central Hudson Gas and Electric Corp.* v. *Public Service Comm. of N.Y.*, 447 US 557 (1980). Ironically, this came at a time when the U.S. courts were engaged in something of a retreat from their constitutional commitment to the protection of commercial speech. See *Posadas de Puerto Rico Associates* v. *Tourism Co. of Puerto Rico*, 478 US 328 (1986).

42 W. Shakespeare, *As You Like It*, Act II, sc. vii.

43 N. Postman, *Amusing Ourselves to Death* (New York: Penguin 1985), 128. This is an insistent theme in much sociological literature. See, for example, S. Ewen and E. Ewen, *Channels of Desire: Mass Images and the Shaping of American Consciousness* (New York: McGraw-Hill 1982); and R. Williams, *Problems in Materialism and Culture* (London: NLB 1980).

44 See S. Ewen, *All Consuming Images: The Politics of Style in Contemporary Culture* (New York: Basic Books 1988). The impact of the mass media in shaping the political process in the image of commercial consumption is well documented. See, for example, D. Lazert (ed.), *American Media and Mass Culture: Left Perspectives* (Berkeley, CA: University of California Press 1987); and E. Herman and N. Chomsky, *Manufacturing Consent: The Political Economy of the Mass Media* (New York: Pantheon Books 1988).

45 See supra, ch. 2.

46 See *Hunter* v. *Southam Inc.*, [1984] 2 SCR 145 and *First National Bank* v. *Bellotti*, 435 US 765 (1978).

47 See *Re Rocket and Royal College of Dental Surgeons of Ontario.* [1988] 64 OR (2d) 353, 376 per Cory J.A. and *Re Klein and the Law Society of Upper Canada*, [1985] 50 OR (2d) 118. These 'advances' in the protection of corporate rights and freedoms are put in critical context when set against the treatment of unions. Whereas corporations are deemed worthy of constitutional recognition, the labour movement has received short shrift from the courts. See *Reference re Public Service Employee Relations Act, Labour Relations Act and Police Officers Collective Bargaining Act*, [1987] 1 SCR 313 and supra pp. 47–9.

48 See R. Sharpe, 'Commercial Expression and the Charter,' *University of Toronto Law Journal* 37 (1987), 229, and S. Braun, 'Should Commercial Speech Be Accorded Prima Facie Constitutional Recognition under the

Canadian Charter of Rights and Freedoms?', *Ottawa Law Review* 18 (1986), 37.

49 See for example, *Buckley*, supra note 34.

50 A. Camus, *Resistance, Rebellion and Death* (New York: Knopf 1961), 104.

51 See Postman, supra note 43, 138–41, 155–63.

52 D. Cornell, 'Toward a Modern/Postmodern Reconstruction of Ethics,' *University of Pennsylvania Law Review* 133 (1985), 291, 378. See also F. Michelman, 'Foreword: Traces of Self-Government,' *Harvard Law Review* 100 (1986), 4, 33. For an excellent introduction to the epistemological implications of a dialogic ethic, see *Anti-Foundationalism and Practical Reasoning* E. Simpson ed., (Montreal: Academic Publishing 1987).

53 R. Bernstein, *Beyond Objectivism and Relativism* (Philadelphia: University of Pennsylvania Press 1983), 163.

54 See supra ch. 6.

55 C. Gilligan, *In a Different Voice: Psychological Theory and Women's Development* (Cambridge: Harvard University Press 1982), 29.

56 See J. Habermas, *Toward a Rational Society* (Boston: Beacon Press 1971) and *Legitimation Crisis* (Beacon Press 1976), and R. Rorty, *Philosophy and the Mirror of Nature* (Princeton: Princeton University Press 1979).

57 R. Rorty, *Contingency, Irony and Solidarity* (Cambridge: Cambridge University Press 1989), 39–40, 133.

58 Ibid. 57.

59 T. Nagel, *The View from Nowhere* (New York: Oxford University Press 1986), 67. For a first cut at articulating and defending this theoretical position, see A. Hutchinson, 'The Three "R"s: Reading Rorty Radically,' *Harvard Law Review* 103 (1989), 555.

60 R. Unger, *Law in Modern Society: Toward a Criticism of Social Theory* (1976), 206.

61 For a succinct account of this divergence, see R. Parker, 'Issues of Community and Liberty,' *Harvard Journal of Law & Public Policy* 8 (1986), 287. In this sense, I plead guilty to Chris McCrudden's charge that I am an advocate of 'non-hierarchical constitutive communitarianism.' See C. McCrudden, 'Community and Discrimination,' in J. Eekelaar and J. Bell (eds.), *Oxford Essays in Jurisprudence* (Oxford: Clarendon Press 1987), 224. This could only be an indictable offence under a liberal regime of jurisprudence, and, as such, my work is committed as an act of civil disobedience.

62 For a thorough critique of liberalism, see, for example, R.P. Wolff, *The Poverty of Liberalism* (Boston: Beacon Press 1968); R.M. Unger, *Knowledge and Politics* (New York: Free Press 1975); and J. Spragens, *The Irony of Liberal Reason* (Chicago: University of Chicago Press 1981).

63 See S. Bowles and H. Gintis, *Democracy and Capitalism: Property, Community and the Contradictions of Modern Social Thought* (New York: Basic Books 1987), 13.

64 See K. Marx, 'A Critique of Political Economy' in D. McLellan (ed.) *Karl Marx: Selected Writings* (Oxford: Oxford University Press 1977), 330. This point was strongly reinforced by Engels, who stated that 'the cohesive force of civilized society is the State, which in all typical periods is exclusively the state of the ruling class, and in all cases remains essentially a machine for keeping down the oppressed, exploited class.' See F. Engels, *The Origin of Family, Private Property and the State* (Chicago: C.H. Kerr 1884), 755. See also G.A. Cohen, *Karl Marx's Theory of History: A Defence* (Princeton: Princeton University Press 1978), and R. Miliband, *The State in Capitalist Society* (New York: Basic Books 1969).

65 See V.I. Lenin, *State and Revolution* (New York: Vanguard Press 1917), 375–89, and I. Balbus, *Marxism and Domination* (Princeton: Princeton University Press 1982), 109–21.

66 L. Panitch, 'The Role and Nature of the Canadian State' in *The Canadian State: Political Economy and Political Power* (Toronto: University of Toronto Press 1977).

67 See supra ch. 6.

68 Unger, supra note 60, 193.

69 In pointing to an adumbrated theory of the state, I have tried to weave together an eclectic selection of material. See, for instance, A. Gramsci, *Selections from the Prison Notebooks* (London: Lawrence & Wishart 1971); J. Habermas, *Legitimation Crisis* (1976); M. Foucault, *Power/Knowledge* (C. Gordon ed.) (Brighton: Harvester Press 1980); R. Unger, *Politics* (1987); and C. MacKinnon 'Feminism, Marxism, Method and the State: An Agenda for Theory,' *Signs* 7 (1982), 515, and 'Feminism, Marxism, Method and The State: Towards a Feminist Jurisprudence,' *Signs* 8 (1983), 635. Some have claimed that these writers fall within the Marxist tradition. See M. Mandel, 'Marxism and the Rule of Law,' *University of New Brunswick Law Journal* 35 (1986), 7, 13. It seems to me that there are sufficient differences to place them outside such a canon. Nevertheless, I do acknowledge that there are many similarities between the critique offered here and that of Marx in his earlier work. See Marx, supra note 64.

70 See G. Hodgson, *The Democratic Economy* (Harmondsworth: Penguin 1984).

71 For a general survey of the constitutional status of Crown corporations, see A. Lucas, 'Judicial Review of Crown Corporations,' *Alberta Law Review* 25 (1987), 363.

72 See W. Stewart, *Uneasy Lies the Head: The Truth about Canada's Crown Corporations* (Toronto: Collins 1987), 22–34, 209–12.

73 See J.J. Rousseau, *The Social Contract* (M. Cranston ed. 1968), 28–9. This theme is taken up and pursued by G. Frug. See 'Administrative Democracy,' *University of Toronto Law Journal* 40 (1990), 554.

74 'Commencement Address' (July 7, 1978) *National Review* 838.

75 See R. Dworkin, *A Matter of Principle* (1985), 335–97, and A. Meiklejohn, *Political Freedom* (New York: Oxford University Press 1965).

76 See, for example, B. Ackerman, *Social Justice in the Liberal State* (1980).

77 While agreeing with much of my critique, Rosemary Coombe chastises me for my 'pessimistic and fatalistic attitude' and encourages me to be more 'sensitive to the critical role that mass culture plays in shaping potentially salient forms of democracy.' See Coombe, 'Publicity Rights and Political Aspirations: Mass Culture, Gender Identity, and Democracy,' *New England Law Review* 20 (1992), 1221, 1271–81.

78 *Attorney-General* v. *Guardian Newspapers*, [1987] 2 WLR 1428.

79 *Gay Alliance Toward Equality* v. *Vancouver Sun*, [1979] SCR 435.

80 *Trop* v. *Dulles*, 356 US 86 at 102 per Warren C.J. (1958).

81 M. Glendon, *Rights Talk: The Impoverishment of Political Discourse* (New York: Free Press 1991), 182.

82 A. Phillips, *Engendering Democracy* (Cambridge, UK: Polity Press 1991), 15.

83 See I. Young, 'Polity and Group Difference: A Critique of the Ideal of Universal Citizenship,' in C. Sunstein (ed.) *Feminism and Political Theory* (Chicago: University of Chicago Press 1990) and *Belonging: The Meaning and Future of Canadian Citizenship* (W. Kaplan ed.) (Montreal: McGill–Queen's University Press 1993).

84 *Speech*, supra note 31, 1416.

85 M. Ignatieff, *The Needs of Strangers* (London: Chatto & Windus 1984), 141–2.

CHAPTER 8 IN WAITING

1 W. Wordsworth, *The Prelude* (London: E. Moxon 1850), Bk. xi, ll. 140–4.

2 A. Gramsci, *Selections from the Prison Notebooks* (Q. Hoare and G. Nowell-Smith eds.) (London: Lawrence & Wishart 1971), 276.

3 D. Beatty, *Talking Heads* (Toronto: Carswell 1989), 119.

4 See E. Wolgast, *The Grammar of Justice* (Ithaca, NY: Cornell University Press 1987).

5 See T.S. Eliot, *Murder in the Cathedral* (New York: Harcourt, Brace 1935),

44 ('The last temptation is the greatest treason / To do the right thing for the wrong reason.').

6 See E. Said, *Representations of the Intellectual* (New York: Pantheon Books 1993).

7 J. Handler, 'Postmodernism, Protest and the New Social Movements,' *Law and Society Review* 26 (1992), 695, 724.

8 Ibid. 727. A central motif of that book was the need to stake out a narrow and precarious ledge of criticism that ran 'the considerable risk of succumbing to the secure comforts of traditional jurisprudence or straying too far into the wilderness of political irrelevance.' A. Hutchinson, *Dwelling on the Threshold: Critical Essays on Modern Legal Thought* (Toronto: Carswell 1989), viii.

9 C. Castoriadis, 'Socialism and Autonomous Society,' *Telos* (1980), 91, 104.

10 A. Macleish, *The Hamlet of Archibald Macleish* (Boston: Houghton Mifflin 1958).

11 C. West, 'The Limits of Neopragmatism,' in M. Brint and W. Weaver (eds.) *Pragmatism in Law and Society* (Boulder, CO: Broadview Press 1991), 124–5. See C. West, *Prophetic Fragments* (New Jersey: Africa World Press 1988) and *The American Evasion of Philosophy: A Genealogy of Pragmatism* (Madison: University of Wisconsin Press 1989).

12 See A. Harris, 'Race and Essentialism in Feminist Legal Theory,' *Stanford Law Review* 42 (1990), 581, and M. Radin, 'Pragmatism and Feminism,' *Southern California Law Review* 63 (1990), 1699.

13 See H. Gates, 'Statistical Stigmata,' *Cardozo Law Review* 11 (1990), 1275, 1289.

14 See R. Rorty, 'Priority of Democracy to Philosophy,' in M. Peterson and R. Vaughan (eds.), *The Virginia Statute for Religious Freedom* (Cambridge: Cambridge University Press 1988), 274. Rorty reiterates this radical commitment in urging that we have 'faith in ourselves – in the utopian hope characteristic of a democratic community – rather than asking for reasons or back up from outside.' R. Rorty, 'Education without Dogma,' *Dissent* (1989), 198, 201.

15 S. O'Connor, *I Do Not Want What I Haven't Got* (1990) Chrysalis/Ensign CD, VKW-41759.

Cases

Adderley v. *Florida*, 398 US 39 (1966) 193
Andrews v. *Law Society of British Columbia*, [1989] 1 SCR 143 83, 151
Attorney-General v. *Guardian Newspapers*, [1987] 2 WLR 1428 214

Black v. *Law Society of Alberta*, [1989] 1 SCR 591 148
Blathwayt v. *Lord Cawley*, [1976] AC 397 135
Borowski v. *Canada*, [1989] 1 SCR 342 52
Brown v. *Louisiana*, 383 US 131 (1966) 192–3
Brown v. *Allen*, 344 US 443 (1953) 162
Brown v. *Board of Education*, 347 US 483, (1954) 67
Buckley v. *Valeo*, 424 US 1 at 48–9 196

Central Hudson Gas and Electric Corp. v. *Public Service Comm. of N.Y.*, 447 US 557 (1980) 198
Co-operative Committee on Japanese-Canadians v. *A-G for Canada*, [1947] AC 87 17
Committee for the Commonwealth of Canada v. *Canada*, [1991] 1 SCR 139 54, 194
Committee for the Commonwealth of Canada v. *The Queen*, [1991] 1 SCR 139 194
Cornelius v. *NAACP Legal Defense and Education Fund*, 105 S. Ct. 3439 (1985) 193

Daigle v. *Tremblay*, [1989] 2 SCR 530 52, 109, 143–4
Dandridge v. *Williams*, 397 US 471 (1970) 100

Edwards v. *Attorney General for Canada*, [1930] AC 124 30
Edwards v. *California*, 314 US 160 (1941) 176
Entick v. *Carrington* (1765), 95 ER 807 17

First National Bank v. *Bellotti*, 435 US 765 (1978) 200
Food Employees Local 590 v. *Logan Valley Plaza*, 391 US 308 (1968) 193

Ford v. *Quebec (Attorney-General)*, [1988] 2 SCR 712 32, 47, 149, 198

Gay Alliance Toward Equality v. *Vancouver Sun*, [1979] SCR 435 45, 214

Hague v. *C.I.O.* 307 US 496 (1939) 192
Harris v. *McRae*, 448 US 297 (1980) 107
Harrison v. *Carswell*, [1976] SCR 200 80, 87
Hudgens v. *NLRB*, 424 US 507 (1976) 193
Hunter v. *Southam*, [1984] 2 SCR 145 32, 83, 95, 131–2, 200

Irwin Toy Ltd. v. *Quebec (Attorney-General)*, [1989] 1 SCR 927 32, 51

Kask v. *Shimizu*, [1986] 4 WWR 154 40

Lavigne v. *O.P.S.E.U.*, [1991] 2 SCR 211 151
Lloyd Corp. v. *Tanner*, 407 US 551 (1972) 193
Lumley v. *Gye* (1853), 118 ER 749 141

Marsh v. *Alabama*, 326 US 501 (1946) 193
McKinney v. *University of Guelph*, [1990] 3 SCR 229 144
Minister of Justice of Canada v. *Borowski*, [1981] 2 SCR 575 119, 143
Minnick v. *California Department of Corrections*, 452 US 105 (1981) 192

National Citizens' Coalition v. *A.G. Canada* (1984), 11 DLR (4th) 481 (Alta. Q.B.) 149

Ontario Human Rights Commission v. *Simpson-Sears Ltd.*, [1985] 2 SCR 536 48
Osborn v. *Bank of the United States*, 22 US 738 (1824) 11

People's Pleasure Park Co. v. *Rohleder* (1909), 61 S.E. Rep. 794 32
Perry Education Assoc. v. *Perry Local Educators' Assoc.*, 460 US 37 (1982) 193
Phillips v. *Social Assistance Appeal Board* (N.S.) (1986), 76 NSR (2d) 240 40, 148
Posadas de Puerto Rico Associates v. *Tourism Co. of Puerto Rico*, 478 US 328 (1986) 198
Professional Institute v. *Northwest Territories*, [1990] 2 SCR 367 34
Pruneyeard Shopping Centre v. *Robins*, 447 US 74 (1981) 193
Public Service Employees Relations Act, [1987] 1 SCR 313 34

R. v. *Big M Drug Mart*, [1985] SCR 295 33, 131–2
R. v. *Lerke* (1986), 25 DLR (4th) 403 (Alta. CA) 146
R. v. *Morgantaler*, [1988] 1 SCR 30 52, 105, 179
R. v. *Oakes* [1986] 1 SCR 103 50, 68
R. v. *Rahey*, [1987] 1 SCR 588 137
R. v. *Sullivan*, [1991] SCR 489 31
Race Relations Board v. *Charter*, [1973] AC 868 135

Racial Relations Board v. *Applin*, [1975] AC 259 135
Retail, Wholesale and Department Store Union, Local 580 et al. v. *Dolphin Delivery Ltd.*, [1986] 2 SCR 573 83, 129
Roncarelli v. *Duplessis*, [1959] SCR 121 17

Slaight Communications v. *Davidson*, [1989] 1 SCR 1038 49
Salomon v. *Salomon & Co.*, [1897] AC 22 31
Schachter v. *Canada*, [1992] 2 SCR 679 148
Silano v. *The Queen*, [1987] 5 WWR 739 (B.C.S.C.) 148
Société des Acadiens et du Nouveau-Brunswick v. *Association of Parents for Fairness in Education, 50 Branch*, [1986] 1 SCR 549 48
Southern Pacific Co. v. *Jensen*, 244 US 205, 222 (1917) 61, 149
Switzman v. *Elbling*, [1957] SCR 285 17
Symes v. *Canada*, [1993] 4 S.C.R. 695 42

Tremblay v. *Daigle*, (1990), 35 McGill LJ 633, 652 103, 115
Trop v. *Dulles*, 356 US 86 (1958) 214

United States Postal Service v. *Council of Greenburgh Civic Ass'ns.*, 453 US 114 (1981) 193

Virginia State Board of Pharmacy v. *Virginia Citizens Consumer Council*, 425 US 748 (1976) 198

Wheeler v. *Leicester City Council*, [1985] 2 All ERR 1106 (H.L.) 45
Wilson v. *B.C. Medical Services Commission* (1988), 55 DLR (4th) 171 (B.C.C.A.) 151

Index

Abel, Albert 77
abortion 52–5, 85, 104–21, 179–81
Ackerman, Bruce 15
Acton, Lord 57, 58, 87
animal rights 34–5
Arbuthnot, Dr 88, 121
Aristotle 84, 93
Atwood, Margaret 108, 120–1, 169

Baum, L. Frank 154, 182
Beatty, David 64, 66–75, 86, 133, 169
Beckett, Samuel 3, 21, 27, 154, 228–30
Beetz, Jean 77
begging 95–102
Blondin, Charles 125
Burke, Edmund 11

CBC 21
Charter of Rights 3–7, 15–19, 23–4, 28, 30–56, 58–60, 66–71, 86–7, 88, 95, 128–47, 164–5, 167–9, 177–8
– Section 1 19, 48–55, 68–70, 193–94, 198
– Section 32 130–1, 144–7
– Section 33 (override) 19, 24, 198

Chrétien, Jean 24
citizens 30, 152, 172, 187, 210–11, 214–17, 226–8
civic dialogue xii
civil rights 35–6
Cohen, Adam 96–102
commercial speech 198–202
Conklin, William 66, 76–84, 86
Copelon, Rhonda 107
Coraf 3–7, 12, 18–19, 22–5, 27, 172, 221–2, 230
corporations 32–4, 41, 124–8, 152–3, 199–202, 209–10, 311–14

Daigle, Chantal 109–14, 115–20, 144
democracy
– and citizenship 98, 147, 152–3, 170–2, 210–11, 214–17, 226–8
– and dialogue xii, 24–7, 166–9, 173–4, 185–90, 202–6, 212–14, 215–20, 226–8
and society xii, xiii, 24–7, 57, 74–5, 98–9, 107–8, 122, 170–2, 195–6, 210–11, 227–8
Dennis, Davis xi
Derrida, Jacques 78
Dicey, A.V. 10, 11, 124

Dickson, Brian 77, 80, 87, 131, 144
Diefenbaker, John 17
Dworkin, Ronald 6, 10, 14–15, 24, 92, 133, 169, 184, 186, 188, 212

Eliot, T.S. 223
Ely, John Hart 36
equality 37–8, 39–43, 44–8, 94–5, 148–9, 216

fetus 30–1, 53–4, 104–6, 143
formalism 60–6, 75–8, 86–7, 162–3, 171–2, 182, 229
France, Anatole 101
free speech 45–7, 51–2, 189–98, 212–14, 217–18
freedom of association 43–4
freedom of religion 47–8, 49–50, 150
French Revolution 224
Fiss, Owen 15, 195–7, 220

gay men xii, 31, 86, 95, 214
Gilligan, Carol 205
Globe and Mail 211
Glorious Revolution of 1691 10, 223

Habermas, Jurgen 205–6
Hand, Learned 123
Handler, Joel 224–5
Hayek, Friedrich 10, 12
Hershkoff, Helen 96–102
Hobbes, Thomas 10, 36, 91, 104, 132
Hogg, Peter 137–8
Hort, Herbert 9–10, 160
Hugo, Victor 95
Hume, David 11

idols 31
Ignatieff, Michael 220
indeterminacy 6, 24, 28–56, 72–3, 83–4, 89, 103–5, 115–18, 159, 173
individualism 89–95, 100–1, 103–4, 122, 185–90

Jackson, J. 176
jury 172

Kant, Immanuel 91
Kymlicka, Will 65

Langille, Brian 155, 157–65, 167
Larkin, Philip xxii
Laskin, Bora 77, 79–82
Lederman, William 77
legalism 7–12, 26, 139–40, 226–8
legitimacy 20–4, 57, 58–87, 123–5, 155–6
Le Guin, Ursula 104
lesbians 31, 95
Les Misérables 95, 99
liberalism 7–15, 28–9, 36, 64–6, 69–70, 89–95, 97–101, 103–8, 123–5, 131–6, 166–9, 174, 185–90, 190–8, 202–3, 204–6, 206–8, 215–16, 220, 225–8
liberty 7–15, 43, 44–8, 53–4, 92–3
Locke, John 10, 14, 36, 91, 132, 186

MacLaine, Shirley 61
Magna Carta 10–11, 223
Manning, Preston 64
Marx, Karl 101
Marxism 155, 174–8, 207–8
Mill, J.S. 10, 36, 124
Monahan, Patrick 64
Mulroney, Brian xii, 18, 64

Native people xii, 8, 41, 85
natural rights 4, 62–3, 64–5, 134

Nedelsky, Jennifer 155, 165–6, 168, 183, 204
Nelson, Lord 148
Nietzsche, Friedrich 99

objectivity 6, 22–3, 61–2, 66–8, 69, 86–7, 165
O'Connor, Sinéad 230

Paley, William 11
patriation 15–17, 77
People's Package 15–19, 23
Pigeon, Louis-Phillippe 77
Plato 78
postmodernism 20–1, 155, 159, 173, 224–8
Poswas, Justice xi
pragmatism 155–9, 160, 165–72
public/private 106, 124–5, 128–36, 137–42, 147–53, 192–4, 213–14

rationalism 77–8, 165, 186, 223–4
Rawls, John 187, 205–6
REAL Women 64
rights
– contents of 35–8
– and litigation 106–7, 177–82
– and rights-holders 29–35, 118–20
– scope of 38–44, 96–102, 119–21
Rodell, Fred 25
Rorty, Richard 187, 205–6
Rothman, Barbara 104
Rule of Law 7–12, 14–15, 63–4, 134, 173
Russell, Peter 77

scepticism 72–4, 164–5, 175–8
Schneider, Elizabeth 199
Shakespeare, William 199
Slattery, Brian 156–7
smoking 38
socioeconomic rights 36–8
Solzhenitsyn, Alexander 211–12
South Africa xi, xiii, 174
Spender, Dale 189
Stevens, Wallace 32
Stone, Christopher 34

Taylor, Charles 65
Trakman, Leon 155, 166–72, 183, 204
trade unions 33–4, 43, 50, 85, 129–31, 149, 151
Tremblay, Guy 110–14, 144
Tribe, Laurence 15
Thompson, E.P. 174

United Kingdom 174
United States xii, 10–12, 16–19, 192–3

Waiting For Godot 3, 21, 27, 221–2, 228–30
Wilson, Bertha 77, 106–7, 145–7
Wittgenstein, Ludwig 157–8, 160, 163
Wodehouse, P.G. xii
women 30, 41–2, 44, 103–21
Wordsworth, William 22

Yeats, W.B. 57